Financial Fitness In 45 Days

THE

COMPLETE

GUIDE TO

SHAPING UP

YOUR PERSONAL

FINANCES

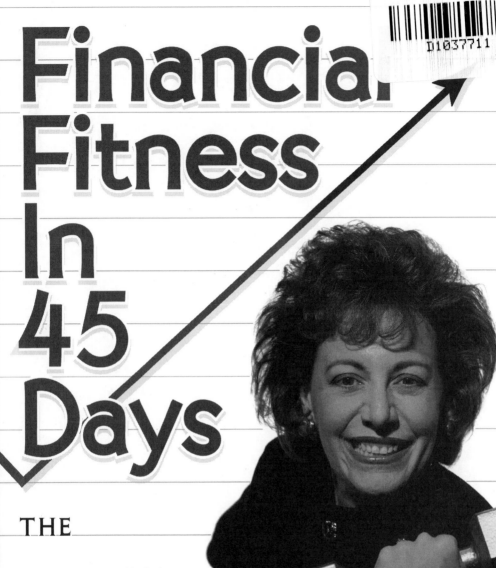

Lorayne Fiorillo

Financial Fitness In 45 Days

THE COMPLETE GUIDE TO SHAPING UP YOUR PERSONAL FINANCES

Lorayne Fiorillo

Entrepreneur Press

Entrepreneur Press
2392 Morse Ave., Irvine, CA 92614

Managing Editor: Marla Markman
Book Design: Sylvia H. Lee
Copy Editor: Julie Flick
Proofreader: Alison Steiner Miller
Cover Design: Mark A. Kozak
Illustrations: Peter Bennett
Indexer: Ken DellaPenta

Cover Photo:
Photo© John Emerson

This publication is designed to provide accurate and authoritative
information in regard to the subject matter covered. It is sold with the
understanding that the publisher is not engaged in rendering legal,
accounting or other professional services. If legal advice or other expert
assistance is required, the services of a competent professional
person should be sought.

Library of Congress Cataloging-in-Publication Data
Fiorillo, Lorayne.
    Financial fitness in 45 days: the complete guide to shaping up your
personal finances / by Lorayne Fiorillo.
        p. cm.
    Includes index.
    ISBN 1-891984-12-8
    1. Finance, Personal.   I. Title.
    HG179.F532 2000
    332.024—dc21   99-052450

Printed in Canada

09 08 07 06 05 04 03 02 01 00   10 9 8 7 6 5 4 3 2 1

Please read the following disclosures before beginning the book:

To my parents, who taught me I could do anything;
my husband, Bill, who believed that I could do anything;
and my son, Max, for whom I would do anything.

Acknowledgments

This book is the story of every client I've ever been fortunate enough to serve and every audience I've ever been lucky enough to address. Without them, there would be no career, no stories, no book.

Thanks to all the experts who helped me by sharing their time and tips. Steve Norowitz and his staff at T. Rowe Price and Associates made my life easy by providing excellent work sheets and studies with no strings attached.

A special thanks to the people at my firm, especially Frank Beyer, the best boss anyone could ever have. When he wasn't running interference for me, he assumed the role of head cheerleader and psychologist. And thanks to my assistant, Bobbi Sherrill, who kept everything together, read chapters, and made her friends and relatives read them, too. Vinny DiPierro and Noah Sorkin gave this book their undivided attention, losing several weekends to make it the best it could be.

To my colleagues at the National Speakers Association, who supported me and ensured me that my writing and speaking could indeed help people reach their financial goals.

To my family, who somehow put up with me, especially my husband, Bill, who baby-sat endlessly and lived through a huge mess in his office and a grouchy, exasperated wife; my mother, Lucille, who took care of my son, cheered me on, and provided witty and thought-provoking commentary; my father, Mike, who bragged so incessantly about this book that I had no choice *but* to finish it; and Max, who can't wait to have momma all to himself—finally.

For the ever-patient staff at Entrepreneur Media, who made this idea a reality, the greatest thanks to Rieva Lesonsky, who believed in it and in me; Marla Markman, who asked tons of questions and helped me to clarify the book's content; and Julie Flick, who patiently copy edited, re-edited and re-edited again, chapter after chapter.

Finally, the greatest thanks to Melanie Weining, my assistant for three and a half years, who read every chapter, made copious notes, corrected even the most minute errors, and cheerfully put up with tantrums, doldrums and exaltations. She worked as hard as I did to write this book. If you're laughing while you're doing the workbook exercises, it's because Melanie put so much of her kind heart and soul into them.

Table Of Contents

Introduction

Welcome to our financial workout. Unlike a spa program, we won't be setting an appointment for a massage and there won't be a selection of light cuisine to choose from. Our program aims to help you shave those extra dollars from your credit-card bills, crunch those investment numbers and whip your portfolio into shape. You'll be building your investment muscles, and you don't even have to leave home to do it.

Whether you're a novice investor or already have a few bull and bear markets under your money belt, buying this book may be one of the smartest money moves you've ever made. *Financial Fitness in 45 Days* helps you make short work of a tedious task: figuring out and putting together an investment strategy. Most of all, it helps you take the bull (if you'll pardon the pun) by the horns and get started . . . now. Just think: In 45 days you'll be ready to make the most of your financial future. When was the last time $19.95 did that for you?

Why 45 days? Behaviorists tell us it takes 30 days to turn a behavior into a habit, 45 days to break an old habit and start a new one. After spending 45 days with me, I hope I'll have revamped your money style. After all, if you can get firmer abs in 30 days, a lean, mean portfolio in 45 days should be a snap!

"Wait a minute," you might say. "Why should I spend 45 days when other people say it only takes nine steps to reach financial freedom or just one minute to become a money manager . . . even for dummies?" First, I assume you're not a dummy, or you wouldn't be reading this book. As for nine days or one minute or any promises out there, they may very well work. But what I know for sure is this: Unlike many financial authors, I am a financial advisor. I have more than 600 individual clients, people just like you. This book isn't based on research I did in the lab or things I've read; it's the stuff I say to my clients every day. Reading this book is just like talking to me, only slower.

You'll notice this book doesn't get into the psychology behind how people deal (or, more likely, don't deal) with money. Most people don't have the time to psychoanalyze their financial status; they just want to improve it. Think of this book as financial behavior modification: You won't find out why you spend everything you make or why you don't have enough money to retire—you'll just stop spending that money and get enough saved and invested properly so you *can* retire. I'm not saying that in 45 days you're going to work out all your deep-rooted money problems, but if you set—and achieve—some goals, perhaps the problems will be a little less daunting.

You'll find the book organized like a workout. The first six days are a money warm-up; you'll be asked to take a look in the mirror and do some self-analysis. What spots need a little work? What are you proud of?

For Days 7 through 9, you'll check out the equipment you'll be working with, covering fixed income, stocks and mutual funds in a most general way. Then the real workout begins!

During Days 10 through 13, you'll learn about specific fixed-income investments; Days 14 through 18, concentrate on stocks; and Days 19 through 24, put mutual funds through their paces. After these sessions, you'll be ready to get into some advanced investments, which you'll run through on days 25 through 33.

The next five days give you the chance to put it all together with my strategies for investment success. Then on days 39 through 42, you'll learn how to smooth the road to retirement and estate planning.

Finally, in your three-day cool down, you'll learn how to maintain your financial fitness by keeping the right company—joining an investment club and picking the right financial advisor. You'll wrap up your workout with the most common investment mistakes to avoid.

Don't skip any chapters . . . you just may find some new twists on old ideas. When you've finished each day's workout, test your knowledge with the corresponding exercises in the bonus workbook, *Mental Gymnastics*, starting on page 285. You'll notice that not every day has an exercise. Special emphasis is placed on areas that my clients have found most useful. After all, this is financial fitness in 45 days, not 45 years! To find out how you did, turn to the answer key, starting on page 355.

As you go through the chapters, be on the lookout for five different types of tip boxes:

Healthy Habit

Look for this box to reveal ideas on how to invest more efficiently or make better investment decisions.

Trainer's Tip

Here you will find insightful thoughts from investment experts.

Money Missteps

Heed the warnings in this box to avoid common pitfalls and investment mistakes.

Smart Stretch

Here you will find helpful information and other sources for more details.

Joggin' Jargon

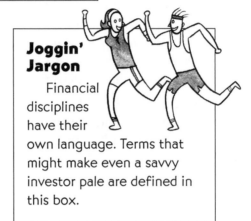

Financial disciplines have their own language. Terms that might make even a savvy investor pale are defined in this box.

If you're not familiar with a term or can't remember whether a bull market is good or bad, consult the glossary on page 277 for a quick refresher.

To make the most this book, you should:

● Get a calendar to check off each day.

● Read each chapter.

● Do the workbook exercises.

● Celebrate . . . you're on your way toward financial independence!

All work and no play doesn't do much for Jack (or Jill). While money is serious business, *Reader's Digest* may have put it best: Laughter is the best medicine. While you should have respect for your money, facing your dollar bills the same way, folding them tenderly and kissing them good night won't make you richer . . . it didn't work for Midas, and it probably won't work for you. The key to learning and remembering is to enjoy what you're doing as you're going along.

Humorist Art Buchwald was the commencement speaker when I graduated from Georgetown University. His talk was peppered with stories and anecdotes, and he got his points across to us as we laughed in the sunshine. He finished his talk with this comment: "When you think about this day, you may not remember what I said, but you'll remember that you laughed." Funny, I recall not only that I laughed, but his sage advice as well.

Successful investing, like most of life, is a process of sifting the wheat from the chaff. There is no one way to make money in the financial markets. The idea is to know enough to ask the right questions, understand the answers and recognize when something (or someone) is a rip-off. This is not to say that you don't now or never will need help from an expert in financing your retirement, saving for your children's college education or planning your estate. This book is not meant to take the place of professional advice, but to prepare you to make the most of what information comes to you by way of newspapers, magazines, newsletters, the Internet, TV, radio and those who proffer financial advice.

As you start this book, consider the widely quoted words of Napoleon Hill: "Think, and grow rich" . . . and remember my own, less widely quoted version: "Do, and grow richer."

See you at the "gym"!

Eyes On The Prize

Setting your financial goals

> "Obstacles are those frightful things you see when you take your eyes off your goals."
> —Henry Ford

They say that nature abhors a vacuum, and when it comes to money, that vacuum can become so strong that it can pull in even the savviest among us. Dave and Julie sat in my office for a periodic financial review, their net worth statement proudly nestled between them. The bottom line? Together they were worth more than $1.2 million. "When can I retire?" the exhausted executive queried. "Tomorrow," I replied. After a few seconds of stunned silence, he looked down at the page and exclaimed, "Oh, no. I've got to have at least $2 million!" Why? No reason he could come up with; just to have it. It didn't matter that he would probably never spend all he had already amassed or that his wife stood to inherit at least an additional $650,000.

He was convinced that he had to have $2 million, "even if it kills me." Let's hope not, but with his level of stress, you never know.

What are your financial goals? Do you want to retire 10 years early? Save enough to send your kids to college without taking out any loans? Change careers and do what you love instead of what you must to survive? Maybe all these things; maybe something else entirely. One thing is for sure, though: Before you gear up to learn all kinds of practical information that can help you become financially fit, you'd better spend some time figuring out what financially fit means to you.

Can't Buy Me Love

Believe it or not, many people with perfectly wonderful net worths panic, sure that they won't have enough. Enough for what? For a penthouse on Park Avenue, a ski chalet in Chamonix and a pair of BMWs in the driveway? If those are your goals, you'd better read fast, and save and invest even faster. But most people can retire in comfort and have fulfilling lives without a seven-figure net worth. The first step to defining your goals is to realize that you don't have to be rich to have a great life.

First, don't believe everything you hear about financial goals. Many companies are spending a lot of money to make you feel like you have to work, work, work and save a ridiculous amount of money or you won't be able to educate your children, live in a house you can enjoy, travel the world or retire in comfort. Balderdash! On Day 5 you'll see what kind of house you can afford; Day 29 will help you figure out what it will take to send your children to college; Day 40 deals with determining the sum you'll need to retire. You may be pleasantly surprised. Promise yourself (and me!) that you will suspend any negative thoughts on the amount of money you'll have to stash away until you've seen what you really need.

Second, most people don't spend their golden years working under the golden arches unless they want to: Yes, Virginia, Social Security will probably be

Healthy Habit

It's great to have goals, but there's a much greater chance you'll reach them if you write them down, step by step. Checking off the steps makes your journey more fun, and once you've committed to your goal in writing, you're more likely to achieve it.

there for you, too. Studies have shown that most people don't live in expensive nursing homes for years and years. You probably don't need a million dollars to retire.

Third, when it comes to their money, many people put the emphasis in the wrong place. They spend most of their time worrying about whether the market is up or down and bemoaning the fact that they didn't get in on the latest Internet initial public offering (IPO) instead of spending their time doing what really makes a difference: saving more, cutting their debt and investing their assets properly. If you learn nothing else, learn that you can't predict the market; you can only predict what you can save, and no amount of worrying will change that. A wise person once said that worry is interest on a debt that may never come due. Don't waste time fretting about the market—use your energy to make better financial decisions.

Fourth, remember that life is short, so eat dessert first. That doesn't mean go out and spend everything you make. What it does mean is stop working so hard to earn all that money you probably won't need for the future that you have no time for your friends and family, have no hobbies or interests and are in awful physical and mental health. Even if you live to be 100 (which you probably won't if you live this way), what good will it do to be as rich as Croesus if you have no one to share it with and nothing fun that you like to do? Getting financially fit means you'll have more time to do the things you like to do because your money is doing the hard work, not you.

The Road Less Traveled

If you've ever been to a motivational seminar, you've probably heard this mantra: "If you don't know where you're going, you'll probably end up somewhere else." Money management is no different from life management—if you want to reach your financial goals, you've got to figure out what they are. Most people spend more time planning their annual vacation than they do planning their financial future. Why? Maybe because most vacations have a specific start date, a preset budget and an obvious goal—to enjoy yourself! Think of financial goal-setting as planning a vacation: Decide where you'd like to go, gather relevant information and carefully plan your route. In fact, financial goal-setting is even more rewarding than a vacation, because vacations only last for a short time—but setting and reaching your financial goals can provide benefits that last a lifetime.

To get started, turn to today's first workbook page and get out a pencil. Go somewhere quiet and spend some time daydreaming about financial goals you'd like to reach. Jot down anything that comes to mind . . . no censoring allowed. For the rest of our 44 days together, whenever you have a brainstorm and come up with another financial goal, write it down.

Some vacations last a weekend; others involve a trip around the world in 80 days. Likewise, while some goals are short term, others focus on periods far in the distance. Here's how to break down your goals:

- **Short-term goals can be achieved in a year or less.** Maybe it's paying off your credit-card bills, building a deck on your house or buying a new car. Find out what these goals cost and divide the amount by 12. Use tomorrow's Income, Outgo work sheet to see if you can afford to save for your goal over 12 months. If not, consider moving it to intermediate goals.

- **Intermediate goals can be achieved in anywhere from one to five years.** Here you might put buying a home or a second home, starting a business or remodeling your kitchen. These goals are bigger and more expensive, but they're usually not of vital importance to your financial health—you can be more flexible about these than about short-term goals.

- **Long-term goals are those you plan to achieve over your lifetime, like funding your children's education or saving for retirement.** These goals require the most planning, but since you have a relatively long time in which to achieve them, you can take them step by step.

If wishes were horses, beggars would ride . . . right down Wall Street. Unfortunately, just wishing for a goal doesn't make it any more accessible. For the next 44 days, you'll learn the tools to make your financial dreams come true. It's a lot more efficient than wishing on a star.

DAY 2

Where's Your Money At?

*The basics
of budgets*

My mentor, Irvin McNeil, was quite a guy. He spent hours trying to teach me how to trade index options (no luck) and financial futures (no hope). What I did learn from him was how to understand and learn from my clients.

After months as my devoted tutor, Irvin decided it was time to put me in front of some real, live potential clients. Mind you, I had spent my formative financial advisor years as a New York Yankee in the Tarheel State. Irvin, a native of North Carolina's small towns, seemed unperturbed about juxtaposing me with some of "his people."

That afternoon we went for a drive in the country . . . what Irvin called "God's country" and what I considered *another* country. Past field and stream, cows, chickens, pigs and horses, we pulled onto a dirt road by an old farmhouse. Wearing our best navy-blue suits, we stepped gingerly into the parlor of a house that seemed to have predated the Mayflower. The homeowners sat on two straight-backed chairs (lacking only a pitchfork between them), leaving their couch to us.

In broker school, I thought I had learned all the right questions, so I dove right in. "What sort of investments have you made in the past?" They looked at each other, puzzled. "How have your investments fared?" More concerned looks. Still, I pressed on: "What do you consider your best investment so far?" Both looked at Irvin, who promptly kicked me and said, "Where's your money at?" They both smiled and pointed . . . I thought at us, but no, at the couch. That old, lumpy, uncomfortable, threadbare couch was stuffed not with upholstery, but with *money*!

You may wish you had such a stash, but the truth is, you're probably stuffing money in places every bit as unprofitable as that old couch—without even realizing it. If you sincerely want to start investing and can't imagine where the money is going to come from, don't start ripping up your upholstery or pulling out your hair. Here are a few more constructive places for you to look.

Bend And Stretch

Let's face it. Who would rather save their money for later than buy something they really want now? Not need, mind you; want. America may be the land of the free, but it's also the home of the consumer. Nothing gets done until somebody buys something, so spending is more than the national pastime: It's downright patriotic. It creates jobs, stimulates the economy, and is certainly a better hobby than spraying graffiti on subway cars. The only problem with profligate spending is that while purchasing enough to keep the gross national product on an upswing, you're probably buying more than you need, and you never get around to saving and investing. Not only are you squandering money, but you've also spent all your time getting the best deal on that down comforter for the king-sized bed that you haven't yet purchased. So let's consider making a lifestyle change.

The procedure we're about to follow looks a lot like something that is often considered a bad word: budget. Like a diet, anyone who has ever been on one knows that if it works at all, it's short-lived. Lifestyle changes, on the other hand, can make a permanent difference, especially if you build in a couple of places where cheating is allowed.

First, how do you effect a lifestyle change? If you sincerely want to be rich, let's start out with a little coaching. Grab a copy of *The Millionaire Next Door: The Surprising Secrets of America's Wealthy* (Pocket Books) by Thomas J. Stanley, Ph.D., and William D. Danko, Ph.D. Compiled by two former professors who spent more than 20 years studying the habits of the rich, this book is a most enlightening experience. Throughout its pages are examples of millionaires that made it the hard way—they earned it.

You're no different: According to Stanley, rich people do lots of things you probably wouldn't associate with wealth, like buying a used car instead of a new one, paying very little income tax, and, most surprising of all, living well below their means. If you're like me, as you read, you'll find yourself cringing at opportunities missed and stupid mistakes made. Of course, not everyone will want to drive a Ford pickup or leave his or her corporate job for the life of an entrepreneur. But a little inspiration goes a long way: Think of it as a little dollar sign on your shoulder, making you think before you whip out that Visa card.

> **Trainer's Tip**
>
> "Whatever your age, whatever your income, how much should you be worth right now? From years of surveying various high-income/high-net worth people, we have developed a simple rule of thumb [that is] more than adequate in computing your expected net worth: Multiply your age times your pretax annual household income from all sources except inheritances, then divide by 10. This, less any inherited wealth, is what your net worth should be."
>
> —*Thomas J. Stanley, Ph.D.,*
> *co-author of*
> The Millionaire Next Door

Reach For The Dough

So you say you're just squeaking by, barely covering the necessities of life for yourself and your family. Every paycheck disappears before you've had a chance to save a dime. At year's end when you get your W-2 form, you wonder where all the money has gone.

Before you stomp into your boss's office to demand a raise, consider giving yourself one. For one week, write down everything you spend. That means everything, from the quarter you put in the parking meter to the dollars you spend on a roll and coffee. Don't leave out anything: a tank of gas, your kid's field trip, a can of soda, lunch with your colleagues, cigarettes, a beer with friends, money you pay the baby-sitter or tip the newspaper boy. You get the picture. At the end of the week, total up your expenses. Bet you never thought you spent that much money on, well, nothing. If you want to have money to invest, start by taking a sack lunch three days a week and save $10.

If you *do* decide to storm the boss's office, be sure you have a savings plan intact first. If you don't, you will spend every bit of that hard-won raise (and more). Remember: Nature abhors a vacuum, and she'll suck every cent from your wallet if you let her.

Tighten Up

No money to save at the end of the week, month or year? Here are 10 action steps you can take toward making your money dreams come true:

1. **A dollar saved.** Take a dollar out of your wallet every day and put it in an envelope. At the end of the month, deposit it into your bank account. Now the process has begun, and you haven't felt a thing. After six months, increase it to two dollars a day. At the end of the month, deposit this into your bank account and have that account drafted to invest in a mutual fund or a stock.

   Why bother with a sum so small? There's nothing like a little compound interest to make even the smallest sum interesting. Take all your spare change and put it into a piggy bank (if you have kids, let them make the deposit . . . participating may help them get into saving, too). At the end of the month, have a celebration, open the bank, and add this money to your investment account. This can also be a great way to start saving for your children's college education.

2. **Goodbye, ATM.** ATM cards are the downfall of many a well-intentioned saver. It's so easy to just get a little

Healthy Habit

Using coupons can really save money, if you do it right. Don't clip deals on things you never use; you'll just waste time and money. Organize your coupons into categories using a coupon organizer (about $1), and keep it in your car, purse or jacket pocket. Check the grocery store circulars before you shop, and make use of their specials when you plan your menus. Your family will eat better for less.

Up, Up And Away!

At the top of most people's list of things they'd like to do is travel. You don't have to put your wanderlust away for another day, just take advantage of off-season deals, such as the following.

- **Cruises:** Sail at half price when cruise lines move their ships from the Mediterranean to the Caribbean (September and October).

- **The Big Apple:** Half-price theater tickets and relatively cheap hotel rooms are easier to find when New Yorkers are summering at the Hamptons (August).

- **Florida:** Bienvenito à Miami for a whole lot less in the autumn (October to December).

- **Australia, New Zealand and the Far East:** It's wintertime there, but a fine time to avoid the crowds (June through September).

If you're looking for the best airfares, check out *Best Fares* magazine (800-880-1234), where access to hundreds of discounts cost $59.90 per year. Or browse www.bestfares.com for constantly changing "Snooze you lose" information.

---

money that you can blow your plan in a second. Having your ATM card at the ready is like holding out chocolate cake to a chocoholic . . . you just can't resist. If you must use the evil card, instead of making frequent trips, limit your access to one trip per week, take out only what your preset budget will allow, and make that money last.

3. **But it was on sale.** I remember my mother coming home with us after a full day of shopping. Laden with purchases, she announced to my father that she had saved a ton of money. His reply? "You would have saved more if you hadn't bought any of it." Now, no one's saying you can't do a little recreational shopping, but why not avoid the impulse purchases? Make a list of things you'd like to have but don't need, and buy them when they go on sale. When you get them on sale, write down their original price and what you've saved. Add half the savings to your investment account. (You still need a little something for your next sale, right?) The real key to saving money here is to avoid buying anything that isn't on your list.

4. **Pay now, buy later.** In case the buying list sounded too good to be true, you need to wait until you have the money *before* you buy. That's right. Don't whip out your credit card until you know you can pay it

off. Some people solve this problem by paying cash (you know, that funny-looking green stuff) instead of using credit cards. But if you aren't ready for the life of the ascetic, we won't force you . . . yet.

5. **The art of the deal.** Face it, if you were born to shop, you cannot and probably will not change who you are. The key here is to make your eye for the deal work for you, not against you. If you're a Christmas junkie, set a maximum amount that you can spend, and shop after the holiday for next year's cards, wrapping and ornaments. And be wary of buying mammoth sizes of perishable products. Part of that huge can of tuna may go to waste when you can't face another tuna noodle casserole. (Maybe that's why mammoths are extinct.)

6. **Time is money.** In addition to the basic necessities of life, like housing, utilities and other fixed expenses, your list of essentials may include items like gardener, housekeeper or baby-sitter. Could you do without these services? Probably. Should you? This comes down to the question, What is your time worth? In some cases, it may actually be a question of what your sanity is worth. While you could possibly earn more money (there's always that trip to your boss's office, or to your own office if you're the boss), time lost is gone forever. If you hate cleaning the toilet or mowing the lawn, why spend time doing it? Instead, to save money on these items, consider having them done less frequently.

7. **Interest-free loans to Uncle Sam.** Expecting a tax refund? Congratulations! You're doing Uncle Sam a big favor . . . giving him an interest-free loan, and you didn't even get a thank-you note! Make that money work for you by checking your W-2 form and changing your withholding to the correct number of deductions. At tax time, many experts say it is better to pay a small amount than to get a big

And Your Goals Will Set You Free

If you're too busy looking at the sidewalk, you'll miss all the scenery. Managing your money is like that: If you wait to pay off all your bills before you start saving for your goal, you may never reach them. Instead, consider putting some money toward your goals *first*. Then make sure the rent and utilities are paid, the food is bought and the bills brought up to date. Buy fewer new clothes or cook whatever is on sale, but pay yourself first.

refund. To avoid penalties, be sure you pay at least what was withheld the prior year, and consult a tax advisor before you make any changes.

8. **Sock it to your retirement account.** Take advantage of any retirement plan offered by your employer. By participating in qualified retirement plans, contributions may be tax-deductible up to certain annual maximum limits (consult your plan administrator for more information), and some employers match a portion of their employee's contributions. Your savings grow without being taxed until you take the money out at retirement (a procedure known as "tax deferred"), making these accounts especially efficient. Not covered by an employer's plan? See Days 39 and 40 for details on retirement plans.

> **Smart Stretch**
> Stop junk mail before it starts. To have your name removed from mailing lists, write to the Mail Preference Service, Direct Marketing Association, P.O. Box 9008, Farmingdale, NY 11735-9880. Include the different spellings of your name that are used in junk mail solicitations. To limit the number of telephone solicitations received, write to the Telephone Preference Service, Direct Marketing Association, P.O. Box 9014, Farmingdale, NY 11735-9014.

9. **Junk that junk mail.** You've made the commitment and have stopped spending weekends at the mall—but that's only half the battle. It's nearly impossible to ignore those tempting offers that come almost daily in the mail. Oh, the agony . . . only an ogre would deny you that precious Gorgonzola knife, the stainless steel fondue pot, those pleated microfiber golf pants with the matching Greg Norman shark hat— especially when it's all on sale. Get rid of temptation by tossing that junk mail before you open it.

10. **Pay yourself.** Finished making all the payments on your car, revolving credit line, whatever? Don't stop making them—just make them to yourself. Have a mutual fund or stock investment program draft the same amount of money from your bank account. You won't miss it, and you'll be one step ahead.

At first, defining your budget sounds ugly, scary and complex. It doesn't have to be! Here are four ways to make it easier:

1. Establish specific, achievable goals. (For example: "Save $2,000 for the down payment on a car by next summer.")

2. Figure out how much you're spending each month.

3. Reconcile your net income with what you're spending. If you come up with a negative number, it's time to cut down on a few expenses.

4. Continue to write down all your "outgo" . . . you'll be amazed at how those small amounts add up!

Whew! How was that for a warm-up? While your juices are flowing, turn to today's section of the workbook and learn how to stretch a dollar even further.

Tame It
Or Toss It

Getting organized

> "For the first 25 years of my life, I wanted freedom. For the next 25 years of my life, I wanted order. For the next 25 years of my life, I realized that order is freedom."
> —Winston Churchill

One day during my first year as a financial advisor, I was "broker of the day." As such, new clients who walked or called in were assigned to me. Just before lunch, the receptionist called me to the front to meet a disheveled older man carrying a shoebox tied with a frayed piece of string. Apologetically, he asked me if I could help him. "I need to get some money," he explained. "My daddy needs to go to the doctor. He sent me here with these papers. Are they worth anything?"

We went back to my cubbyhole to sort through the documents, amidst the sidelong glances of other brokers. In the box were papers all right . . . hundreds of shares of blue-chip stocks, government and municipal bonds, and zero-coupon securities. My shock must have been apparent, but it was

Healthy Habit

If you can't seem to part with your newspaper clippings collection, get a scanner and store them in your computer. To save space on your hard drive, download files to disks.

also misinterpreted. "I just knew it," he sighed. "It's not worth anything, is it?" "Are there any more where these came from?" I asked. "Why, yes," he said. "There's a whole bunch under my daddy's bed." Not only could my new client take his daddy to the doctor, he could have bought the hospital!

Not everyone has a wheelbarrow full of old stock certificates hidden under their beds. But let's face it: People put money in curious places, and I don't mean in the secret drawer of your grandma's rolltop desk, those hollowed-out bug-spray containers, or the swiveling bookshelf that reveals a secret compartment when you look cross-eyed at the portrait of Great-Aunt Agatha. You could check out every coin-operated phone in the airport, shake out all your pocketbooks and go through the pockets of your jeans, but you'll probably come up with more lint than dough. Effective investing starts with organization, so get ready to clean out those drawers, sort through those piles and root around in your files.

Systems Check

"An organized desk is the mark of a sick mind," or so the card says. Who am I to question the wisdom of Hallmark? But if your desk, office and file cabinets are organized in a way that only Pandora could love, it's a fair bet that you're losing money and wasting time. With a little effort, you could put a system in place that could actually save you time (I figure at least 84 hours per year)—and time, as we all know, is money.

If you need a personal trainer to dig you out of your closet, find that proposal you're sure you sent last week, or compile those receipts you need for next week's audit, take some advice from Agatha Christie's famous detective, Hercule Poirot: "Touch nothing"—more than once, that is! If you want to whip your desk into shape, make a decision about each piece of paper that crosses your desk the *first* time it comes along.

Organizational experts suggest that you toss it, delegate it or save it. But how you decide depends on your personality. Organizational specialist Rebecca Rhodes, president of Carolina Training Consultants, a company that specializes in all types of corporate and individual training, is convinced that people follow patterns learned over the years, patterns that are very hard to break. Some people place incoming information in files. Others stack it in neat piles. Some spread it all over their desk, office, home, car . . . you name it.

What's a poor slob to do? If you don't want to change or don't want to spend the time and energy, you can hire someone to organize you. An expert can set up a system compatible with your personality, then come in periodically to maintain it. Surprisingly, this method is quite cost effective (remember those 84 hours?).

No matter who gets you organized, following are a few financial necessities that must be dealt with.

I'm From The IRS, And I'm Here To Help You

Your friendly neighborhood IRS agent is probably not the person you'd want to have organizing your files and office. To beat them to the punch, not to mention to save money on your taxes, you've got to take control of your receipts. It's scary to think of all the money that slips through your fingers because you can't remember where you spent it.

To begin with, keep receipts in one place—in your organizer, wallet, briefcase or purse; then file them as soon as you reach your home or office. For business entertainment expenses, on the back of each receipt, write:

- whom you entertained and your business affiliation;

- the date you were with them;

- the business purpose;

- the total amount spent; and

- where the event took place.

If you can deduct your car as a business expense, keep a small diary in the car to record every business trip and the

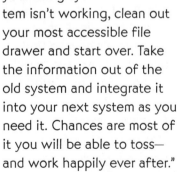

Trainer's Tip

"Don't waste time organizing information you will never use. If your filing system isn't working, clean out your most accessible file drawer and start over. Take the information out of the old system and integrate it into your next system as you need it. Chances are most of it you will be able to toss—and work happily ever after."

—*Barbara Hemphill, author of* Taming the Paper Tiger: The Painless Way to Manage Paper mileage. This record is required if you take your automobile as a deduction.

Keep track of any self-employment expenses in a separate file. Also keep track of any self-employment income, whether you receive a 1099 form or not. Employers are not required to send a 1099 form to anyone who earns less than $600 per year, but they may report your earnings to the IRS. If you haven't included these amounts in your reported income, you could be subject to additional taxes and penalties.

Since 1995, charitable donations must also be substantiated by a receipt. A canceled check is no longer sufficient, no matter how pure your heart or sanctimonious your gift. Make a separate file for these receipts, too.

How long should you keep your receipts and tax returns? Many preparers suggest keeping receipts and backup records for at least three years. In the case of fraud, though, all bets are off, and the IRS can go back as far as it sees fit. It wouldn't hurt to keep tax records indefinitely in case you ever need them. If you lose a tax return, the IRS can (usually) replace it for a nominal fee.

Which Way To Your IRA?

Smart Stretch

Every year, people move and leave behind phone deposits or small bank accounts. This unclaimed property amounts to billions of dollars. Here's how to find money you may have "mislaid": For a free brochure, *Unclaimed Property Information*, send a self-addressed, stamped business-sized envelope to Division of State Lands, 775 Summer St. NE, Salem, OR 97310. Or search online at www.intersurf.com/~naupa.

Do you have individual retirement accounts at every bank and brokerage firm in town? This is not a good way to diversify your money, and it can interfere with your investments' performance. Many firms charge annual maintenance fees that range from $10 to $50 for accounts that are inactive or under a certain size.

Transferring assets directly between institutions is not a taxable event and may actually make your money perform better. How? If you know where all your money is, you can allocate it properly among stocks, bonds and other investments. Monitoring it will be easier, and changes can be made quickly in response to market shifts. And when you begin to draw funds out at retirement, having just one account can simplify things immeasurably.

If for no other reason, consider consolidation to cut down on all the statements you've been losing . . . oops, I mean filing. Save a tree.

Before making your consolidation decision, however, keep in mind that transferring money may involve transfer expenses, setup fees and other transaction costs. Also, when consolidating, be sure that your account value is below that institution's maximum insured amount. For example, bank accounts are insured up to $100,000. Some brokerage accounts carry federally backed insurance on up to $100,000 cash and $400,000 in securities.

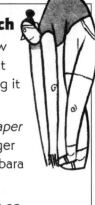

Smart Stretch

Want to know more? Two great books on getting it all together:

- *Taming the Paper Tiger* (Kiplinger Books) by Barbara Hemphill

- *Two Weeks to an Organized Life* (Dell Publishing) by Lucy Hedrick

It's 10 O'clock. Do You Know Where Your Assets Are?

OK, admit it: If you died right now, your heirs would have to hold a séance to figure out where everything is. Your executor should be a master with paperwork, not a master sleuth! Don't hide the key to your safe deposit box in an old coffee can 40 paces due north of the backyard oak tree. By the time your heirs need it, the tree may have been cut down and part of your treasure map may be lost. Unless Robert Louis Stevenson is your executor, put a labeled key in a drawer, file or box where your executor can find it when the inevitable occurs.

In your safe deposit box, keep:

- Certificates for stocks, bonds or other securities if you feel you must hold them in your own name. (These can be expensive and time-consuming to replace, so don't lose them!)

- A list of your brokerage, retirement, bank and annuity accounts, with account numbers, phone numbers and a contact person, if any.

- Confirmations from your brokerage firm that show you have purchased any U.S. Treasury, corporate or municipal securities. Since most recent issues of debt securities are "book entry," meaning they exist only in a computer, your confirmations will help if you ever need to prove ownership.

- A list of all money owed to you, including outstanding personal loans, rents and business loans. (Don't worry too much about money owed by you. If fire destroys your mortgage, credit cards or car loan contract, your creditors will replace them, never fear!)

- The deed to your house; passport; birth certificate; adoption papers; Social Security card; all documents related to marriage, separation or divorce; licenses; military service records; citizenship papers; and important family health records—in short, anything that proves who you are and where you came from.

- Life insurance policies.

- Gold, silver or platinum bars or coins; these can melt in a fire. Most homeowner's insurance policies will pay up to $250 for all currency that

Lift Those Papers

To get your incoming financial mail flow under control, try this exercise:

1. Commandeer several hanging file folders and a box big enough to hold them all.

2. Toss all junk mail immediately.

3. Open all bills and write their due dates on the envelopes. Place them all in a file labeled "To Be Paid" that you go through weekly, paying those that are due the following week.

4. Place all financial-related materials in a file marked "Money Makers" as they come in.

5. Take your money file and this book to a quiet place whenever you have downtime. Rip out investment articles that look interesting and stick them into the appropriate chapter.

6. Keep this book and your additions with you to read as you stand in line at the grocery store, wait for your child to come up to bat or hang out on hold for a client.

7. Make notes in the margins of this book or in your workbook. This is a great way to make the most of your time and really personal-ize your investment knowledge.

8. After you've read something, either take notes on it and toss it or just toss it. You have the knowledge, so heave-ho.

9. Make files for other topics and information that you want to keep track of, culling through periodically and tossing what you haven't used.

is lost, stolen or destroyed. This may not even cover that one Confederate coin Great-Uncle Elmer gave you.

- Expensive jewelry you don't wear often.
- Sterling silver flatware.
- A copy of your will, power of attorney and any trust documents.
- Pictures and records of the contents of your home. That way, if your home burns down or is burglarized, you won't have to compile a list from memory.
- Certificates of authenticity and appraisals on artwork.

You may decide that keeping all this in a safe deposit box means too huge a box or too much hassle. A fireproof in-home safe is another increasingly popular solution. In the long run, however, these may prove as expensive and sometimes more difficult to access in the case of a fire, hurricane, tornado, earthquake or flood. If you go the safe route, make sure a copy of the combination and an extra set of keys are in a different location (such as in a safe deposit box).

You Can Bank On It

What do you do with all those canceled checks? Some people weed through them, saving only those they think they'll need; others keep them all. As president of "Pack Rats Anonymous," I vote for the latter solution. After all, you never know when a canceled check could come in handy:

- You say you've paid a bill; they say you didn't.
- Your ex-spouse says you missed an alimony-child-support payment.
- You are audited by the IRS (canceled checks can sometimes be substituted for receipts).
- If you sell your house or a second home for a profit, some kinds of improvements can cut the size of your capital gain or increase the size of a deductible loss.
- To collect in full on insurance claims, it's helpful to be able to prove what you paid for it (your cost basis).

For the slovenly among us, getting organized seems like hard penance. If you're tired of having St. Anthony as both your personal trainer and patron saint, you, too, can experience the miracle of finding what you're looking for without a legion of angels. Remember those 84 hours you just saved? You can put them to better use praying for the stock market to go up.

Charge Of The Not-So-Light Brigade

Managing your credit

> "Credit is what enables people to spend money they don't have, to buy things they don't need, to impress people they don't like."
> —Joey Adams, columnist for the New York Post

Brenda and Bob got rich the hard way—through a lawsuit settlement. Bob had been injured so severely on the job that he could never work again. Things rapidly progressed from bad to worse, and soon he and Brenda went from working poor to indigent. Their attorney was sure that if they could wait six months, he could double their award through a jury trial. Poverty didn't allow this "luxury," and they settled out of court for $1.25 million.

Their needs were simple: a house for themselves, cars for themselves and their son, and a condo for their son to live in while at school. With these purchases paid for with cash, their monthly income needs would be small: no more than $3,000 per month. The remainder of the money would be invested to pay for future medical bills and a comfortable life. No problem. Enter credit cards.

Flush with their newfound wealth, Brenda and Bob started to spend, first a little, then a little more, then a lot more each month. Cautions, warnings, even threats didn't stop them. After 18 months, they had spent everything they owned, borrowed against their house, and were, once again, dirt poor. So much for credit cards.

Not everyone is awash in debt, but it doesn't take long to work up a powerful appetite for shopping. Like any addiction, you've got to nip it in the bud, Bud. Making the most of consumer credit is a vital part of financial fitness, and if used correctly, it can help you reach your financial goals. So get ready for some crunching—of your credit, that is.

Taking Credit

Credit is a thing of beauty and a joy forever. And forever may be how long it feels like it could take you to get rid of your credit card balances. But credit is a lot more than Visa, MasterCard and American Express . . . there's another whole world to Discover, if you will. Credit allows you to buy a house, redecorate the living room with no money down and 12 months to pay, and drive off in a new Lexus with 0.9 percent financing. As Popeye's friend Blimpie might have put it, credit allows you to gladly pay tomorrow for a hamburger today.

Getting credit can be deceptively easy: You sign up for a credit card, and off you go. As you buy and pay off your credit cards, your car loan, your mortgage, you develop a credit profile, known as a credit rating. The more assiduous you are in making payments, the better your credit rating will be. The better your credit rating, the more credit you can assume. Credit ratings are not necessarily connected to your level of income, but to your pattern of consistently paying bills on time.

Despite the pile of offers you might receive from credit card issuers, without a

Smart Stretch

Search this database for the best deals on credit cards: www. bankrate.com.

credit history, getting that first credit card can be impossible—no credit history, no credit card; no credit card, no credit history. To break this classic Catch-22, open a checking and savings account and get a revolving charge account from a large retail establishment. Make some small purchases for which you could easily pay cash, and pay them off promptly.

In a few months, apply to your bank for a credit card. Again, keep purchase amounts small and pay them off promptly. Now take out a small loan that you really don't need. (If this sounds illogical, that's because it is: Lenders seem to only want to lend to people who don't need the money. Once you've proved that you're part of this group, the world can become your credit oyster.) Pay the loan off early, and *voilà*, a credit rating, and a good one at that.

Even if you've declared bankruptcy, credit is often available through a secured credit card. Designed for people with bad credit or no credit history, these cards require a deposit, from 500 to several thousand dollars. If you don't make your payments, the issuer can use your deposit to pay your bill. Annual fees and interest rates are high, but you can establish a payment history that will show you're serious about improving your credit.

Once you get a credit rating, to make good use of it, be careful about how you use it. Your mother was right—don't play with matches, and don't mess around with your credit rating. If you thought getting a good credit rating was tough, repairing a bad one is twice as hard.

Trainer's Tip

"Whenever you apply for credit, immediately they check your credit rating. One sign of a bad credit rating is lots of third-party checks on it. So if you apply for lots of cards, your credit rating will look bad. Don't bounce from card to card."

—Pete Hisey, Editor,
Credit Card News

A Loan Again? Naturally

Credit cards aren't the only loan in town. Obviously, you wouldn't buy a house on your credit card. Loans come in two flavors: secured and unsecured. Secured loans are backed by collateral, like the mortgage backed by your house. Credit cards are examples of unsecured loans, as they are backed exclusively by your promise to pay. Secured loans have lower rates than unsecured loans because the risk to the lender is less. The bank can repossess your house and sell it to someone else, but who's going to want your used washer and old sneakers?

Money is available from various institutions, including commercial banks, savings and loans, and credit unions. Two lending options should be avoided at all costs: finance companies and pawnshops. Finance companies are probably the most expensive of traditional lenders because they cater to those with bad or nonexistent credit. Pawnshops pay very little for your treasures and have very quick repayment requirements; if you can't pay, your item can be sold to repay the broker. If at all possible, avoid these two options.

If you own a home or have a portfolio of securities, these assets can be used as collateral for a secured loan. Home equity loans, which allow you to borrow against the value of your home, and margin accounts, which allow you to borrow against the value of your portfolio, can provide larger sums of money than credit cards, and at lower rates. In some cases, interest on these types of loans is tax deductible; consult your tax advisor for more information. Borrowing from these sources can be easy, but if you borrow too much or can't afford to make your payments, you could lose your house or your portfolio. Never borrow more than you can pay back within 12 months.

> **Healthy Habit**
>
> Pay off your credit cards faster by paying more than the minimum required amount. Make a deal with yourself to pay off anything that's gone at the end of the month, including food, entertaining, gifts, vacations, and so on. This will help keep your balance in line.

It's All In The Cards

If you've been charging like the Light Brigade, get ready for some changes in the credit-card industry—and not all of them are good news for those who shop till they drop. Issuers will approve fewer cards for those applying for their most attractive rates; introductory, or "teaser," rates will edge up from an average of 9 percent to 10 percent; and solicitations to those with marginal credit records will fall dramatically. Those who pay bills late or not at all will see some issuers lowering their credit lines; other issuers will punish these accounts with high interest rates, reduced grace periods and higher late fees.

Having too many credit cards can be dangerous to your financial health. Too many open lines of credit can impair your ability to apply for the best rates and could cause some issuers to declare you a high-risk account and charge you a much higher interest rate. If low mortgage rates are tempting you to refinance your home, excessive credit lines can stymie your application. As a rule of thumb, avoid owing more than 20 percent of your gross income on credit cards, and keep your total available credit under 35 percent of your gross income.

Even if you've forgotten what cash looks like and hoard your frequent-flier miles like a miser, you don't have to give up your card collection. Following are some strategies you can't afford to pass up.

Card Sharps

The trick to getting the most from your credit cards is to select the ones that are right for how you spend, pay and keep track of your purchases. If you have an impeccable credit history, a low total outstanding

Are You Credit Card Savvy?

Follow this flowchart, and see if you're using the right credit cards.

| Do you have impeccable credit history, low total outstanding debt and keep a balance each month? | Do you pay your balance in full each month? |

| You should have low-rate credit cards (below 15 percent and *not* teaser rates) and no rebate cards! | You should ignore interest rates and go for no-annual-fee cards and rebate cards. |

| Make sure you never owe more than 20 percent of your gross income. | Make sure your total credit line on all cards is under 50 percent of your gross income. |

| Call and ask for details about penalty interest. | Make sure there is at least a 25 day grace period from the moment you make a purchase. |

debt and consistently small balances on your accounts, consider low-rate credit cards. They offer limited services and below-average credit lines, but you can expect to pay one-third to one-half the average interest rate. If you pay your balance in full each month, your card's interest rate doesn't matter. Choose a card with no annual fee or one with rebates.

"I can get it for you wholesale" is the battle cry of the shopper's republic—and "I can get it for you free" is even better. Cardholder rebates started in the 1980s with the introduction of airline credit cards and the creation of Discover card's cash-back program. Rebate cards come in many varieties. In addition to airline mileage cards, there are telephone company calling cards, automobile rebate cards, gasoline rebate cards, grocery rebate cards, investment or savings rebate cards and more. The key is finding the best deal.

Smart Stretch

For more information on managing credit, check out these resources:

- *Downsize Your Debt* (Penguin Books) by Andrew Feinberg
- *Money Troubles: Legal Strategies to Cope With Your Debts* (Nolo Books) by Robin Leonard
- *Invest in Yourself: Six Secrets to a Rich Life* (John Wiley & Sons) by Marc Eisenson, Gerri Detweiler and Nancy Castleman

First, select a card with rebates on something you really use; then compare the interest rate and annual fees to other cards you carry or that are available. Rebate cards can really pay off as long as you pay the bill in full each month. On the other hand, if you carry a balance of more than $3,000, you'll almost always be better off finding the lowest-rate card available. Paying an 18 percent interest rate on a rebate card that earns a 1 percent cash-back bonus is no bargain compared to paying a 12 percent rate with no cash-back program.

If you carry a balance, you can still benefit from a rebate program by transferring the balance each month to a low-rate card or credit line. This can help you avoid interest rates of 17 percent or more on some rebate cards. With so many cards to choose from, this is easier than it sounds. But keep track of when you switched; if you stick with a card for too long, you may end up paying an even higher rate on your balance than before you switched.

Make the most of your rebate cards by limiting their number to one or two. Some gas cards give a maximum rebate annually. When you've reached it, stop using the card. And some frequent-flier programs have expiration dates you need to be aware of. Check these fine points before you sign up for a card.

If your wallet is lost or stolen, don't panic. If you notify card issuers within 48 hours of your loss, in most cases you'll only be liable for $50. Can't figure out which cards disappeared? Make copies of all cards, front and back, and keep them with your important papers. Write the phone contact next to each card's image so you'll know who to call in an emergency. In case you lose this, better make two copies. . . .

Pandora's Box

Before jumping ship to a new card, beware the offer that sounds too good to be true. Study the lowly disclosure box that appears on the back of every credit-card application. If any of the following conditions fly out of that box, put a lid on that offer—fast!

- **Penalty interest.** If you fail to meet the requirements of the account (by exceeding the credit limit or making late payments, for example), your interest rate can rise, sometimes to as high as 30 percent. Credit card issuers don't have to spell out when these rates go into effect, so before you sign up, call and ask about potential penalties.

- **High annual fees.** There are so many low-fee and no-fee cards out there, why pay through the nose?

Keep Your Head Above Water

How do you know when you've got too much debt?

- You can't seem to make any headway with your bills.
- You're losing sleep worrying about where the money will come from.
- You need a second job to pay your bills.
- You can't make your minimum payments or can make only the minimum payments.
- You don't know how much you owe.
- You can't afford to pay cash for anything.
- You're at the limits on your cards.
- Your payments are always late or you're missing payments.

- **Little or no grace period.** If your card doesn't have a grace period, you'll start paying interest the day you make a purchase.

- **Balance transfer restrictions.** Some cards limit the amount you can transfer from one card to another. Others set a "teaser rate" at a low interest level for the first six months or year you have the card. Watch out when this rate expires.

- **Cash-advance terms.** Cards may charge higher interest rates for cash advances; find out before borrowing.

Healthy Habit

To check up on your credit, request a copy of your credit report from one of these reporting companies:

- Experian: (800) 682-7654
- Equifax: (800) 685-1111
- Trans Union: (800) 916-8800

Give Yourself Some Credit

Whether you charge a lot or a little, credit can be your friend, as long as you keep up your end of the bargain. To stay on friendly terms, make sure you always use less credit than you can afford, make payments promptly, keep track of what you owe, don't exaggerate when applying for credit, and if you should have a problem and are not able to make payments, notify your creditors immediately.

Of course, no one is perfect, and sometimes your outgo may exceed your income. If you're carrying huge balances on your credit cards at high interest rates and have run out of cards to switch to and money to pay with, seek credit counseling. You'll learn how to budget and pay off your debt. Based on your needs and income, the service will interact with your creditors and establish a payment schedule. You pay the service, and they pay your bills. Nonprofit services are available through the Consumer Credit Counseling Service at (800) 388-2227.

Avoid debt-consolidation loans if possible. Unlike counseling services, this is a very expensive route to take. If you've gone beyond all help and nothing is working, bankruptcy is the last resort. Pick up *How to File for Bankruptcy* (Nolo Books) by Stephen Elias.

Don't let your bills get you down. Just because you may not be solidly in the black doesn't mean you will never be. When you're about to make a purchase, stop for a few seconds to figure out why you're buying whatever you're buying. Are you shopping because you're depressed? Bored?

Celebrating? There's nothing wrong with any of these reasons as long as you're aware of why you're doing what you're doing. Some people say that the way to start respecting your money is to treat it nicely, facing all bills the same way and placing them neatly in your wallet. I don't care whether your money is folded or wrinkled, or whether you place it lovingly in your wallet or shove it in . . . just as long as you leave it there.

DAY 5

Home Workout

The key to home mortgages

Maya is smart, savvy and single, a senior vice president for a multinational firm and a person who is probably the definition of "nobody's fool." So how did she get rooked out of $20,000 on a house deal that went bad?

Enter the house of her dreams, a turn-of-the-century (dilapidated) charming (filled with asbestos and radon) center-hall colonial (leaking roof, chipping lead paint . . . you get the picture). Nonetheless, she saw the potential and put down a very large earnest money deposit—vital, her realtor assured her, because another person was interested in the property (funny, no one had been interested during the previous six months it had been on the market). Thinking smart, Maya noted in the contract that the purchase was contingent upon the house passing inspection and that repairs would total no more than $5,000.

Sure enough, two inspections and three contractors later, the news was in: The minimum cost to make required repairs ranged from

$10,000 to more than $25,000. Deal over, earnest money returned, right? Wrong. The sellers, two attorneys in the middle of a nasty divorce, decided that repairs could be done for less than $5,000. After threatening litigation, they kept the earnest money and sold the house out from under her for more than Maya had offered. Maya got her own lawyer, but the jury is still out. Judge Wapner, where are you?

Never fear—not everyone makes a huge gaff when buying a home, but having bought a few, I've made my share of stupid mistakes. Fortunately, you don't have to repeat my errors. Today we'll spend the day away from the gym and concentrate on a home workout.

Homeward Bound

Whether you're ensconced in Scarsdale or housed in Houston, your home is your castle, and for many people, it represents their largest investment. Whether you're buying your first home, trading up to a bigger place or making plans for a little hideaway at the beach, you'll find it's quite a workout—and it pays to have the right form.

Everyone wants to buy a house, right? It's kind of like a chicken in every pot, a truly American institution. No one would want to rent when they could own . . . or would they? Deciding which way to go is your first step. Renting has its own rewards. If you don't plan to stay in the house for more than four years, you may not have a chance to recoup the closing costs. If interest rates are high, it may be cheaper to rent than to buy. If liquidity is a problem or you've got a bad credit rating, getting a mortgage may be out of the question (but you can fix that . . . take another look at Day 4). You may not want to deplete your savings on a down payment, you may be in a lower tax bracket (making the tax incentives of a mortgage less enticing) or you may be unable to afford the continual maintenance that a house requires. (They don't call it a money pit for nothing.) Finally, some markets may be so hot that even the worst properties are selling for a fortune. You may decide it's better to rent now and buy later.

Smart Stretch

Check these sources for more information:

- *Home Buying for Dummies* (IDG Books Worldwide) by Eric Tyson and Ray Brown

- *How to Buy a House, Condo or Co-op* (Consumer Reports Books) by Michael C. Thomsett

Isn't It A PITI

If you decide to buy a home of any kind, one key to success is to be realistic. True, houses can provide status, privacy, tax advantages and an investment that could appreciate over time, but finding the perfect situation is more difficult than finding the perfect gym—and locating your home sweet home is only the beginning.

Before you start perusing the local real estate section, figure out how much home you can afford. There's no sense in looking at $400,000 houses when the most you can afford is $250,000. Don't know what you can afford? Never fear, banks and savings and loans have very strict lending rules on how much of your gross income can be dedicated to PITI, or principal, interest, taxes and insurance.

To get a thumbnail sketch of what kind of monthly payments a lending institution might believe you can afford, here's how to figure it: First, any debt that you must carry for longer than 10 months goes against you. This includes car loans, revolving credit and other long-term obligations. For conforming loans, those less than about $250,000, lenders use a PITI ratio of 28/36: No more than 28 percent of your monthly gross income can go to PITI, and no more than 36 percent can be spent on PITI plus any other debts that take longer than ten months to pay, including debts like car and student loans. Nonconforming loans, like jumbos used by well-heeled clients or loans on unique properties, may have a PITI ratio of 33/38, depending on the client's credit history, additional assets or relationship with the lender.

Smart Stretch

Real estate commissions are fixed, right? Maybe not: You could get a rebate on your purchase or sale. Some real estate companies have referral relationships with insurance carriers, credit unions or other membership organizations, offering a rebate to buyers or sellers who are members of or who use their affiliates. Also try America's Realty ReferralNet (www. clnet.com.arrdft.htm), a service that offers rebates of several hundred dollars to buyers and sellers.

Mr. Smith Builds His Dream House

What's your dream house? You may not be building a new structure, but before you waste a lot of your time and your realtor's, decide on your priorities. Do you have school-aged children? If so, check for playgrounds, schools and traffic patterns. Would you like a shorter commute to work or easier access to mass transit? A walk or short drive to shopping or houses of worship? Do you want to entertain more or do you dream of a vegetable or flower garden? Do you need lots of closets? Bathrooms? Bedrooms? A pool?

Finally, what style of house do you prefer? If you'd prefer a century-old stucco mansion with a copper tile roof, looking at a contemporary ranch or an English Tudor will get you nowhere. Experts suggest making a list of seven to 10 priorities and looking only at houses that have most of them. Thinking of a fixer-upper? A grand idea, provided you can do the fixing up or you have oodles of money to throw to someone who can. (Stay away from those copper roofs, trust me.)

Most people can afford one thing but desire another. If you find the house that makes your heart beat fast, don't give up too easily. Maybe the house is worth home manicures and pedicures, washing the dog yourself or eating out only twice a month instead of twice a week. Whatever you do, never plan to use your savings to make the mortgage payments. Avoid becoming so house-poor that you have to scrimp on savings. If possible, consider making a larger down payment to lower your monthly expenses.

Get Your House In Order

Once you've found the house you'd like to buy, the next step is to, well, buy it. Not so easy. When I bought my first house 15 years ago, the contract was a brief two pages. Last summer our contract dragged on for seven pages . . . of small print. Prior to delivering your John Hancock, read the contract carefully. Remember that most contracts were written by the selling agency (not your ally) or a state or local association (not your foe, but not necessarily your ally, either), and that with the exception of some standard phrases, most contracts can be amended.

For starters, make sure the names of buyer and seller are correct, and check the description of the property and the financing details. Insist on a home-inspection clause stipulating that if the inspection report is not approved by the buyer, the contract may be canceled and the earnest money returned immediately. Unless you can afford to pay cash for your house, add a financing contingency clause that gives the rate at which you intend to finance your loan and the time in which you intend to find financing. If a mortgage can't be found, this can often be another out for the buyer.

Interested in keeping the refrigerator, carpets or window treatments? Say so in the contract. Unless you're really in a buyer's market, avoid making a contract contingent on selling your current residence. Most sellers do not look kindly on this type of contingency. Before you sign on the dotted line, consider paying a real estate attorney to review the contract and make recommendations.

Wait a minute, you might be saying, didn't Maya do all these things? You bet, but just because someone signs a contract doesn't mean they will honor it. There are all kinds of creeps in the world, and you may run into one of them.

Home Sweet Home Inspector

You know how important a home inspector is, but how do you find the best one? Evan Grugett, president of home-inspection firm Evan Grugett Associates, offers these tips:

- Select an experienced, independent, professional home inspector, not someone who will also offer to make the necessary repairs on the home. Look for membership in the American Society of Home Inspectors (ASHI). Members must have completed no fewer than 250 fee-paid inspections using ASHI standards and passed written examinations.

- Determine what is and is not covered by the inspection and how long it should take.

- Ask what kind of report you will receive. A combination narrative and checklist is best. The report should be very specific to your house. Do not accept a boilerplate report.

- Accompany the home inspector on the inspection. This is essential! A veteran home inspector will tell you a lot about the house.

Re Fi? Ho-Hum

If you already have a home but are paying high interest or you're thinking of moving up to the house of your dreams, low mortgage rates can give you some options. Some people are refinancing junkies. They move from lender to lender, rate to rate, in search of mortgage nirvana—the lowest possible rate on the perfect loan. This is all well and good if that's how you like to spend an afternoon (or two or three), but even if refinancing isn't your idea of an Olympic sport, if your objective is to lower your mortgage payments or pay off your loan faster, refinancing can help.

But don't plan a visit to your lender just yet: Refinancing costs cut into your savings. Orientation fees (typically 1 percent of the mortgage amount), appraisal costs, attorneys' fees, underwriting fees, tax service fees, surveys, discount points, credit reports, application fees, title insurance, document preparation and other miscellaneous fees that vary from state to state can make breaking even a far-off goal. So before you begin compiling the collection of tax returns, bank statements and credit references needed to refinance, be sure you'll actually save money.

Experts have varying opinions on when it makes sense to refinance. If you'll be in the house a long time, though, it could be worth it. To figure out the number of months it will take to recoup your costs, divide your monthly savings into the total closing costs. For example, if you hold a $100,000 30-year mortgage at 8 percent, your payments are about $733 per month. Refinancing at 7 percent would drop your monthly payment to about $665, saving you $68 per month. If your closing costs came to $2,200, it would take 32 months for you to recoup the cost of refinancing—a smart move if you plan to stay in your house longer than that.

Another reason to refinance is to shorten the length of your loan. If you can make the higher payments, in the long run you could save big. Here's an example: If you have a $100,000 30-year mortgage at 9 percent, your monthly payments are $804. If you stay in the house for the term of the loan, the house will cost you $289,664. If you refinance and get a shorter, $100,000 15-year mortgage at 7¾ percent, your monthly payments go up to $941. If you stay in the house for the term of the loan, however, you will pay $164,429. The moral of the story? If you can afford the higher payment, you could save $125,235. With results that good, you could almost buy yourself another house!

Let's Make A Deal

You've decided refinancing will save you a bundle in the long term, so who ya gonna call? All your friends are talking about how they just got the world's best interest rate; newspapers and TV ads are hawking fabulously low rates, with loan applications taken over the phone and approval in just an hour. You can't get your dry cleaning done that fast.

It's tempting to start your search with the lowest advertised rate, but real bargains begin at home with your current lender. "It's not necessarily the interest rate that makes refinancing attractive, but the additional costs that do—or, preferably, don't—go along with it," cautions Jim DeMare, loan officer at Market Street Mortgage Corp. "A super-low rate can take a lot of your equity if it involves high costs that are included in your new loan. If the rate offered by your current lender is attractive, you may save on closing costs, appraisals, title insurance and the like."

If your lender can't or won't compete for your business, it's time to enter the refinancing zone. Talking with bank loan officers can lead to a great deal. Banks sometimes lower their rates to get a chance at a new customer's future business, including auto loans, lines of credit, credit cards, checking and savings accounts and business accounts.

Mortgage bankers offer deals that they finance themselves; mortgage brokers, on the other hand, act as middlemen between you and the lender. If your application fails at one lender, mortgage brokers can try others with whom they have a relationship. If your credit report is spotty, this may be your best choice. Some mortgage brokers also act as mortgage bankers, able to bid your loan out or take it on themselves.

> **Trainer's Tip**
>
> Edward Dixon, public affairs officer at Citibank, suggests as a rule that consumers not consider refinancing if there is less than a 2 percent difference between the old and the new mortgage rates. Says Dixon, "Closing costs would eat up your potential savings."

Although the Bailey Brothers Building and Loan is no longer in existence, your loan can still have a wonderful life at a midsize bank or thrift. Some are especially competitive in the adjustable rate area. Commercial banks and some large brokerage firms have begun aggressive credit programs to service their best clients. If a jumbo loan is what you're after, they can do the deal easily.

Build Up Your ARMs

When interest rates are low, most borrowers focus on fixed-rate loans. When rates are less attractive, adjustable-rate mortgages (ARMs) can be a better idea. If you're sold on a house with monthly payments that seem to put it out of reach, the lower payments of an ARM could help you close the deal. But don't position that easy chair in the corner just yet. While the initial rate may be alluring, ARMs rise when interest rates increase, and the increase can be a doozy!

ARMs change their rates on a schedule. Some fix an initial rate for a certain period before converting to annual adjustable loans. Schedules include 3-1, 5-1 and 7-1. That means the loans are fixed for three, five or seven years before converting to a one-year adjustable. Interest rates on ARMs can run from about half a point to several points less than fixed-rate loans. Should you decide to stay in your home, some lenders provide a conversion option that allows you to switch to a fixed loan—for a fee, and provided you do so before your loan begins to adjust.

ARMs are not for everyone, but if you're planning to live in your home for just a few years or to increase your earnings, they could save you money.

Home is, above all, where the wallet is. Of course, you should really, really like the house you're going to buy, but don't let love at first sight draw you into a money pit. Buying a home is a huge financial undertaking, a major investment and a big business deal. Treat it like one, and you'll take advantage of the opportunity instead of letting it take advantage of you.

Your Money Or Your Life

Get the right life, health and disability insurance

> *"Life is short. Eat dessert first."*
>
> —Anonymous

Ellen had found herself on the short end of the stick one too many times. After buying an insurance policy that was supposed to pay itself off in 10 years but did not, Ellen decided to take matters into her own hands. Instead of blindly accepting advice at face value, she and her financial advisor called the insurance company and told them she wanted to change the policy to one that could lower or eliminate future payments. Lo and behold, because the company wanted to keep her account (and, no doubt, to avoid a lawsuit), Ellen was allowed to convert her old policy to a new policy at no additional cost. In fact, all the accumulated cash value of her old policy could be used to pay the premium on the new policy. And, best of all, as Ellen put it: "I'm glad I took the time to get this right because a mistake would have been disastrous.

And now I know that I can understand these policies and get the right one for me."

Buying insurance can be both tricky and intimidating, but getting the right policy can provide for your heirs and give you peace of mind. It's not hard to do, but it does require time and attention. The process is like buying a pair of running shoes—the array of choices is overwhelming, but you need to find the perfect fit. Before you consider taking a policy for a jog, here are some things to look for right out of the box.

Roads That Should Be Less Traveled

While you can buy insurance against just about every possible risk, only a few make sense. First off, don't buy insurance that you don't need. This includes life insurance for your children, unless your child earns an income that is vital to your family's survival. Some parents use insurance as an investment to save for college, but there are better ways. Others are told that their children should get insurance now, since they may not qualify for it later. In most cases, that just doesn't happen. Credit insurance policies are designed to cover your credit card, car loan and mortgage payments if you die or can't work. Coverage is far more expensive than regular life insurance and should be avoided unless you can't get life insurance for medical reasons.

Healthy Habit

Looking at permanent insurance illustrations? Ask to see additional illustrations reflecting other variables. If you are shown an illustration reflecting "current dividend scale" or "% growth," request a second illustration showing these rates 1, 2 or 3 percent less. This will better demonstrate the required premium to keep the policy from lapsing.

Planning on renting a car? Make sure you have adequate insurance, but don't pay twice. If you have auto insurance on your vehicle back home, you may be covered. Check with your insurance agent before you decline the rental car company's insurance. Some credit card issuers restrict insurance benefits to gold or platinum holders; some cards don't cover certain countries or types of cars. Finally, don't use a debit card to rent a car without checking specifics from the issuer. Many debit cards do not provide the same types of services as credit cards.

Extended warranties on inexpensive appliances are a waste of money. (They'll probably break *and* become obsolete immediately after your policy has expired.) Thinking of saving money at the vet through a health insurance policy for Fido? Make sure your vet will accept such coverage, and then consider how much you'd be willing to spend if Fluffy got really sick. Unless you plan to spare no expense, routine care can probably be paid for from your savings.

Look Lifely

Now that you know what to avoid, you're ready to get the most out of your insurance dollars—starting with life. The purpose of life insurance is to provide for your loved ones' financial needs in the case of your death. If your net worth exceeds the maximum individual exclusion amount (you'll learn about this on Day 41), insurance policy proceeds can also be used to pay estate taxes, helping your heirs to lighten this additional burden.

Insurance falls into two categories: term (or temporary) and permanent (or cash value). The former provides a death benefit only; the latter, a death benefit plus

Smart Stretch

Looking for information on term insurance without having a salesman parked in your living room? These sites may make comparison shopping a bit easier:

- Quotesmith: (800) 431-1147, www. quotesmith. com

- AccuQuote.com: (800) 442-9899, www. accuquote.com

- RightQuote: www. rightquote.com

- Quicken InsureMarket: www.insuremarket.com

There is no charge for these services; they are compensated by the insurance companies they quote.

a savings feature. Term insurance covers a specific period, anywhere from one to 20 years. This type of insurance is especially useful to cover expenses that you know will be coming up, like a college education, medical school tuition or a mortgage payoff; anything that would be difficult or impossible for your family to fund without your earning power. Premiums on these policies are cheap when you're young but increase with age, and the policies are typically renewable (usually at a higher premium). Term insurance is appropriate for the young who can't afford high premiums and aren't currently looking to invest, or for people who have other assets and want to be certain that specific monetary goals can be met without them.

Cash value insurance provides a death benefit plus a choice of investment options. There are three types of cash value policies: whole life, universal life and variable life. Although the initial premium on a cash value policy is higher than that of a term policy, it doesn't increase as long as the policy stays in force. Unlike term insurance, cash value policies allow the insurance company to invest the premiums. The cash value that results can be borrowed from the policy or used to pay the premiums or increase the death benefit.

Of the cash value types of insurance, whole life has been around the longest. Insureds who have more cash flow and who can afford the higher initial premium often consider whole life. The insurer invests your premiums; you have no control over how your money is invested. This is considered the most conservative type of cash value policy.

Universal life policies invest a portion of the premiums in fixed-income accounts. The better the account does, the more you can borrow, the faster your premiums are paid or the quicker your death benefit grows. If you can afford the initial premium and seek a relatively conservative investment opportunity, look into universal life.

Variable life allows policyholders to invest a portion of the premium in an array of managed accounts. Typically, the better your account performs, the higher your death benefit, but this varies with each insurance company. These policies also carry a minimum death benefit; in case the portfolio hits the wall, your beneficiaries won't be left standing in the middle of the track. Insurance purchasers who don't mind ups and downs and some uncertainty could benefit from variable life. The opportunity to invest your premiums in various managed accounts can be great, but can also be confusing. Be sure to read the prospectus before investing.

No matter what kind of insurance you select, as my mama told me, "you'd better shop around." Premiums on term insurance can vary widely, as can the options on whole, universal and variable life policies. Make sure the ink is dry on your new policy before you cancel the old. If you've settled on term insurance, consider a policy that guarantees level premiums for the length of the policy. For example, if you buy a 20-year level term policy, your annual premiums should stay the same for the entire 20 years. If you decide on an annual renewable term policy, make sure you can renew each year without a health exam.

To Tell The Truth

When it comes time to fill out that insurance application, tempting though it may be, don't lie. Insurers have ways of making you talk, or at least making your medical records cough up accurate information. If you get coverage under fraudulent means, your insurer can cancel your policy at any time. Worse, if you die or are disabled and have lied on your application, an insurer may deny your claim.

When determining what premium an insured will pay, life insurance companies have at least three price categories: Preferred, the lowest premium for those who represent the lowest risk; standard, an average price for standard risk; and substandard, the highest premium for those with the highest risk. Whatever your risk level, if you die within two years of buying a policy, life insurance companies will usually conduct an investigation to rule out the possibility of suicide to obtain insurance proceeds.

Life insurance is a complicated business. To make the most of your money, avoid these common blunders:

> ## Trainer's Tip
>
> "Buying permanent life insurance? Don't go with the lowest bidder. Permanent life insurance is not quoted at a guaranteed price; your quote is an estimate. This estimate is based on the company's projected mortality costs, rate of return on premiums, and administrative costs. All of these will vary over time. If you pay the guaranteed premium, then you have probably paid the insurer too much."
>
> —James Addison Weaver, ChFC, CLU, CFP

- Insurance policies are not savings accounts, investment accounts or retirement accounts. They are insurance accounts, and don't let anyone try to tell you otherwise.

- Many policies have addendums for optional coverages that insure against specific situations, like accidental death, in which the death benefit is doubled. If you're thinking of taking a ride on this rider, don't. While "double indemnity" was a nice title for a movie, it's usually a waste of money, as are other optional coverages. Most are costly and unnecessary.

- Planning to use your policy as a tax-free savings vehicle? Make other plans: The provisions that allow policyholders to make tax-free withdrawals can change at any time.

- Cash value policies project the value of your policy under different interest rate scenarios in illustrations that accompany any proposal. Read the prospectus and the footnotes on the illustrations when the policy is delivered. Depending on your state of residence, you have 10 to 20 days to return the policy for a full refund if you decide you don't want it. This is usually referred to as the "free look" period.

Running Downhill

Most people have life insurance, figuring that someday they will die. On the other hand, many of us lack disability insurance—an unforgivable (and expensive) error. While death is a catastrophe for your loved ones, disability can be an even larger financial problem. If you can't work, you need to have a source of income, and the right type of disability insurance can help you secure it.

Before selecting a policy on your own, check to see if your employer has one. Workers' compensation coverage will cover you for accidents occurring on the job only. If you break your leg skiing or have a car accident while out of town at your cousin's wedding, you may not be covered. Company-sponsored disability insurance, however, may fill the bill. Find out when your coverage begins, your benefit amount, time before benefits start, and the cost (if any) to you. This insurance can help supplement your income should you become disabled, but benefits are often short-lived. Remember, too, that benefits paid from employer-provided policies are taxable.

Whether or not your employer provides disability insurance, this type of coverage should be a priority. To figure out how much you need, do a quick financial inventory. Take a look at your net worth statement, and calculate how long your savings would last if you had to invade them in an emergency. Don't panic—this is what insurance is for.

Several companies provide disability insurance, so talk to a few agents before signing up. Keep in mind, premiums increase with age, risky hobbies or self-employment. To get the most for your money, consider the following:

Money Missteps

All agents are not alike. Captive agents sell only one company's products, while independent agents sell policies from several companies. Both are reputable, but independent agents may offer more choices.

- **Length of coverage.** This is the time during which you will receive benefits. Policies can cover one year, up to a specific age, or for the rest of your life. The shorter the benefit period, the less expensive the policy.

- **Policy renewal period.** A policy that is guaranteed renewable can't be canceled, and premiums on your policy can't be raised unless they're raised for all similar policies. These policies provide a fixed benefit at a fixed premium. Consider a policy that is guaranteed until age 65.

- **Elimination period.** This is the time that you are disabled before benefits can begin. Elimination periods can begin at 30 days or can be much longer. The longer you can wait to start receiving benefits, the less expensive the policy. If your employer covers you for disability or if you have large savings or a working spouse, consider a longer waiting period.

- **What is a disability?** If this sounds like a no-brainer, think again. While disability to you may simply mean not being able to practice as the butcher, baker or Wall Street deal maker that you are, to an insurance company, a much broader definition may be applied, like not being able to work at *any* job. Many professionals opt for the more expensive option of defining disability as the inability to work at their own occupation.

> **Healthy Habit**
>
> Check out any insurance company before you sign up. Information on company ratings is available at the library, or you can call a rating service for more information. Standard & Poor's will provide a free rating over the phone (212-208-1527); A.M. Best charges $2.50 per minute (900-420-0400). Why such scrutiny? You want to be sure they can pay your claim, right?

- **Amount of benefit.** Think in terms of replacing part of your income, not all of it. Why? Unlike your regular income or benefits from employer-sponsored disability plans, benefits paid to you from a disability policy you purchase for yourself are not taxable. Consider a maximum benefit of 65 percent to 70 percent of your current income. To lower the premium, go back to your net worth and figure out how much you'd need to pay your bills and put groceries on the table, then work from there. Some people take into account potential Social Security benefits, but these can be hard to qualify for, so include them in your calculations at your own discretion.

To Your Health

Young and healthy? Why spend the money on health insurance when there are so many other things you need, right? Wrong. Good health is great, but good health insurance is almost better. Unfortunately, affordable health insurance is hard to come by, and not having at least some coverage can be financially devastating.

Any policy you select should cover at least 80 percent of doctor and hospital bills after your deductible is paid. To reduce your premiums, raise your deductible. Your policy should also have a maximum lifetime benefit of at least $250,000 and cover all diseases.

If you have a serious pre-existing condition, health insurance may be more difficult to secure. In many states, Blue Cross and Blue Shield, Aetna, Prudential and other insurers offer quality coverage for a competitive price. Many HMOs and individual insurers offer open-enrollment periods several times per year. Health insurance may also be available though professional associations or your local chamber of commerce.

Jogging In Place

Introducing fixed income

> *"Gentlemen prefer bonds."*
> —Andrew Mellon

Carolyn and Jimmy are antique collectors first, investors second. Living in the rural South, they've amassed a great collection of "stuff"—and a pretty nice bond portfolio, too. Their financial guru, LeeRoy Lookabill, has built their portfolio around one idea: Never risk your safe money. Sure, this sounds easy, but when technology stocks made instant millionaires of what seemed like half the population, LeeRoy didn't change his mind. And when tech stocks turned tail and ran the other way, Carolyn and Jimmy kept buying their antiques . . . with the dividends from their nice, safe bond portfolio.

Though past performance is no guarantee of future results, historically, investing in common stocks has proved to have the best potential to build and protect wealth over the long term. But like Carolyn and Jimmy, many investors, afraid of losing their principal, invest heavily in lower risk debt securities. Whether you choose individual securities or managed funds, if you're looking to bond your portfolio, today we give a brief overview of fixed-income and short-term investing. (More in-depth information will follow on Days 10 through 13.)

Getting A Fix

First, why are these securities called "fixed income"? Bonds are debt securities issued by organizations to finance various projects. All bonds have certain features in common, including coupon, maturity, face value or par, and credit quality rating. When you buy a bond, the issuer promises to pay a certain rate of interest (called the coupon), often semiannually, for a certain period of time (until the bond matures). The principal is also called the par, or face value.

Two major rating services, Moody's and Standard & Poor's, assign letter ratings to bonds to give investors an idea of a bond issue's quality and the issuer's ability to make timely payments of interest and principal (see the following chart).

How Does Your Bond Rate?		
Credit Risk	**Moody's**	**Standard & Poor's**
Investment Grade		
Highest Quality	Aaa	AAA
High Quality	Aa	AA
Upper Medium Grade	A	A
Medium Grade	Baa	BBB
Below Investment Grade		
Lower Medium Grade (somewhat speculative)	Ba	BB
Low Grade (speculative)	B	B
Poor Quality (default possible)	Caa	CCC
Extremely Speculative	Ca	CC
No Interest Being Paid Or Bankruptcy Petition	C	C
In Default	C	D

If you're considering an investment in bonds, don't look exclusively at the interest rate paid. Think of bonds as you would a loan. Your brother-in-law may not be very good at paying back loans (if he were a bond, he'd get a lower quality rating), so if you were going to lend him $10,000 for five years, you'd ask him to pay more interest than if he had a great repayment history. And you probably wouldn't want to lend him money for 30 years. Bonds are the same: The longer the maturity or the lower the rating, the more interest you should receive.

Bonds are issued by corporations, the federal government and its agencies, state and local governments, and foreign governments. For a rundown on each of these categories, read on.

In Good Company

There are several types of corporate bonds; they're classified based on the collateral that backs the payment of interest and repayment of principal. Corporate bonds can be secured by real estate (mortgage bonds), equipment (equipment obligations), stocks and bonds (collateral trust obligations), or the general credit of the issuing company (debentures).

Corporations can retire debt prior to maturity in several ways, including calling in their bonds and converting them into other securities. If your bonds are called or converted, you'll receive your principal back and interest payments will cease or change. (Convertible bonds are covered on Day 13.)

Corporations with lower quality ratings need to offer greater incentives to investors in the form of high yields. These higher-yield, lower-rated bonds are often called "junk bonds" because there is a greater risk to investors' interest and principal. (More on this on Day 12.)

Cry Uncle

The federal government, like corporations and state and local governments, borrows funds (through the sale of Treasury securities) to conduct its business. Since Treasury securities are backed by the U.S. government, they have the highest safety rating.

There are three kinds of Treasury securities: bills, notes and bonds. *Treasury bills* are short-term securities with maturities of one year or less. They are issued at

Smart Stretch

"Treasury Direct" lets investors buy U.S. Treasury bonds, bills and notes directly from the Treasury without paying $50 or more per transaction to a broker. Minimum purchases have also been reduced, making access easier than ever. For more information, call (800) 943-6864 or check out the Web site: www. publicdebt.treas.gov. Note that this service is best for those who plan to buy and hold until maturity. Traders can get faster service from a broker.

a discount from face value, and they are issued in minimum denominations of $10,000, with $5,000 increments available above $10,000. *Treasury notes* are intermediate-term securities, with maturities ranging from one to 10 years. Denominations range from $1,000 to $1 million or more. *Treasury bonds* are long-term investments, with maturities of 10 years or longer, issued in minimums of $1,000.

Treasury securities can be bought directly from the U.S. Treasury or from banks or brokerage firms. Agencies of the U.S. government also issue securities. These are not obligations of the Treasury; instead, they are issued and backed by government agencies. Because of this implied but inherent backing by the federal government, they are considered to be of the highest credit quality.

You may have heard of the "Mac" family—Ginnie, Fannie and Freddie Mac, otherwise known as the Government National Mortgage Association, Federal National Mortgage Association and Federal Home Loan Mortgage Association, respectively. Of these, only Ginnie Mae is backed directly by the U.S. government. Ginnie Maes sell in minimum denominations of $25,000, while Freddie Mac and Fannie Mae offer smaller denominations. All three of these securities are based on pools of mortgages and are called "pass-through securities" because the interest and principal paid monthly by homeowners is passed through to investors.

But, Wait, There's More

Here are some more bonds for you to consider:

- **State and local government bonds.** Home is where the heart is, and it's also where investors can find interest-bearing investments free of state and federal income taxes. If you purchase municipal bonds in your home state, the interest earned on these bonds is free of state taxes. Interest from bonds issued by the Commonwealth of Puerto Rico is tax-free in all 50 states. For some investors, however, this income may be subject to the federal alternative minimum tax, a flat tax applied to wealthy taxpayers to ensure they pay at least some tax. (Learn more about tax-free investing on Day 11.)

- **Foreign government bonds.** Foreign governments issue bonds to finance their projects, too; sometimes interest rates are higher than those of U.S. government bonds. But before you invest, be sure you understand the inherent risks in foreign securities, including currency fluctuations and political and social instability.

- **Inflation-indexed bonds.** These bonds offer a rate of return that is guaranteed to be above inflation. With a Treasury-backed inflation-indexed bond, if inflation rises, the Treasury will credit additional money to the bondholder's principal at the same rate that inflation increases, as measured by the Consumer Price Index. The coupon does not change, but it is paid on the larger principal amount. This subjects the holder to current tax on the inflation-adjusted coupon interest payments.

- **Step-up bonds.** These are corporate bonds with coupons that rise or fall in predetermined increments as inflation increases. The principal remains the same, but bondholders receive higher monthly or semi-annual payments. Some bonds reset their coupon, changing their rate of interest regardless of the level of interest rates, while others reset when certain inflation benchmarks are reached.

Dangerous Curves

If you're considering adding a fixed-income component to your portfolio, it helps to become friendly with the yield curve. This graph plots the interest rates of bonds of the same quality with maturities ranging from the shortest to the longest. Usually the curve is positive; the shorter a bond's maturity, the lower its yield. This makes sense because most of the time, investors who are willing to tie up their money for a longer amount of time are rewarded for doing so by receiving more interest. An inverse yield curve is relatively unusual and occurs when short maturity bonds pay higher interest. An inverse yield curve often signals an economic reversal or recession.

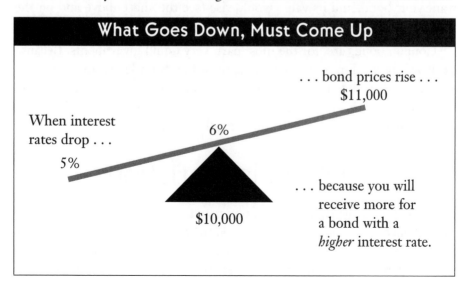

What Goes Down, Must Come Up

. . . bond prices rise . . .
$11,000

When interest rates drop . . .

6%

5%

$10,000

. . . because you will receive more for a bond with a *higher* interest rate.

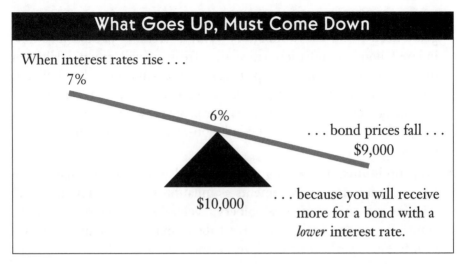

What Goes Up, Must Come Down

When interest rates rise . . .

7%

6%

. . . bond prices fall . . .
$9,000

$10,000

. . . because you will receive
more for a bond with a
lower interest rate.

Yield curves are important when buying bonds because they provide a way to determine whether a bond is a good deal or not. Most yield curves are based on Treasury securities, so if you're considering a bond with 10 years to maturity and a lower credit rating, the yield should be higher than that of a comparable Treasury bond.

When considering any kind of fixed-income investment, remember that bonds trade inversely with interest rates. In English, it goes like this: Say you're buying a bond today, selling at par, with a 7 percent coupon. If interest rates rose, all the new bonds being issued might pay an interest rate of 9 percent. Would you rather have your bond or a new, higher-paying bond? Of course you'd want the new one, and so would everyone else, causing the value of your bond to fall. If rates fell, on the other hand, and all the new bonds were paying 5 percent, theoretically, everyone would want your bond, and its value would rise (see the chart above and on the previous page).

Coupon bonds are, for the most part, very liquid investments. Because of their relationship to interest rates, most bonds trade at either a premium or a discount to their par value once they have been issued. Understanding the relationship of bonds to interest rates will help you decide when it's worthwhile to buy or sell bonds.

Outrunning Inflation

If safety is your major concern, you may think your best bet is to invest in fixed-income securities, spreading your investments among several types of bonds or even sticking with U.S. government securities. But after inflation is taken into account, this risk-free concept becomes questionable.

According to research firm Ibbotson Associates, over the long term, Treasury bills barely outperformed inflation, earning an annual 3.7 percent return while inflation increased at 3.1 percent per year. In fact, after taxes and inflation, many T-bill investors actually experienced a negative return. The key to investing wisely in fixed income is to vary the types of fixed investments and to add a smattering of growth to protect your portfolio from inflation.

Stock It To Me

A basic guide to equity investing

> "Don't gamble; take all your savings and buy some good stock and hold it till it goes up, then sell it. If it don't go up, don't buy it."
> —Will Rogers

Kate never bothered with money until her husband passed away. At the ripe young age of 75, she found herself with lots of statements and lots of bills and lots of things she didn't understand. When I first met with her, she told me that she was an old lady and she couldn't learn how to invest in stocks now. On the contrary, I assured her, we'll keep talking, and you'll understand stocks in no time.

After many conversations, we got to know each other better, and Kate started to feel more confident about her portfolio. But I knew I had done it when she called me one day and had this to say: "Lorayne, I was reading this article from *Barron's*, and I think that based on their dividend yield, low P/E relative to the S&P and the possibility that interest rates could fall, utilities look pretty good right now." Thank you, Kate the stock maven.

The stock market seems a mysterious place to the uninitiated, but as Kate learned, you only need a little guidance through the basics to begin unraveling the secrets of equities. Stocks, as represented by Standard & Poor's weighted index of 500 stocks, have clearly outpaced inflation and taxes, with an average pretax total return, including reinvested dividends, of more than 11 percent per year from 1926 to 1998, according to research firm Ibbotson Associates.

There's no guarantee this trend will continue, but consider that this 72-year period includes times of war and peace, growth and decline, bull and bear markets, inflation and deflation. Common stocks clearly provide the potential to fulfill your objectives of building and preserving wealth.

Taking Stock

Buying stock in a company means buying part ownership in that business. As a shareholder, you receive capital appreciation (the difference

Caught In The Web

Looking for access to the financial world at the click of your mouse? Here are some Web sites that *Barron's*, the Dow Jones business and financial weekly magazine, rates at the top of the heap. These sites provide information quickly and in a well-organized format.

- Microsoft MoneyCentral: www.moneycentral.com
- CBS MarketWatch: www.cbs.marketwatch.com
- Yahoo! Finance: http://quote.yahoo.com
- CNNfn: www.cnnfn.com
- Quicken.com: www.quicken.com
- Morningstar.com: www.morningstar.com
- TheStreet.com: www.thestreet.com
- ZD Interactive Investor: www.zdii.com
- Stockpoint: www.stockpoint.com
- The Motley Fool: www.fool.com

Smart Stretch

Many companies have dividend re-investment plans (DRIPS) that allow investments of as little as $10 to $25 without paying brokerage fees. Call the investor relations department at the company you are interested in to find out if they offer this program.

The DRIP Investor is also a great source of information; write to 7412 Calumet Ave., Hammond, IN 46324 for details.

between your purchase price and the current market value) and/or dividends (generally a quarterly payment that represents a percentage of the company's earnings). Of course, stock prices and dividends can fall if the company doesn't do well.

Stocks can be classified into several broad categories:

- **Blue-chip stocks** are the high quality stocks of major companies; they generally have long, unbroken records of earnings and dividend payments.

- **Growth stock** companies are those whose sales, earnings and market share are expanding faster than the industry average and the economy in general. These companies usually retain most of their earnings to finance expansion and pay few, if any, dividends to shareholders.

- **Defensive stocks** are from companies that provide necessary services, such as electricity and gas; essential goods, such as pharmaceuticals; or staples, such as food or soft drinks. Due to the constant demand of these products, these stocks typically provide a degree of stability during periods of recession.

- **Income stocks** are generally attractive to people seeking current income, particularly seniors and retirees of all ages. Income stocks, often the province of utilities, usually pay high dividends in relation to their market price, providing shareholders with greater quarterly income.

- **Cyclical stocks** are those of companies whose earnings are tied to the business cycle. When business conditions are good, the company is profitable and the common stock price usually rises. When conditions decline, the company's earnings and stock prices generally fall. Steel, cement, machine tools and automobile companies are considered cyclical stocks.

- **Seasonal stocks'** performance fluctuates with the seasons. For example, retail companies' sales normally increase at Christmas and the beginning of the school year.

Avoiding The Pitfalls

Many investors who manage their own portfolios make common mistakes that lead them to the false conclusion that it's impossible to make any money in the stock market. These mistakes include:

- failure to establish clear objectives
- selecting securities that are not consistent with objectives
- purchasing too many or too few securities
- taking profits too soon
- failing to minimize losses promptly
- buying a stock based on a "tip" rather than investigating its merits
- not adjusting to changing market cycles
- not fully exploring alternative investments
- failing to follow a disciplined approach

Birds Of A Feather

Individual stocks can be purchased on their own or through many different vehicles, whether actively managed, as in the case of mutual funds (see Day 9 and Days 19 through 23) or individually managed accounts (see Day 24), and passively managed, as you'll find in index funds (see Day 21). Various "associations" of stocks are quite familiar, including the Dow Jones industrial average (DJIA), or Dow. This grouping is comprised of 30 common stocks chosen by the editors of *The Wall Street Journal* as representative of the New York Stock Exchange and of American industry. The Dow is a weighted average, giving more weight to some stocks than to others; that's why its movements are often so sharp when one large component either rises or falls precipitously. The Dow is considered a bellwether indicator of the direction of the stock market, thus its place, front and center, in media reports.

However you like your stocks, understanding what they are and how they work is an important first step to making your money work as hard for you as you do to get it.

DAY 9

Mutual Admiration

Managing money with mutual funds

Bill had invested about $25,000 in a set of mutual funds over a period of about six years. The funds had grown to $50,000 when he needed to tap them to buy an office for his practice. He withdrew $15,000 and then forgot all about those funds—the statements took too long to decipher, and he wasn't planning on using the money anyway, so why worry about them?

One day Bill heard some analysis of world markets and decided to move a bit into South American equities. Since he knew almost zilch about individual companies in these countries, he decided to sell some of his mutual fund shares and move the money into funds investing in the South American market. The surprise was mine: The value of the account had grown to more than $86,000 in four years, with no additional investments—a nest egg Bill didn't have to sit on to incubate!

I've been telling people for years that mutual funds provide an anchor for their portfolios—in a positive sense, that is. Bill's experience shows just how solid that anchor can be.

At last count, more than $3 trillion was invested in mutual funds, and the number of funds is larger than the number of stocks listed on the New York Stock Exchange. There is probably only one thing more prolific than the number of mutual funds, and that's the number of publications that rank, explain, praise and berate them.

But what are mutual funds, and why is everyone so excited about them? Mutual funds are created by investment companies that invest a pool of money contributed by a group of investors in certain ways to achieve particular objectives. Funds have a lot going for them. They provide easy access to professional money management and lots of opportunities to diversify your money in different markets and types of securities. Funds usually have smaller minimum requirements than other types of investments and generally take less time and are more convenient than investing on your own in individual stocks. What funds don't provide is any kind of guarantee: As with any investment, there's risk involved. That said, mutual funds have a place in many portfolios.

Read It Or Weep

You've heard it a million times, but let's say it once slowly, all together now: "Read the prospectus before you invest or send money." Why bother with the mumbo-jumbo of a fund prospectus? Think of it like going on a date. Your friends may have fixed you up with their idea of Ms. or Mr. Right, but you won't know just by looking at him or her. After spending a few hours together, you'll have a better idea of what he or she is like and whether you want to repeat the experience.

Reading a fund's prospectus can tell you a lot about it. The prospectus includes information on the fund's objectives, fees and expenses, the kind of investments it makes, how and when dividends are paid, and how to buy and sell shares. You'll also find out how often the fund trades its securities, how performance figures are figured, your rights as a

Smart Stretch

An Investor's Guide to Reading the Mutual Fund Prospectus is available from the Investment Company Institute, 1400 H St. NW, Washington, DC 20005, (202) 326-5800. The first copy is free.

Joggin' Jargon

What's the difference between a fund's yield and its total return? Yield is the income per share that the fund pays its investors. Not every fund pays a dividend, so some funds have little or no yield. Total return is the per-share change of the fund based on its net asset value (NAV). The total return includes the yield plus any capital gains and appreciation in the share price.

shareholder, and the name and address of the fund's advisor and transfer agent. Prospectuses do not usually include a list of the fund's investments, the names of the fund's directors or the name of the fund's investment advisor.

Sadly, many investors invest first and read the prospectus later. Reading a fund's prospectus isn't as exciting as reading a John Grisham novel, but reading it before you invest can save you a lot of headaches. Pretend you're studying for a test and see what you can learn from a prospectus. Circle all the passages you don't understand and make notes in the margins. Who knows, you may get a lot out of it after all.

Fund Money

While all funds have some things in common, how and in what they invest can be anything but similar. (On Days 22 through 24, we'll take an in-depth look at mutual funds, but today we'll just get the basics and terminology down.) There are many categories of mutual funds, but here are some of the most common.

Money-market funds invest in short-term IOUs from industry and government agencies. Dividends are usually accrued daily and often credited monthly. These funds are designed to have low price volatility. An investment in the fund is not guaranteed or insured by the FDIC or any government agency. Although the fund seeks to preserve the value of your investment at $1 per share, it is possible (though not likely) to lose money invested in a money-market fund.

Income funds seek high current income by investing in a variety of securities that pay dividends and interest. These funds can invest in government and corporate bonds, utility and high-dividend stocks, preferred stocks and convertible bonds. Some funds may include all or a number of these securities, while others are dedicated solely to government bonds. Because of their relatively high income compared to funds that invest exclusively in equities, these funds are somewhat insulated from some of the stock market's volatility, although they are often more sensitive to interest rate changes.

Stock funds come in a large variety of styles and flavors. In general, there are two styles of equity investment: growth and value. Both styles of management have their devotees; a balanced portfolio should consist of a bit of each. (For more on value vs. growth, check out Day 16.)

Value funds invest in companies with low prices compared to earnings, but which pay a relatively high dividend and whose price compared to book value is low. Growth funds, on the other hand, seek capital appreciation by investing in companies whose earnings are growing at a rate higher than that of other companies in their industry or higher than that of the stock market as a whole.

Growth funds generally invest in large, well-established companies. Sometimes called "blue chip funds," some pay dividends, although income is usually a secondary consideration. Aggressive growth funds take this concept a step further, striving for maximum capital appreciation—making them the riskiest of equity funds. They may concentrate on small-company growth issues or stocks in volatile market sectors. To achieve the highest possible returns, these funds may use speculative techniques. The greater the potential profit, the greater the potential risk.

Balanced funds strive to manage risk by dividing their investments among stocks, bonds and cash. They usually invest in higher-grade securities and may be appropriate for investors who seek moderate returns and lower risk.

International and *global funds* provide access to markets outside the United States, allowing investors access to foreign securities that trade on foreign exchanges. While global funds may invest in both U.S. and foreign securities, international funds deal exclusively in securities outside the United States. Funds may invest in well-established markets, such as those in Europe; provide access to emerging markets in third-world countries; or employ both strategies.

Both types of funds allow investors to benefit from changing trends abroad. Remember, though, that foreign investing is subject to certain risks, such as cur-

> **Money Missteps**
>
> Don't pay tax on your own money. If you're planning to put your year-end bonus into your favorite mutual fund, check with the fund to find out when they plan to distribute dividends and capital gains, both of which are taxable. If you invest right before these payouts, your distribution will include part of your recent investment.

rency fluctuation and social and political changes. (You'll learn more about foreign investing on Day 26.)

Total return funds seek long-term appreciation by investing in securities that provide a combination of dividends and capital gains. They are frequent choices in retirement plans.

Bond funds invest in a mixture of different types of bonds or in a single category. The categories include U.S. government, mortgage-backed, investment-grade corporate, high-yield corporate, and foreign bonds of all of the previous categories. Bond fund share prices move in the opposite direction of interest rates. When interest rates rise, share prices fall. In addition, the longer the average maturity of the bonds held in the fund's portfolio, the higher its yield and the more volatile the fund's share price.

Specialized funds, or *sector funds*, concentrate on a particular industry or region, such as health care, real estate investment trusts (REITs), utilities, precious metals, commodities, technology or any number of areas of interest. Since they aren't diversified outside their particular areas of interest, they may be more volatile than more diversified funds. (More on REITs on Day 27.)

No matter what kind of fund you choose, unless it's a money-market fund, mutual funds are a long-term investment. Plan on keeping your money invested for a minimum of three to five years. Although funds provide professional management and diversification, they are not risk free. Some, in fact, are very risky indeed. Buying shares of a fund does not mean that you are guaranteed to become wealthy, just as entering a dance contest doesn't mean that you're going to win. Funds provide an opportunity to make your money work, and the more you know about them, the better choice you can make.

DAY 10

Special Treatment

High dividends with preferred stocks

> *"The safest way to double your money is to fold it over once and put it in your pocket."*
> —Kin Hubbard, tax expert

Minnie has a hard job. Her daughter Jamilia was disabled in an accident 10 years ago and now must have full-time care. In addition to making sure her daughter is well cared for in a special health-care setting, she must manage the proceeds of a lawsuit to be sure that Jamilia will be well cared for the rest of her life.

Unlike many people who can't face such difficult responsibility, Minnie, a woman in her 60s, has risen to the challenge. Even several years of low interest rates haven't gotten her down . . . she's become an investor in preferred securities. High-rated preferred stocks have augmented the level of income in Jamilia's account and allowed Minnie to get the best care for her daughter. That's special treatment.

For investors who seek high yields and frequent payments, preferred securities can help build a portfolio's income. If you're not familiar with this type of security, it's something of a cross between a common stock and a bond. For years, large institutions were the biggest investors in preferred stock, although new twists on the old formula of preferreds are making them more accessible and more interesting to individual investors.

Like common stock, preferred stock represents ownership in a corporation. On a company's balance sheet, it appears under the "equity" section. Unlike common stock, preferred stock usually pays a set dividend, similar to the way bonds pay a set interest payment. If a company's assets are liquidated, preferred stock holders are usually paid before common stock holders, but after debt holders, making preferred stock more attractive to safety-conscious investors than common stock, but less secure than bonds.

Preferred stocks are rated by Moody's and Standard & Poor's rating services to give investors a basis upon which to judge their credit quality. They usually have higher dividends than their common cousins, making them more attractive to those looking for Mr. Yieldbar. Most preferred stocks are listed on major exchanges, making it easy to sell at what the market deems is the price of the moment. Yet preferred stock is not for everyone. As Professor Harold Hill once said, "You gotta know the territory."

On the downside, like any fixed-income security, many preferreds offer little protection from inflation. If interest rates rise, although you'll continue to receive payments, your purchasing power decreases. And to add insult to injury, the share price of your stock would probably fall. This scenario may not be a problem if you intend to hold your position, but if you should decide to sell, you may get back less than you invested.

Unlike bonds that have a set maturity, preferreds can exist forever—or until called by the issuing company. Most preferred stocks issued today have call dates, at which time the issuer can call, or redeem, the shares at a predetermined price. Investors who buy a new issue of preferred stock often have call protection for five years; the company can't call their stock for this period, but any time afterward, the shares are fair game. Many preferreds are called either at the issuing price or at a slight premium. Some companies issue convertible preferreds that convert into a set amount of underlying common stock . . . at the company's convenience, of course.

The Misfits

Part of the beauty of preferred stocks is their predictability: a set dividend, a perpetual life span, predetermined payment dates. Unfortunately, it's the privilege of some preferred stocks to change their minds. In addition to standard, callable, and convertible preferred stocks, there are adjustable rate, cushion and cumulative varieties.

As with any fixed-income investment, rising interest rates are bad for preferred stocks. Not only will the dividends buy less for investors as the price of goods and services rise, but the share price is also affected. If you're worried about rising inflation, consider *adjustable-rate preferreds*. Here's an example of how this type of stock works: XYZ stock adjusts its dividend each quarter based on 85 percent of the highest yield of the three-month, 10-month or 30-year Treasury bond. Let's say the 30-year Treasury offers the highest yield of 7 percent to maturity. Multiply this rate by 85 percent to reset the dividend to an annual rate of 5.95 percent (7 percent x .085 = 5.95 percent). If the stock has a $25-per-share par price, the dividend paid is $1.48 ($25 x .0595 = $1.48). This rate is in effect for one quarter only, then the process is repeated. Almost all adjustable-rate preferreds have a collar, or a minimum and maximum interest rate to which the dividend can be reset.

Should you need a more reliable dividend, *cushion preferreds* could provide just the kicker you're looking for. Due to the interest rate sensitivity of perpetual preferred securities, the idea here is to purchase the higher coupon issues that have a greater likelihood of being redeemed on a yield-to-call basis. By purchasing higher coupon issues, you can collect a larger dividend payment and effectively lock in the rate.

Dividends on preferred stocks are paid from a company's earnings. No earnings, no dividend. What's a preferred investor to do? Before you invest, find out if the stock is *cumulative preferred*. If a company should run into difficulty and its dividends run into arrears, cumulative preferred stock must pay its shareholders all dividends owed before it can resume its dividend payments on common shares.

Some Like It Monthly

Both common and traditional preferred stocks pay dividends quarterly. Income-oriented investors who need monthly payments can buy an assortment of issues that

Healthy Habit

Today's preferred stocks are affordable to most investors, as many trade at $25 per share and are generally listed on major stock exchanges. It's easy to follow their price and to buy and sell these securities.

allow them to receive payments as needed. By purchasing one issue that pays January, April, July and September; another that pays February, May, August and November; and yet another paying March, June, October and December, all the months are covered. Some investors shy away from this idea because it seems too complicated. If that's the case for you, several new classes of preferred stock may be just the ticket.

In recent years, new forms of preferred securities have been created that are especially interesting to individual investors. Their income payments are generally higher than traditional preferred, and their frequency of payment, credit quality, small investment per share and NYSE listing appeal more to individuals than institutions.

Monthly income preferred securities (MIPS) represent an interest in a special-purpose company which exists solely to issue preferred securities and lend the proceeds to its parent company. Distributions are made monthly, and while they are not direct obligations of the parent company, that company does guarantee their payments. QUIPS, or quarterly income preferred securities, are much the same as MIPS but with quarterly payments.

Smart Stretch

Preferred securities are part of many mutual funds, and several funds invest exclusively in them. For more information on such funds, check out www.morningstar.com.

Trust originated preferred securities (TOPRS) are very similar to MIPS. A TOPRS is a special-purpose business trust that exists solely for the purpose of issuing preferred securities and then lending the proceeds to the parent company through the purchase of a long-term debt or debenture from the parent. TOPRS' characteristics are similar to QUIPS, except when it comes to taxes. TOPRS holders receive a 1099-OID, unlike QUIPS and MIPS holders, who receive a K-1. Consult your tax advisor to find out which is best for you.

Quarterly income debt securities (QUIDS) and monthly income debt securities (MIDS) are two additional new types of preferred securities. They are direct obligations of the issuing companies and make payments quarterly and monthly, respectively.

The Bus Stops Here

Large corporations, like insurance companies and banks, have long been fans of preferred stock. The primary reason it is so attractive to them is that 70 percent of the dividends received are not taxable. To qualify for this tax benefit, the company receiving the dividend must be a domestic tax-paying entity and hold the preferred security for at least 46 days.

The benefit works like this: A corporate investor in the 35 percent tax bracket would pay only 10.5 percent of the preferred dividend in tax and keep the remaining 89.5 percent. Assuming a dividend of 8 percent, the corporation's 89 percent becomes an after-tax yield of 7.16 percent. If you

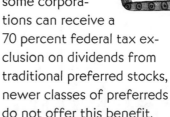

Money Missteps

Don't throw out the old for the new! While some corporations can receive a 70 percent federal tax exclusion on dividends from traditional preferred stocks, newer classes of preferreds do not offer this benefit.

compare this to the after-tax yield on a corporate bond, where the dividend is taxed at 35 percent, the same 8 percent becomes an after-tax yield of only 5.2 percent. These tax benefits aren't limited to giant corporations, either. Any C corporation can qualify. Ask your tax and financial advisors how you can apply this benefit to your company's portfolio.

Whatever their shape and size, preferreds, like diamonds, can be an income-oriented investor's best friend.

DAY
11

Packing A Punch

Hate taxes?
Fight back with
municipal bonds

Some people love risk and thrive on it—and others avoid it whenever possible. Jeremy and Talia want their money to make money, but not at the expense of their sanity. Big drops in the value of their stock portfolio make them uneasy. Their solution? Bonds . . . municipal bonds.

Jeremy and Talia invest primarily outside their retirement accounts, so taxes are an important consideration. With retirement as their primary investment objective, immediate income isn't important. For their situation, insured zero coupon municipal bonds fill the bill nicely. By choosing bonds that start maturing when Jeremy is 55 and building a ladder of bonds maturing every year until Talia retires 10 years later, they know they will have enough money for their basic needs.

According to his projections, Jeremy can retire early and pursue some of his hobbies, while Talia can work less or more as she desires. Best of all, when the stock market wobbles, Talia and Jeremy feel secure. Because they aren't relying solely on their stock portfolio, they can wait for its long-term appreciation to make their financial situation stronger.

Whether you share Jeremy and Talia's desire for security or just want a good way to lessen the bite of taxes, municipal securities may be just the tool you're looking for. Smart investors know that diversification is the one-two punch that can help secure long-term financial success. But all too often, municipal bonds aren't recognized for the jewels they are. So why municipal bonds?

Float Like A Butterfly

"Munis," as municipal bonds are affectionately called, have long been allies of investors who want to have their interest and save on taxes, too. Today's municipal market is large and diverse, with more than $1.2 trillion in outstanding issues— and that makes it easy to diversify a tax-free portfolio.

Municipal bonds are debt instruments issued by cities, counties, states and other municipal entities to pay for public works, including water and sewer projects, hospitals, schools, roads, bridges, tunnels and airports. As fixed-income securities, they

Joggin' Jargon

Alternative minimum tax (AMT), an alternative method of figuring income tax, is aimed at those who take a large amount of deductions. The interest paid by certain municipal bonds is subject to this tax; find out if it applies to you before you buy.

provide a steady income from semiannual interest payments.

These bonds are usually issued in one of two categories: general obligation or revenue. General obligation bonds are backed by the full faith and credit of the city, state or county that issues them. Payment of interest and repayment of principal is backed by the issuer's taxing power. These bonds are especially attractive for conservative investors—you know the rating of the issuer when you buy the bond.

Revenue bonds are issued by utilities, schools, toll roads and hospitals, and payments are based on the stream of revenues from the issuing facility. Because interest and principal payments are based on the success of the issuing facility rather than on the taxing power of a municipality (They can always raise taxes, but raising tolls might be a different matter!), revenue bonds are often considered more risky than some general obligation bonds. For accepting higher risk, investors in these bonds often receive a higher rate of interest.

Like any good boxer, these bonds are flexible and light on their feet, providing investors an opportunity to own long- or short-term securities with maturities ranging from several months to 30 years or more. Municipal bonds are some of the most widely traded fixed-income securities, which is great if you want to buy or need to sell. Millions of new municipal bonds are issued every year, but if you can't find any new ones that you like, the secondary market, where bonds are re-sold, provides many opportunities. (Like all bonds, if you sell before maturity, you may receive more or less than you invested.)

Put Up Your Dukes

Perhaps the most attractive feature of munis to many investors is their tax-free status, which has been at the heart of municipal bonds since the adoption of the Income Tax Amendment in 1913. Interest earned on these bonds is generally free of federal tax, and if you live in the issuing state, free of state and local taxes, too. (Capital gains, however, are subject to tax, and certain investors are subject to alternative minimum tax.) Municipal bond issuers are happy about the tax-free status, too, as it allows projects to be financed at lower interest rates.

Some investors, however, are turned off to municipal bonds because of their paltry yield. After all, why invest in a 30-year municipal bond paying only 5.25 percent when you could have a Treasury bond of the same maturity yielding 6.13 percent? You don't have to be a rocket scientist to figure that one out . . . or do you? To compare a taxable bond with a municipal bond, use this simple formula: tax-free municipal bond yield ÷ (1 - your federal tax bracket) = taxable equivalent yield. Financial advisors are fond of saying that it's not what you earn on an investment—it's what you keep. To understand the full impact of taxes on yields, let's put the aforementioned investments in the ring to see how they compare (see the chart below). Shake hands and come out fighting!

Contestants: 30-year AAA-rated municipal bond yielding 5.25% vs. 30-year Treasury bond yielding 6.13%	
Yields from municipal bonds after taxes are taken into account:	
An investor in the 39.6% federal tax bracket:	8.69%
36% tax bracket:	8.2%
31% tax bracket:	7.61%
28% tax bracket:	7.29%
After-tax yield for the Treasury bond: 6.13%, regardless of the investor's tax bracket	

The winner and heavyweight champion? You guessed it: For high-income investors, municipal bonds generally provide better after-tax returns. The secret is to look beyond the initial coupon at the after-tax yield before you duck away.

It's All In The Footwork

Bond defaults are rare, but notorious defaults like those in Orange County, California, have made some investors wary. So where should investors look for value in the municipal market? Consider the insured municipal market. Here, issuers with poor credit quality buy insurance

Healthy Habit

All states don't treat interest on municipal bonds the same. Illinois, Iowa, Kansas, Oklahoma and Wisconsin generally charge state taxes on interest; Florida, Nevada and Texas levy no state or local income taxes.

that guarantees investors the timely return of their principal and interest. About 40 percent of the new-issue muni market is insured municipal bonds. While these bonds pay a marginally lower yield, they often maintain their market value better than bonds that are not insured.

Munis are insured by four companies: Ambac, MBIA, FGIC and BIGI. The insurance is good for the life of the bond, and there is no charge to the investor. Once insured, these bonds will carry a AAA rating by Moody's and Standard & Poor's. For example, if yields on 10-year AAA-rated insured bonds are about 4.45 percent, yields on A-rated munis of the same maturity could be about 4.6 percent. While there's nothing wrong with an A-rated bond, why take the additional risk for only 15 basis points?

Down For The Count

Most investors are familiar with coupon bonds, those that pay income on a regular basis. But municipals come in another variety: the zero coupon. Like all zeros, these bonds are purchased at a steep discount. But unlike regular zeros, no capital gains taxes are due if you hold the bond to maturity.

Of course, there's a downside in this seemingly perfect tax-free compounding world. Because zero coupons don't pay interest, they are more volatile than current coupon bonds and therefore may not be suitable for all investors. You will see many fluctuations on your statements, so be prepared to buy and hold these securities.

Whether you invest in current coupon or zero coupon bonds, an important feature of all municipals is their rating. For a review of how bonds are rated, see Day 7.

Heavyweight Or Welterweight?

Regardless of their popularity, municipal bonds are not for everyone. Investors in the highest tax brackets will benefit the most from the savings on taxes, as the chart on the next page illustrates:

Savings Grace				
Tax Bracket	**Municipal Yields**			
	4%	**5%**	**6%**	**7%**
28%	5.56%	6.95%	8.33%	9.72%
31%	5.8 %	7.25 %	8.69%	9.92%
36%	6.25%	7.82%	9.83%	10.14%
39.6%	6.62%	8.28%	9.94%	11.59%

Those in the highest bracket (39.6 percent) get the full punch of tax-free interest. An investor in the 36 percent bracket would have to buy a taxable security yielding 7.82 percent to match a municipal security yielding only 5 percent. When the savings on federal and state taxes are combined, it's a jab that would make all the George Foremans proud.

Municipal bonds offer investors tax-exempt income, a relatively high degree of safety and a wide variety of styles and maturities. They're one way to give your money a fighting chance.

DAY 12

Trash Collectors

*Junk bonds—
they're anything
but garbage*

> *"Junk bonds
> are equity
> in drag."*
> —Lawrence Summers,
> secretary of
> the Treasury

Yoshi was a widow when her broker left our firm and I inherited her account. For a widow, she had quite an account. One quarter was invested in blue-chip stocks; the remainder was positioned in junk bonds. Not a junk bond fund—individual junk bonds. While yields topped 10 percent for most of the securities, their credit ratings were far below investment grade . . . OK if you can afford to speculate, but not, as they say, for widows and orphans. I couldn't get the point across to Yoshi (some things just don't translate well), so I tried to explain through her son. While he understood, his mom liked the danger, so off they went. Fortunately, no bonds defaulted, and Yoshi kept getting high interest payments until the bonds were called. Then I repositioned the money . . . whew!

Used sparingly in a diversified investment portfolio, junk bonds can be part of a great workout routine. So even if you can't make it to the gym, you can burn a few calories by taking *in* the trash.

Think the risk isn't for you? Don't flip that page—junk bonds have come a long way, baby. The last many investors heard about junk bonds, or, as they're called in polite society, high-yield corporate securities, might have been in connection with leveraged buyouts, corporate raiders, the predator's ball and the infamous Michael Milken. The late 1980s and early 1990s saw the unraveling of the high-yield corporate bond market due to overly aggressive issuing of debt from the lowest ranks of corporate society.

While millions of dollars were lost on those highly speculative issues, these bonds look as different now as Milken does without his toupee. Yet many investors still avoid these securities, fearing default and spurred on by the impulse to put everything in stocks. History shows that junk bonds offer high returns relative to both stocks and bonds: According to *Worth* magazine, since 1991, mutual funds investing in this sector have produced average annual returns of 10.6 percent, beating most other bond categories and the performance of plenty of stock funds, too. Investors in search of diversification instruments would be well to look into the possibilities offered by high-yield securities.

Toxic Securities

High-yield securities are those that offer historically high payouts. They come in several flavors, including preferred stocks and foreign government, municipal and corporate bonds. These securities are considered to be below investment quality, earning them a rating below triple B, the lowest standard of investment-grade securities. This lower credit rating means an increased chance that the issuer may not be able to make interest and principal payments as promised. Because of the possibility that these securities may default, potentially costing investors both interest payments and principal, the yields proffered are higher than investment-grade bonds of similar maturities.

There are two types of junk. "Fallen angels" are bonds that are issued initially

Healthy Habit

If a big position in junk bonds sounds too risky, divide your fixed-income money into several investments and make junk bonds a part of your total. You'll get to try out high-yield bonds without taking too much risk. Ease into the position slowly by adding to it monthly until you've reached the desired percentage.

as investment grade, but through their underlying firm's financial difficulties, lose their investment-grade credit rating. The second type of junk bonds are those issued by companies which themselves are rated lower than investment grade. Robust earnings can rescue either type of security from the junk heap, and an increased rating could result in profits for bondholders. On the other hand, in either situation the fate of the issuer could turn down, taking the bonds into default and the bond's holder into a tax loss.

Taking In The Trash

You don't have to go to the bottom of the barrel to find good value and high interest rates. Today, many "junk" bonds are of significantly higher quality than those issued during their heyday in the late '80s and early '90s. During the recession of 1990, about 10 percent of outstanding bonds defaulted. Five years of good economic times dropped that number to only 1.6 percent in 1996.

Although the quality of bonds is much better, this is no time to become complacent. Part of the reason behind the improvement is that banks are lending to firms that would otherwise be in financial trouble . . . which means if the spigot closes, default rates could rise. Currently, though, many experts expect the default rate to remain low and losses infrequent.

Historically, retail firms and grocery store chains were big issuers of high-yield corporate debt. A larger variety of industries issue this type of security today, including financial services, cable and telecommunications, and cyclical industries like forest products, steel and our old friend retail.

Healthy Habit

Invest in high-yield bonds through a mutual fund. If you own anything less than a round lot ($1 million) of an individual bond, you will probably have difficulty finding a bidder for your bond if its credit deteriorates. In choosing a fund, investigate its record. Top performers in bull markets sometimes wind up at the bottom in bear markets because they take the biggest risks.

Sifting Through The Rubbish

An initial foray into high-yield securities can be daunting, and as with any

Put Out The Trash

Is your junk fund too trashy? Watch out for:

- Yields much higher than the average junk fund
- A large portion of the portfolio invested in bonds rated CCC or below
- The use of leverage to increase yield
- Small portfolios concentrated in a few issuers or a few sectors
- Extensive use of noninterest-paying securities (like zero-coupon bonds)

investment, don't put all your eggs in one basket. The simplest plan is to mix and match within your fixed-income portfolio. Consider investing a large portion of your allotted sum into high-grade Treasury bonds of intermediate maturity, which, although they tend to underperform other types of bonds in a stable rate environment, will give your portfolio a core of stability. Then perk up your portfolio with a portion of high-yield corporate bonds, which generally pay a hefty yield compared to their safer fixed-income brethren.

If this sounds like a good idea, don't go it alone. Most experts recommend that small investors, those with less than six figures to place in any particular class of investments, stick with managed accounts. While individual bonds may sound scintillating, if you select five issuers and even one goes bankrupt, you could sustain a severe loss. Instead, select a mutual fund with a substantial track record. Albert Fredman, professor of finance at California State University, prefers standard mutual funds over closed-end funds because the latter often use leverage and can be more difficult to understand.

As with all mutual funds, there are different strokes for different folks: For the more aggressive, funds that invest in lower-grade junk bonds can provide a potentially higher return, but at a substantially higher risk. For the more conservative, higher-grade junk bond funds can provide income and diversification without betting the ranch. Not all junk funds are created equal, so be sure you read the prospectus before you invest. Some funds may invest in emerging markets, deferred-interest bonds, derivatives or very thinly traded issues, possibly increasing an investor's return, but very definitely increasing the risk. The best way to get the lowdown on a fund? Read its prospectus and annual report.

Yields Are Picking Up All Over

Astute investors might fear the effect of rising interest rates on the value of high-yield bonds. Fredman, however, sees it this way: "If interest rates are ratcheted up, junk bonds have less interest rate risk than Treasury bonds. Junk bonds as an asset class are less risky than stocks because bonds have more security than stocks."

Yet, he also notes that junk bonds share some characteristics with stocks. "If a company is doing well financially, recovering from losses, both its stock and junk bonds will appreciate as it recovers from a setback," says Fredman. "The price behavior of these bonds is based on the earnings of the company"—not exclusively on the direction of interest rates. In a recession, Fredman believes Treasury bonds would outperform junk: "As corporate profits peter out, this hurts junk bonds, but declining interest rates help Treasuries, at least to a point."

From a yield perspective, junk bonds beat investment-quality corporate bonds hands down; they also trade with much richer yields than long-term Treasury securities. In an atmosphere of high price-to-earnings, price-to-book, price-to-cash flow and price-to-dividend ratios on stocks, junk bonds can lend significant value to a diversified portfolio. Much of the risk of junk bonds can be managed by avoiding individual issues and sticking with diversified funds.

Money Missteps

Make no mistake: To get a lot of income, you need a lot of money or you need to take a high level of risk. Historically, global government bond funds, derivative-laden fixed-income funds and other specialty funds have paid well . . . for a while. Sooner or later, however, share prices usually begin to erode, and dividends may also decrease. Be prepared to sell when this happens.

Junkyard Dogs

Junk bonds are definitely not for everyone. Troubles in overseas markets, for example, prove that going for the highest yield available can get you in trouble. Foreign bonds with double-digit yields may sound like love at first bite, but watch out for a bout of indigestion. A high-flying dollar does not a happy foreign investment make, and currency fluctuations aren't all you have to worry about when investing in foreign bonds. Thinking of emerging-market bonds?

Beware too high a concentration in any managed portfolio. While their good years are very, very good, their bad years can be harrowing.

Similarly, high-yield corporates are best for only certain types of investors. Fredman notes that for high-income investors, too much taxable interest may not be tax-efficient. He recommends investing in municipal bonds to avoid paying tax on interest earned. But be wary of individual issues of low-quality municipals, he cautions. "Stick with investment-grade municipal bonds if you'll be buying individual issues with under $100,000," Fredman says. "Most smaller investors should consider a mutual fund if they seek high-yield municipals."

On the other hand, Fredman recommends high-yield corporates as part of a diversified tax-deferred account. Their yields are a bonus to investors in pension or profit-sharing plans, where, he says, "they add stability to a portfolio where people are afraid of a correction." The same goes for IRA and simplified employee pension IRA plans.

When it comes to different ways to diversify your fixed-income portfolio, you may find that NBA players aren't the only ones talking trash.

DAY 13

Ticket To Ride

Cruising with convertible securities

> *"You can't expect to hit the jackpot if you don't put a few nickels in the machine."*
> —Flip Wilson

Gary and his wife, Rose, received a windfall when Gary sold part of his business. How to invest a large sum of money? After divvying it up into various types of stocks and bonds, a small amount was placed with a manager who specialized in convertible securities. Lucky for Gary and Rose, too. When stocks took a hiatus from their run for the roses, the convertible portion held its own and stabilized the portfolio, just like the textbooks said it would!

Who doesn't covet the rush of wind coursing through their portfolio as it cruises down the four-lane appreciation highway? But you'd better buckle your seatbelt to get ready for the inevitable bumps in the road. One way to soften their impact, like Gary and Rose did, is to get behind the wheel of convertibles.

Convertibles are hybrid securities that share characteristics of equities and fixed-income securities, combining the interest payments of bonds with the chance to participate in the upward movement of stocks. They generally come in two models, bonds and preferred stocks.

As the name implies, convertibles can be exchanged for a set number of shares of the underlying common stock at a fixed price that is usually about 25 percent above the stock's level when the securities are issued. The price of convertibles tracks that of the common stock on the way up. But as fixed-income securities, they also pay a fixed interest rate. This interest payment cushions the price on the way down, so convertible securities rarely fall as far or as fast as their common stock cousins. For some investors, it's the best of both worlds.

Investing With The Top Down

Investors can earn money with convertible bonds in several ways. First, the bonds pay income to investors at a fixed rate, like a traditional bond. Second, convertibles can appreciate in value and may result in a gain when the investor sells them. Finally, the bonds can be converted into stock if the price has risen enough to justify the conversion, and sold for a gain. (Of course, like any security, convertible bonds can also decline in value.)

For all this flexibility, investors pay a premium and earn less interest than they would on a conventional bond. Convertibles also offer comparatively less security than straight bonds because their value is linked to the price of the underlying common shares. Unlike conventional bonds, convertibles are debentures—unsecured debt instruments—and are therefore often of lower credit quality than the company's other debt.

Convertible bonds are long-term debt instruments and have features in common with all bonds. They usually sell in $1,000 denominations, pay interest semiannually and have a fixed maturity date. Like many bonds, they are callable. Of course, what sets convertibles apart is their ability to change into common stock . . . abracadabra! Many convertible bond investors track the issuer's common stock, using the bonds to participate in the equity market with some downside protection.

These bonds are not suitable for everyone, as they require knowledge of

Smart Stretch

Looking for help crunching numbers? Try this Web calculator at www.numa.com/derivs/ref/calculat/cb/calc-cba.htm.

several complex factors. So before you decide to take a ride down Wall Street in a new convertible, here are a few things to know:

- **Investment value.** The convertible's value as a traditional bond is known as its investment value. Investment value is determined by comparison to the price of a regular bond whose interest payment, credit rating, maturity and issuer are similar. Keep in mind that convertibles often command higher prices than do comparable bonds.

- **Yield advantage.** Convertibles frequently have higher current yields than common stock. To calculate the yield advantage, subtract the current yield on the common shares from the higher convertible yield.

- **Conversion price.** This is the specified price per share at which the bond could be converted into common shares. This is found in the convertible's legal description.

- **Conversion ratio.** This is the number of common shares resulting from the division of the face amount of the convertible by its conversion price.

- **Conversion value.** What the convertible is worth as a stock at current common share market price is known as its conversion value. You can get this number by multiplying current common share market price by the conversion ratio. Conversion value rises and falls with the common share price.

- **Conversion premium.** The percentage difference between a convertible's actual market price and its conversion value is called the conversion premium. The lower the conversion premium, the closer the convertible is to its value as a common stock.

At first glance, understanding these terms and their permutations may seem like an exercise in futility . . . sort of like trying to replace the head gasket on your 1965 Mustang when you don't even know how to change the oil. But if convertibles are what you'd like to add to your portfolio, you've got to get a little dirt under your fingernails.

The Road To Success

As anyone who has ever owned a convertible can tell you, you've got to plan for those rainy days. Before you invest, make sure you know when the bond is callable. If it is called early, you may not get the chance for appreciation to repay you for the premium you paid. And never buy a convertible unless you like the underlying stock.

Bumps In The Road

Convertibles can give you a smooth ride, but watch out for these potholes:

- Getting in and out of convertibles is more difficult than trading stocks because there are fewer buyers and sellers in the convertibles market.

- Many companies that sell convertibles have lower ratings, either because they have a spotty earnings history or no history of earnings (such as Internet companies). Make sure you know what you're getting into before you drive away in an old clunker.

- Getting accurate prices can be difficult because some convertibles trade about as frequently as Yugos.

- Prices of convertibles are influenced by interest rates *and* earnings reports, so it's sometimes difficult to figure out what these securities are worth.

- Ask your broker if you're being charged a markup on every transaction (as you would with a bond) or commission (as you would on a stock). One or the other is OK, but avoid unscrupulous individuals who charge you both!

Before embarking on a buying spree, consider newer models. Convertibles issued several years ago may have already appreciated along with their stock. If the underlying stock has risen 50 percent, the bond may have appreciated 40 percent already. If the stock falls, the bond could be subject to the same volatility. Instead, buy convertibles selling near par in stocks that you'd like to own. If the stock goes up, you will participate because you own the convertible, but if the stock drops, you have less to lose.

Check under the hood before buying: Select bonds that have a yield different enough from that of the common stock so that market fluctuations won't be so worrisome. Kick the tires of the underlying company, too. Because convertible bonds are subordinated debentures, it's especially important that the issuer has a strong balance sheet—that way you know you'll receive your interest payments in a timely manner. Lower-quality, higher-yielding bonds with a higher default risk are also available, but ask your financial advisor for help so you don't get stuck with a lemon. Finally, consider buying larger issues so illiquidity won't be a problem if you decide to sell or want to buy more.

Other Models

So far we've looked at just convertible bonds, but there are lots of other types of convertible securities you might want to consider as well. In addition to convertible bonds, some companies issue convertible preferred stock. Like convertible bonds, convertible preferred stock is a hybrid security with characteristics of nonconvertible preferred and common stock. It, too, is usually callable, and its conversion value and characteristics are the same as convertible bonds. The major difference is that while convertible preferred stock trades at a premium over both standard preferred and common, the premium is smaller than that of a convertible bond over the common.

If these types of preferred securities seem too sedate and you'd like a racier model, consider PERCing up your portfolio. PERCS, or preferred equity redemption cumulative stocks are preferred stocks that will be exchanged in the future for the issuing firm's common stock. Here, the growth potential lies in its redemption feature. PERCS are redeemed at a specific future date—they are not convertible at the holder's option and cannot be called. They pay a higher dividend than do the corresponding common shares and are redeemable into common shares at a particular price. If the price of the common stock is higher at the redemption date than when the PERCS was issued, the number of shares of the underlying stock that the PERCS holder receives is adjusted downward. There is a ceiling over which the rise in the common share price will not benefit the PERCS holder; therefore, PERCS are most appropriate to investors who seek to receive higher dividends now and who expect the price of the underlying common shares to stay about the same.

Money Missteps

If you're seeking shelter from the storm, don't pick just any convertible fund: There's more to it than fees and performance. To increase returns, some managers add a portion of stocks to the mix, and this can increase volatility—just what you're trying to avoid. Check fund portfolios at www.cbsmarketwatch.com and www.personalwealth.com.

Taking A Spin

Convertibles, like most securities, should be only part of a diversified portfolio. Even after you've mastered the ins and outs of convertibles, you may not want to spend the time to follow them, or you may not want to make the minimum investment necessary, around $10,000 for an individual issue. Fortunately, there are lots of ways to avoid putting all your eggs in one vehicle. One option is convertibles packaged as mutual funds: This way, you can let someone else worry about conversion premiums and call dates! Before you invest, read the prospectus to be sure you understand how the securities will be managed and the manager's objectives. And always remember that past performance is not an indication of future returns.

Whatever road you decide to take, happy cruising.

Healthy Habit

Buying convertibles to insulate a portfolio? Look for those with higher premiums. Those with lower premiums tend to follow their underlying securities and may be almost as volatile.

DAY 14

Picky, Picky, Picky

How to choose a stock

> "Fundamentals answer the question what to buy and technicals answer the question when to buy it. Both must be used to achieve the optimum results."
> —Tom Dorsey, stock analyst

One evening, my husband and I were having dinner at a suburban bistro. During a pause in our conversation, I overheard the waiter and busboy discussing the stock market. Said the busboy, "I sold my Microsoft today." The waiter, who recently arrived from France, asked why. "It's simple," his friend replied, and he proceeded to explain his strategy. I was sure that I had forgotten any French I had ever known, so I asked our budding analyst what was behind his recommendation. What spewed forth was an astounding assortment of ideas: He had all the right words, but when he strung them together, they made no financial sense. Was the trouble my translation or his interpretation? I told him my opinion, noting that Microsoft would probably rise and then split. He politely told me that I really had no idea what I was talking about.

Our conversation reminded me of the story of John D. Rockefeller, who in August 1929 was having his shoes polished outside his Wall Street offices. When his shoeshine boy proffered a few stock tips, Rockefeller decided it was time for a correction. He sold everything—and the rest, well, is history. (Microsoft, by the way, doubled and split.)

Everyone, it seems, has an opinion. Predictions of stock performance and investment timing have been based on everything from the style of women's fashions (shorter hem lines and higher heels are considered bullish) to the level of consumer debt (high debt is considered bearish). Making sense of stocks is tough enough, but to predict the market's next move, you may feel your only hope lies in a combination of tea leaves and divine providence. We'll help take some of the guesswork away: For the next five days, you'll be immersed in the comings and goings of the Street of Dreams, learning everything from how to pick a stock to when to sell one. Maybe you won't need those tea leaves after all.

Theoretically Speaking

There are two general approaches to equity analysis: fundamental analysis and technical analysis. *Fundamental analysis* uses information on economic growth and industry and company statistics to estimate the value of an individual security and the market as a whole. Information is often gleaned from annual reports and studies of a stock's earnings, dividend yield and price compared to earnings. *Technical analysis* assumes that stocks trade with definite and predictable patterns. Technicians use indexes, averages, trends and charts to predict the direction of the overall market and specific stocks. While it really does take a rocket scientist to develop and interpret some of the more esoteric technical data, anyone can understand the basics of technical analysis.

If you're used to talking about bull and bear markets, you're already familiar with some of the components of technical analysis. The use of the terms "bull" and "bear" to signify positive and negative movements, respectively, of the equity markets probably started with the Dow theory, a type of technical analysis named after Charles H. Dow, an editor of *The Wall Street Journal* in the early 1900s. Although originally designed to predict changes in business activity, the Dow theory has become popular as a forecaster of stock market activity. According to this theory, major market trends are confirmed only when both the Dow Jones industrial average and the Dow Jones transportation average reach new highs or new lows.

The odd-lot theory concentrates on the trading activity of small investors. The idea is that small investors (those who buy or sell less than 100 shares) are usually incorrect about when to buy or sell, selling at the market's trough and buying at its peak. Technicians will buy when odd-lot sell orders increase relative to odd-lot buy orders. Sell recommendations are issued when odd-lot buy orders exceed odd-lot sell orders.

The advance-decline theory measures the number of stocks that have increased in price versus the number that have decreased over a particular period. This data is published daily. Generally, more advancing issues compared to declining issues is considered bullish.

Bull Or Bear?

At its most basic level, a bull market is one in which stock prices rise, while bear markets are those in which stock prices fall. Bull markets develop in four phases. In phase one, stock prices are low and investors are exasperated with stocks because of their poor performance or recent decline. Few investors are interested in stocks, convinced that stock prices may never rise again. During phase two, stock prices start to rise and trading activity increases. Corporate earnings increase and the economy looks healthy. People decide that maybe stocks might not be such a bad investment after all and slowly return to stocks.

In phase three, both business and financial markets look great. In fact, everything's coming up bullish. The markets are reaching new highs, and everyone is talking about their portfolios. Your broker is your favorite person—you talk to him or her more than to your spouse. By this time, most stocks are at new highs. The dividend yield of the averages is low compared to historical levels . . . and phase four is right around the corner. The final phase of a bull market is marked by speculation and buying of stocks with no apparent value

> **Trainer's Tip**
>
> "When a stock is trading above its bullish support line, always go long. When a stock is trading below its bearish resistance line, always go short."
>
> —Tom Dorsey, president, registered investment advisory firm Dorsey, Wright & Associates

or earnings. New issues (IPOs) are the hot item of the day, the name of the latest company to go public is on everyone's lips, and stock prices have gone into orbit.

Bear markets are not often marked by a single cataclysmic event (like a market crash) but by a gradual eroding in the fabric of the market. Like its counterpart, the bear is also composed of four phases. Phase one coincides with the last two phases of the bull, where investors who purchased low begin to take profits. Market rallies become less pronounced,

> **Smart Stretch**
> The largest charting and portfolio system in the world can be accessed at the Dorsey, Wright & Associates site at www.dorseywright.com. This site also gives excellent explanations of charts and how to use them.

and there is less potential for making profits. Some technicians call phase two "the panic stage" because stock prices decline sharply. Investors sell shares to avoid even bigger losses as stock prices come back to earth. The faster they sell, the faster and further stock prices fall, so they sell more, and so on. Phase three involves some improvement in stock prices, as prices rise and investors recover from very oversold conditions. Phase four often involves a long slide in stock prices as values drift ever lower until investors decide they are low enough and the buying (and the bull market) resumes.

Just A Technicality

Most investors associate technical analysis with the study of charts and the subjective interpretations of patterns to predict the direction of future stock movements. To be sure, there is a measure of subjectivity here, but chartists swear by their methods. Famous technicians include Robert Prechter, proponent of the Elliot Wave Theory; Tom Dorsey, whose point and figure charts provide many of Wall Street's signals; and Prudential Securities senior vice president Ralph Acampora, whose prediction that the Dow Jones industrial average would rise to 7000 and then to 10000 made him the laughing stock of Wall Street—for a while.

Over periods of time, stocks and stock markets tend to trade within defined ranges. At certain times, the price of a stock may rise to a level above which heavy selling occurs. This is called a resistance level, where a stock is "overbought." At other times, stock or market prices decline to a point where buying increases, stopping the downward trend in price. This is known as an area of support, and the stock is said to be "oversold."

A stock "breakout" occurs when its price increases above a resistance level or declines below a support level. A breakout signals to most technical analysts that whichever way a stock is going, it will tend to continue. (Remember inertia in physics?) Breakouts above resistance are bullish and are buy signals; those below supports are bearish and are sell signals.

Now, if that's all there is to this, it's a lot easier than you thought, right? The trick is to figure out what exactly you're facing. Technicians look for confirmation of a trend from one or more secondary indicators, such as an increase in a stock's trading volume.

Know Your Fundamentals

Fundamental analysis is more familiar to most investors: Famous fundamentalists include Peter Lynch, former manager of the Magellan mutual fund, and Warren Buffett, the Oracle of Omaha. Proponents of this approach believe that by looking at a company's fundamentals, investors can make educated decisions about what stocks to buy.

Of course, the most reliable way to select a stock is to use a combination of techniques. What fundamental investor hasn't bought into a great company based on its low price-to-earnings (P/E) ratio, admirable earnings and enviable market share and watched, dumbfounded, as it sank lower and lower, eventually hitting a price where even its CEO wants to throw in the towel? Had that investor checked the charts, perhaps this road to ruin could have been avoided. If you don't consider yourself a charting specialist, seek out a charting service that interprets the data unemotionally: It's almost as tough to see a flaw in your beloved stock as it is to see one in your child.

Another theory analysts rely on, called portfolio theory, uses sophisticated mathematical methods to understand the workings of the financial markets. In general, these techniques are based on the premise that investors are rational, and that the more risk one assumes, the greater the possibility of higher returns.

Risk, or the deviation of the actual return of a security from its expected return, is measured as a deviation from the mean. The amount of a stock's calculated deviation is called its beta. A stock's beta measures its volatility compared to a

---

Smart Stretch

To learn more about the fascinating world of individual company analysis, check out *The Motley Fool Investment Workbook* (Fireside).

broad index, like the S&P 500. A stock whose beta equals 1 rises and falls in step with the market. If a stock's beta is 1.88, that means if the market rises 10 percent, the stock should rise 18.8 percent. Or to put it another way, the stock movement should be 88 percent greater than that of the market. High betas are great when the market is rising, but because they represent greater volatility, they can be worrisome in falling markets.

No matter what kind of tools you rely on in making your investment decisions, nothing will work all the time—and nothing will miss all the time. In the end, perhaps the Newtonian theory is the most constant: What goes up comes back down.

Healthy Habit

Betas reflect a relationship to the market but do not determine its direction. Investors who think the market is going to go up should have portfolios with betas greater than 1; if they think the market is going to go down, the beta of their portfolio should be less than 1. To find out a stock's beta, check the *S&P reports*, available in your local library.

DAY 15

Circus, Circus

Learning the tricks of the stock trade

An anonymous millionaire reveals the secret to his success: "How I made my fortune? It was really quite simple. I bought an apple for five cents, spent the evening polishing it, and sold it the next day for 10 cents. With this I bought two apples, spent the evening polishing them, and sold them for 20 cents. And so it went until I had amassed a few thousand dollars. It was then I bought shares in Apple Computer—and made *$10 million*."

They split, they merge, they issue shares and buy them back when you least expect it . . . they do everything but wriggle on their bellies like a reptile. What do we speak of? Well, they make up part of the greatest show on earth.

What we're talking about, of course, are stocks. Who has never wondered if a stock will split and whether it's better to buy shares before or afterward? Is a stock buyback as wonderful as it sounds? Ringling Brothers and Barnum & Bailey may have a few tricks under the big top, but nothing can compare to the ins and outs of the "common" stock.

A Star Is Born

What's the fastest way to make money on Wall Street? If you answered "Buy an IPO," you're right . . . and wrong. Initial public offerings have been all the rage, sometimes delivering returns of 100, 200, even 600 percent—the first day. Sadly, however, most investors are left drooling at the sidelines: The ability to participate at the initial offering is often reserved for institutional accounts and a few well-heeled big clients of firms that specialize in underwriting. Occasionally, brokers can wheedle a few shares for their regular clients, but the really good stuff goes to the big guys.

It sounds like a dream—zip in, get a few thousand shares of a "sure thing," and zip out on the first trading day, toting your profits with you. Unfortunately, it doesn't work that way, at least not if you want to play again. Firms that issue stock look down on the aforementioned practice of "flipping" shares; if you do so, you may never get another chance. But don't pack up your money and go home . . . all you need is a little patience.

Everyone focuses on hot IPOs, but what happens when they inevitably cool off? Even shares of eBay lost altitude during the first two years. In fact, of the 600 IPOs that came out during 1996 and the first half of 1997, 77 percent of them had dipped below their offering price sometime during their first year of trading.

The real key to making money in IPOs is to wait for a stock's almost inevitable fall from grace, usually from six months to two years after the offering. Why the dip? When an IPO is issued, the company's principals (owners, venture capitalists and other insiders) agree not to sell for six months to keep the stock price relatively stable. This is called the "lockup" period. After this period, there is usually a second

Healthy Habit

Watch these clues on which IPOs to buy into after the lockup period:

- *Check the underwriter.* Goldman Sachs, Morgan Stanley and Alex Brown have good reputations.

- *Watch for volume.* Daily volume of more than 200,000 shares is key.

- *Look who's talking.* Seek out companies followed by at least five analysts.

- *Read the "red herring,"* also known as the preliminary prospectus, before you invest.

Smart Stretch

The www.ipo. com Web site offers information on initial offerings, including news, prices, filings and withdrawals. You can also find information on particular offerings.

offering of shares, and this is where some insiders sell stock to get their initial investment back. Additional shares may hurt the stock's price, and usually it tumbles. If you liked the stock at the offering, this is the time to get some shares—and you can probably afford more than the paltry 100 that might have been available at the offering.

In The Center Ring

Hurry, hurry, hurry . . . step right up and get your dividends here! After a corporation has earned a profit, it must decide whether to pay a dividend. Utilities usually distribute a large portion of their earnings. Real estate investment trusts distribute almost all their earnings, while growth companies like Microsoft pay no dividends at all.

Whether they're paid in cash or shares of stock, dividends are important to investors. Most companies that pay cash dividends do so on a quarterly basis, although some pay monthly or semiannually. Dividend payments often increase as earnings increase, making some companies' stock more attractive to investors who seek income vs. capital gains.

Who gets the dividend? Holders of a stock on the date of record will receive the dividend. Stocks trade ex-dividend two days prior to the date of record, and purchasers will not receive any dividend unless they own it before it goes ex-dividend. If you miss the dividend, however, never fear; when a stock trades ex-dividend, its price per share is reduced by the amount of the dividend. Stocks that are trading ex-dividend show an "x" next to the volume of transactions in financial newspapers.

Though some investors think otherwise, buying or selling a stock on an ex-dividend day does not necessarily result in a sudden profit or immediate loss. If a stock is selling for $50 per share and declares a 50-cent dividend, the price of the shares will be reduced by the amount of the dividend, making the price per share $49.50 on an ex-dividend date. If purchased prior to the ex-date, an investor would pay $50 and receive the dividend; after the ex-date, the price would be less the dividend payment.

Is it better to receive the dividend or pay a lower price for your shares? That depends. If you buy shares in a taxable account just prior to the ex-date, you'll receive the dividend and have to pay tax on it—which is like paying tax on your own money! For some investors, it pays to buy after the ex-date; consult a tax advisor to decide what's best for you.

If you'll be receiving a dividend, it may be a while in coming. The day the dividend is paid, known as the distribution date, may be several weeks after the date of record. Many companies make payments on a consistent basis, though, so their investors can count on when dividends will arrive.

Instead of paying investors in cash, some companies choose to distribute profits in the form of stock shares. Stock dividends don't change the value of an investor's holdings, although some investors incorrectly believe that a stock dividend increases the assets of the underlying firm. Here's how it works: Company XYZ declares a 10 percent stock dividend. An investor who holds 100 shares at a price of $20 would then own 110 shares with a price of $18.18. The stock price falls because the number of shares has increased. Stock dividends increase the ability of a company to grow by freeing up its cash to invest elsewhere.

Split Personality

There's almost nothing investors love more than a stock that is splitting. Possessing more shares makes you feel like you have more money. But like a visit to a fun house, all is not as it appears. Here's how it works: Say you own 100 shares of XYZ Corporation, with a price per share of $50. If it splits 2-for-1, you suddenly have 200 shares—but at a price of $25 per share. No matter how you cut it, the value of your investment is the same: $5,000.

On the other hand, stock splits perform several useful functions, including increasing a stock's liquidity and dropping the share price to a level where more investors can participate. Many small investors who can't afford stocks trading at $100-plus prices wait for big-ticket stocks to split. Though splits are normally just a mathematical affair, pent-up demand could bounce post-split share prices higher.

There is more than one type of split. The reverse split is used by companies whose share price is very low: They decrease the number of outstanding shares, which increases their price. This is done to attract investors who wouldn't think of buying a stock selling at $2 per share but who might buy shares selling at $20.

Bull markets, those characterized by rising stock prices, often see more splits. Between October 1990 and October 1998, more than half the companies listed in the S&P 500 split their stock. In 1996, 166 New York Stock Exchange-listed companies split their shares, up 26 percent from

Trainer's Tip

"Finding stocks that will likely split their shares isn't as tough as it seems. First, check stocks with a history of splitting. Narrow this field by looking for those that have increasing earnings and good future prospects. Finally, check the stock prices. Stocks often split at about the same price they did in the past."

—*Joseph Tigue, managing editor of* S&P Outlook

the prior year. 1983 saw a record-setting 225 NYSE-listed companies split their stocks.

Splits are generally well-received because they often signal that management is optimistic about a company's future. While past performance is no guarantee of future results, stock splits could be one source of strong market performance. A study done by David Ikenberry, a finance professor at Rice University, found that 1,200 stocks on the New York and American exchanges that split 2-for-1 gained an average of 3.5 percent the day after the split was announced. Prudential Securities' research found that nine of the 14 companies in the S&P 100 index that split their stocks in 1996 have outperformed the index by an average of 8.38 percent.

Should you buy before or after a split? Like most opportunities in the stock market, there are conflicting viewpoints and no guaranteed road to riches. Prices don't always rise after a split; they will often dip initially as some investors sell shares to diversify. And share prices often increase even more in the months before a split is announced than they do afterwards. Stock splits are rewards given to longtime shareholders, so if you like a stock that has split, you should hang onto it. If you can afford to buy shares of a high-profile stock before the split, sometimes you can make some money by selling immediately after, provided the stock rises, of course. This is like putting your head in the lion's mouth, though—if your stock doesn't get up and go, be prepared to stay put or sell at a loss.

To find out which stocks are splitting, check *Barron's* financial newspaper or consult your financial advisor.

Balancing Act

To an unknowing observer, October 27, 1997, started out like any other day on Wall Street. But after a steep drop in foreign markets, the U.S. stock market tumbled, dropping several hundred points before circuit breakers shut the action down. The next day, traders and investors

Perk Up Your Portfolio

You may not have to wait for rising prices to reap the benefits of your stock purchase. Some companies reward their shareholders now. You can often qualify for these perks by owning as little as one share of stock registered in your name. Shares held on brokerage accounts are also eligible, but procedures for claiming awards may differ. Perks can change, so check with the company's investor relations department for specifics.

- Hassle-free holiday shopping is what you get from General Mills (GIS). For a fraction of the regular cost, shareholders can send gift packages filled with assorted General Mills products, plus coupons for meal discounts at The Olive Garden and Red Lobster restaurants. The retail value of the holiday gift box is more than $50, but shareholders can purchase one or more for $19.95 each. The price includes UPS delivery to anywhere in the continental United States; orders are filled on a first-come, first-served basis.

- Anheuser-Busch (BUD) offers shareholders and their immediate families a 15 percent discount on regular admission to its family entertainment parks, including Sea World and Busch Gardens, and a 30 to 50 percent discount on merchandise from its promotional products catalog.

- Every December, Wm. Wrigley Jr. Co. (WWY) sends a box of gum to its shareholders—a sweet way to thank them for their support.

- If you'd like to blast off to Space Mountain, Disney (DIS) has a deal that's not Goofy: Shareholders can get a two-year membership in the Magic Kingdom Club by buying the Magic Kingdom Club Gold Card for $45 (a $14 discount off the regular price). Discounts at Disney stores and on accommodations at selected Disney resorts can save you hundreds of dollars a year, depending on your travel schedule. Shareholders are also eligible for numerous other travel discounts, including cruises and car rentals. Membership cards are usually mailed by February to all registered shareholders who owned stock by the previous December.

awaited the opening with the trepidation of acrobats on a high wire in a hurricane. Stocks opened down, but then bounced back after IBM announced a stock buyback. The announcement seemed to act like a safety net for the plummeting market. In all, 120 companies announced plans to buy back shares of their stocks, and some analysts viewed these announcements as essential to helping stop the market's free-fall.

Share buybacks are seen by many investors as a sign that a company's stock is undervalued. Often the share price rises after the announcement of a buyback; after all, if shares are good enough for a company to buy back, they must be a pretty good buy.

Not so fast. First, while many companies announce share buybacks, they are under no obligation to make good on their claim. Some companies do repurchase shares, reissuing them to employees in the form of stock options. Still others borrow heavily to buy shares, thus replacing equity with debt, leaving investors with a more leveraged company, a weaker balance sheet, and more potential volatility in an economic downturn.

Share buybacks seem enticing, but before you invest, make sure the company's earnings are still growing, not faltering. Repurchase of shares could limit a company's ability to invest in research and development or buy another company.

Now that the properties of stocks are not quite so mysterious, we hope you'll see that this is one act that may have something for everyone. Come one, come all.

DAY 16

Weight It Out

Choosing between value and growth investing

Frederick is a value investor in every way. For one thing, he likes to buy low and sell high. But he's a value person in lots of other ways, too. He loves a bargain, whether it's getting the best price on air fare to Africa, buying a Camry at a few hundred dollars above cost, or picking a stock that no one else likes and holding it until it has its day in the sun.

But Frederick is relatively new to investing, having only started when he retired a few years ago. "I noticed that a lot of my retired friends were making more money than I was with my money invested in the company's retirement account," he says. "I also figured that keeping everything completely safe wasn't going to do me any good." Taking matters into his own hands, Frederick started reading, reading, reading. But not just any articles, and not just articles on stocks. Instead, Frederick divides his research between business magazines that teach him about companies and financial magazines and newsletters that discuss the merits of buying a company's stock. He bounces ideas off his financial advisor, and they work on his portfolio together.

His key to success? Buy something you really believe in when it's low, and be prepared to hold onto it for a while. "Not everything is going to go up like mad right away," he says. "Sometimes you have to be patient." Does Frederick's strategy work? Well, just last year he and his wife, Helen, toured the Far East and spent several months in Germany, and they have just returned from a visit to Australia. Now, that's some way to retire!

Frederick wouldn't be where he is today without knowing the difference between the various types of stocks and how to combine value and growth styles. Getting a handle on this is as fundamental as knowing which machine is for upright rows and which is for abdominal. Are you ready to start today's regimen? Fasten your weight belt!

Feel The Burn

Any weight trainer will assure you that you've got to vary your lifting routine to achieve optimal results. The same is true for your stock portfolio: Both value and growth styles play a part in a successful investment scheme. For all of their differences—and perhaps because of them—these two complementary and equally challenging moves will give your portfolio the strength training it needs to get into shape.

Value investing . . . to some people, them's fighting words. If you've ever been stuck in a stodgy fund or glared at a statement that featured primarily stocks that were "undervalued" when you bought them and have since done nothing but sink still further, all you may really want to know is the quickest way to the next Internet IPO. But before you toss your "losers" over the side and jump headfirst into the next anystock.com, take a look at what's behind these two classes of investing.

Growth investors seek companies whose earnings are compounding at a rate greater than other companies in the same industry and faster than whatever index to which they are compared. Such stocks need to maintain their momentum to keep their prices rising; therefore, they must sustain above-average earnings growth. Investors who favor such companies often pay a high price for the stocks, especially when compared to the company's earnings or book value. To succeed, these investors must anticipate the rate of future earnings growth and discern whether it's enough to justify not only current prices but considerable future price increases.

Some people call this investing style "the greater fool method": You buy at a high price, hoping to later sell at an even higher price to a greater fool. These companies are often found in growing, flamboyant sectors, such as technology, consumer services, health care and consumer staples. Anyone who invested in these sectors during the past several bull market years was anything but a fool: Growth shares outpaced their value counterparts by remarkable margins.

Value investors, on the other hand, measure what a company's stock is worth now, then try to buy it at a price lower than this value. These companies are characterized by a stock price lower than their earnings and book value, but they pay higher dividends than do growth stocks and are more often found in mature industries, including utility, energy, consumer cyclicals (such as retail and home building) and financial companies.

> **Trainer's Tip**
>
> "If you want to find value stocks, consider focusing on cash flow instead of earnings. After all, cash pays bills; earnings don't."
>
> —Jay Kaplan, manager, Prudential Small-Cap Value Fund

The secret to value investing can be summed up in a few words: Buy low, sell high. Despite what the pundits say, you won't be the first to take this unpopular route. Some rather noteworthy value investors have preceded you—strategist Benjamin Graham, mutual fund manager John Neff, and president of Berkshire Hathaway Warren Buffett, to name a few.

Adjust Your Moves

When selecting value stocks, chartered financial analysts Marvin I. Cline and Richard E. Buchwald of Berwind Investment Management LP suggest choosing stocks with at least a few of these eight characteristics:

1. It has a price-to-earnings (P/E) ratio that is at a significant discount to the market's.

2. It has a low price-to-cash-flow ratio. (Some value enthusiasts regard this more highly than P/E ratio.)

3. It sells at a low price compared to its value.

4. Its dividend yield is greater than that of the market.

5. It can be purchased for less than 50 percent to 60 percent of its estimated private market value.

6. It can be purchased at two-thirds of its current net liquidation value (current assets less total debt).

7. It has a high level of corporate insider buying.

8. The company has implemented a stock repurchase plan.

While only a few stocks meet all these criteria, a reasonable number can meet three or more.

Firmer Abs In How Many Days?

Value investing may seem straightforward enough, but does it get results? While past performance is no guarantee of future returns, Kline and Buchwald cite a 1976 study by Benjamin Graham, the father of value investing, in which he concludes that applying value investment principles resulted in an average annual rate of return of approximately 19 percent over the 50-year period from 1925 to 1975—well above that of the general market. Tom Jackson, a Prudential Investments portfolio manager, agrees: "If you follow the value style over the long term," he says, "you could outperform [the rest of the market]."

Jackson conducted a study that concluded that one dollar invested in 1970 in the S&P 500 (with all dividends reinvested) would have been worth $30.20 at the end of 1997, representing a compound annual rate of return of 12.95 percent. The same dollar invested in low price-to-book-value stocks would have been worth $73.27, representing a compound annual rate of return of 16.57 percent. Had that same dollar been invested in a low P/E ratio value stock, it would have grown to $92.66, for a compound annual rate of return of 17.56 percent. (Taxes, fees and commissions are not considered in this example.) Jackson notes that these returns aren't garnered every quarter, or even every year, but that three- to five-year periods may see the potential for such returns. In value investing, time is on your side.

Like all things in life, value is relative. "A value investor," says Janet Lowe, author of *Value Investing Made Easy*, "should study the work of

Trainer's Tip

"Once you can identify a cheap stock, verifying its appreciated value is easy. If you're buying stocks at 50 cents on the dollar, when [the stock's value] gets to dollar-for-dollar, sell."

—Tom Jackson, manager, Prudential Equity Fund

Benjamin Graham." Lowe condenses Graham's ideas for racking up relatively safe, high profits into these six rules:

1. Don't pay too much attention to the overall market. It's easier to find good buys when share prices are generally low, but you can still spot a few bargains even when the market is high.

2. Buy a stock as if you were buying the whole company.

3. Look for signs of specific value (below-average P/E ratios, above-average yields, and earnings that have doubled since 1985 with no more than two annual declines of more than 5 percent).

4. Focus on quality.

5. Diversify with both stocks and bonds.

6. Above all, think for yourself and be patient.

Healthy Habit

To get the right mix of value and growth, consider how much volatility your portfolio can withstand. Unlike growth stocks, value stocks pay dividends that may help smooth out the fluctuations over time. If you prefer to leave roller coasters at the amusement park, shift your weight toward value; if you've got a strong stomach and a long time frame, consider adding more growth.

Push And Pull

How can you get the best of both worlds? You don't have to be Arnold Schwarzenegger to find good stocks at attractive prices in both classes. Value investors concentrate on mature or out-of-favor industries and stocks that present turnaround opportunities. Good growth stocks, on the other hand, are those that belong to the most popular companies, often having the biggest volume and best perceived potential for future earnings growth. Growth and value stocks come in all sizes, from the biggest blue chips to little companies you've never heard of.

Does selecting stocks have you so baffled you're thinking of sticking with free weights? Relax. You don't have to do it all on your own. Muscle over to your nearest Morningstar report for a list of value or growth funds in each sector. Whether you're looking for large-cap, midcap or small-cap funds, there are plenty to choose from. Just read the prospectus before you invest, and remember that past performance is not an indication of future returns. Come to think of it, for a lot of value funds, it would be great if recent past performance was never repeated!

Weighting It Out

To make the most of their investment dollars, value investors buy when stocks are out of favor and prices are low. Seasoned investors are used to a buy-and-hold strategy, sometimes holding and holding and holding while it seems like the momentum investors are having all the fun. So when do you sell? There's an old adage on the Street of Dreams: Buy on the bad news and sell on the good. For value investors, this adage should become a mantra, though many lack the perseverance to do more than chant it.

Does a value workout seem too long and hard? No one is suggesting you have to stick to a single fitness regimen. Like any good routine, diversity breeds satisfaction. What kind of investor are you? Kurt Kazanjian, author of *Wall Street's Picks for 1999* and *Growing Rich With Growth Stocks*, says: "You can spot a value investor a mile away buying what everyone else is trying to sell. They look for stocks making new lows instead of those making new highs. Value permeates their lives—they don't spend a lot on cars, houses or clothes." If this describes your lifestyle, maybe value investing is right for you.

Of course, where the market is headed is anyone's guess. Falling interest rates, slowing economic growth and lower corporate profits are conditions that generally favor value over growth; big earnings increases and economic expansion generally favor growth over value. Not sure what the world is coming to? Stretch your portfolio's muscles by pumping a bit of each.

Small Is Beautiful

Diversifying with small-cap stocks

> "You can never be too thin or too rich."
> —Wallis Simpson

L
ou likes little companies . . . very little companies. In fact, although he's a lawyer by trade and license, he publishes an investment newsletter and even manages a few accounts—not very legal, but it's been pretty lucrative. He's had good luck with his stock picks for one reason: Lou takes the time to thoroughly research companies that interest him. He calls the CEO, asks questions, and translates the information into either a buy or sell recommendation. People who want to invest in individual shares of small companies should do what Lou does. Of course, they should do it legally, but that, Virginia, is another tale.

Everyone knows that bigger is better. Bigger houses and bigger cars are signs of bigger paychecks and bigger successes. The stock market has echoed this theme, with the large companies housed in the Dow Jones industrial average and Standard & Poor's 500 racking up, well, really *big* gains for the past six years. But as comedian Steve Martin once put it, maybe now's the time for everyone to get small . . . small companies, that is.

Why should investors abandon what seems to be a sure thing to embark on what could be a volatile and risky relationship? At first glance, the question seems academic. After all, for the 12 months ending December 1998, the total return of the Russell 2000, an index of small-cap stocks, was behind the S&P 500 by more than 20 percent—one of the worst trailing performances in the history of the index.

But Claudia Mott, director of small-company research at Prudential Securities, notes that now could be the time to take the plunge. "Historically, the average return for the Russell 2000 in the six-month period following 12 months of underperformance is well above 20 percent," she says. "Although many of these periods are overlapping, there have only been three subsequent six-month periods in which the small caps underperformed the S&P Composite." However, the prices of small-company shares are generally more volatile than those of larger, more established companies. So the question is, Should small stocks be a part of your portfolio?

Small Is Beautiful

Why small companies? In addition to their relatively poor recent past performance, several trends have converged to make this sector attractive. Many investors, tired of watching their small-company stock values decline while large-company shares hit new highs, have redeemed shares in small-cap mutual funds to switch to the big guys. This has pressured fund managers to liquidate shares, dropping stock prices still further. The selling eventually ceases, and it is replaced by new investors seeking undervalued sectors. This inflow of funds has somewhat stabilized the price of some of the top small-cap stocks and led to an increase in some mutual fund share prices.

Recent capital gains tax cuts are also good for small caps. While stocks tend to sell off in response to such tax cuts, the reaction is often short-lived. Small-cap stocks have done well in the past when rates have fallen, as seen in the late '70s and early '80s when their performance outshone that of their larger cousins. On the other hand, when rates have risen, small stocks underperformed large ones. Strong economic earnings have been positive for small caps, recessions negative. Most economic sooth-sayers see smooth sailing ahead, a good sign for small companies.

Finally, comparisons between the relative prices of large and small stocks show the latter to be a bargain at current prices. Small-cap stocks appear to be one of the last relatively cheap alternatives in a market that has soared beyond most investors' wildest expectations, further strengthening the case for small companies.

"When you look at the stock market over 75 years, small-cap stocks have outperformed large caps over that 75-year period," notes Randall E. Haase, senior vice president and portfolio manager of the Alliance Quasar Fund. "The last time they outperformed, though, was in 1993. [Unfortunately], people don't have a memory of more than a few years, and people are by nature momentum investors, so all their money is going to large-cap funds."

Little By Little

On the surface, the case for small caps looks good. Although past performance is anything but a guarantee of future returns, a study done by research firm Ibbotson Associates shows that long-term investors in small-company stocks have had a lot to be happy about. Assuming reinvestment of all dividends and capital gains, one dollar invested in 1925 in small-cap stocks would have been worth $4495.99 at the end of 1996. The same dollar invested in large-cap stocks would have grown to $1370.95.

Although some scholars question the ability of small caps to surge past their larger brethren under current conditions, citing the remarkable gains of the 1970s

Trainer's Tip

"Anyone who's not about to retire should have some small-cap exposure. If you're going to buy a fund, you should hold onto it. People have lost some of their investment by trying to pick the right moment to get in and get out. The idea is to get in and hold on for the long term."

—Claudia Mott, director of small-company research, Prudential Securities and early '80s as an aberration, Claudia Mott disagrees. She notes that in the 10-year period from 1986 to 1996, one dollar invested in small-cap issues would have grown to $4.15, while the same amount invested in large companies would return $3.39 to investors—and this in a period that was hardly anything to brag about for small caps.

Even if small caps do outperform large caps over time, the ride is anything but smooth. With the possibility of higher returns comes higher risk; while some small companies may accelerate into outer space, others have been known to come back to earth with a sickening thud.

If you're concerned about taking too much of a risk, a good way to begin investing in small caps is slowly. Consider investing a set amount monthly in a fund, and be prepared to stick with it for the long term. Review the asset allocation of your portfolio, then think about devoting a portion to small caps. Read that prospectus first—and be prepared for a wild ride.

Little Things Mean A Lot

If you prefer to put together your own portfolio of small companies, do so cautiously. Unlike the Dow's components, analysts who follow teeny stocks are few and far between. Information can be scant, too, making it hard to decide not only what to buy, but when to sell. Finally, many smaller issues are quite illiquid, making them difficult to sell.

Experts advise sticking with industries you know. If you own a small company that markets computer software, start in the technology industry. Keep abreast of industry trends through trade magazines, and be sure to get a copy of the annual and quarterly reports of companies you are considering. Look for companies with good management, little or no debt, high ownership of shares by insiders and a unique niche in an industry.

Savvy small-company investors also avoid those with high ownership by institutional investors, such as mutual

Healthy Habit

To pick yourself a peck of small potatoes, look for companies that are cheap (price-to-earnings ratios of 15 and below, based on the previous 12 months' earnings), have low debt (less than 40 percent of total capital) and solid earnings (market value is lower than sales). Screen potential picks with some of the programs listed in Day 43.

funds. Wouldn't you want to go where the pros go? Definitely, but it helps to beat them to the punch. If the shares of a company you like are thinly traded and few in number, the arrival of a mutual fund on the scene could cause share prices to rise—enough for you to get out at a higher price!

As an investor in this volatile sector, once you've picked a company, keep your exposure to it small. Unlike large multinational firms that boast many products and services, the fortunes of a small company may ride on one product. Problems with production or packaging could put it out of business. A diversified portfolio will help reduce your risk.

Whatever you decide, don't fall in love with a small-company stock. You may have put tremendous time and energy into selecting and follow-ing it, but be alert to the changing winds of fortune and be ready to either take your profits or cut your losses. If you don't have the money to buy several companies' stocks, consider a mutual fund. Either way, make room for both growth and value styles in your portfolio. (Review Day 16 for more on investing styles.)

When filling out your portfolio, small-company stocks are yet another way to add diversity while also lowering your risk over time. It's a small world, after all.

Bye-Bye, Love

When to sell
a stock

> "Bears
> make money
> and bulls
> make money,
> but pigs get
> slaughtered."
> —Wall Street axiom

As a member of the press, I often fulfill speaking requests. I once drove two hours to Albemarle, North Carolina—what many might consider a very small town. As I pulled into the packed parking lot of the restaurant where the meeting of the Albemarle Lions Club was to be held, I was sure this was going to be a wasted afternoon. The baby blue decor extended to everything—walls, ceiling, chairbacks; even the ladies' room had a blue hue, which was almost identical to the hair color of some of the meeting's attendees. Determined to make the best of it, I strode into the room in search of the program chairperson.

A warmer welcome was never had, and I barely noticed as an hour flew by, filled with delectable food (crisp fried shrimp, meltingly sweet oysters, tender catfish), genuine fellowship and hilarious conversation. After completing my stock market update, I fielded a lot of astute questions from that "small town" audience. Finally, an ancient attendee raised his hand. As he rose with the help of a cane, a hush fell over the room. He said,

"Young lady, over the years, I've made a lot of money in the stock market." (The whole room was nodding in agreement.) "Today I'd like to share with you my secret of investing: I sold too soon."

Most people have the opposite problem: holding onto a stock too long. Today we'll work out some ways to help you know when you and your stock should part company.

Love Me, Love My Stock

While love may be a many-splendored thing, for some of us, it pales in comparison to a winning stock portfolio. Nothing quite matches the excitement of a new acquisition or the thrill of watching those little numbers grow. But what happens when love (or the market) goes sour? How do you know when it's time to call it quits?

Most professional investors know better than to become emotionally involved with a stock, but it's not always so with the rest of us. We watch one pet investment sit there, up a point, down a point, not going anywhere, while we cringe as another beloved takes a dive, dragging the rest of the portfolio down with it. Knowing when to sell is at least, if not more, important than knowing when to buy. If anyone knew a guaranteed way to buy in at the bottom and sell out at the top, chances are they wouldn't write about it—they'd be on their private island under an umbrella. Still, there are some tell-tale signs that indicate when it's time to dump those losers in favor of building a solid, long-lasting relationship with the stock market.

Look Out Below

Once upon a time, there were some very smart people who invested in strong companies with good balance sheets, solid earnings and high analyst ratings. Everything was going along famously, with stock values gradually climbing . . . until the market corrected and their portfolio came down to earth with a thud. Ugh! Two of my favorite clients gave me a mug that solves the problem: It has a lit-

Healthy Habit

Want to ease the pain of a loss? You can deduct a loss of up to $3,000 a year against your income. Losses greater than $3,000 can be carried forward to future years. If you like the stock and want to repurchase it, be sure to wait 31 days, or your loss won't count. Stock must be held in a taxable account to take this loss, and IRAs and other retirement plans don't count.

> **Trainer's Tip**
>
> "Never try to catch the top or the bottom of a market. Bernard Baruch always said he was not interested in the bottom 20 percent or the top 20 percent. He was just interested in the middle 60 percent."
>
> —Tom Dorsey,
> president, registered
> investment advisory firm
> Dorsey, Wright & Associates

tle spinner with the choices buy, sell, hold—and jump!

If your stocks correct with the market, the most important thing to do is not panic. Now is the time to repeat the mantra "I am a long-term investor" to yourself and to anyone else who will listen. Market corrections are the times that try investors' patience (and pocketbooks), and they will happen to you, so be ready. If you're looking for a guarantee with your investment, buy yourself a dishwasher, not a stock. Even if your stocks are fundamentally fine, the market may be overvalued—and when it corrects, it often takes no prisoners.

If you can't stomach a sharp drop in your portfolio's value, it may be time to reallocate your assets. Consider lightening up on stocks and repositioning your investments to other asset classes, such as cash, bonds or real estate. Should you decide to hold on for the duration, remember that investors who made it through the October 1987 crash lived to love and invest again (and brag about how smart they were, too).

Lift And Separate

You did your research like the pros, carefully selected your stock, and sat back to watch it grow. The share price picked up a bit, then slowly dropped. Undaunted, you doubled your investment, telling yourself that if you liked it at 25, you'd love it at 10, right? Maybe, but don't continue to buy a stock just because the price is low. It may get a lot lower before it goes back up—if it ever does. A low price may be an indication of a problem. After all, if the rest of the population is selling, who are you to disagree? Don't be afraid to fall out of love with your stock . . . a bad selection does not a bad person make. Marriage is for life, but investing doesn't have to be.

Instead, give yourself a set period of time to evaluate the position. Compare the company's earnings with those of other companies in its industry and with an index of similar-sized companies (the Standard & Poor's 500 for large stocks, the Russell 2000 for small stocks). If your stock's earnings are consistently below those of similar companies and its price appreciation lags behind the appropriate index, consider selling. Your money could make more for you elsewhere.

On the other hand, maybe you've picked a winner. After you invested, the price rose slowly and steadily until you were sitting pretty with a nice profit. Recently, however, your stock's growth has slowed; it's no longer the star of your portfolio. Should you stay or should you go? Instead of gazing into your crystal ball or consulting a palm reader, think back to why you bought the stock in the first place. Is the industry still viable? Will economic and interest rate changes positively affect the company or the industry? In short, evaluate the stock as though you were buying it today. If you would still buy it, hold onto it. If you're not sure, sell some of the stock and keep part to evaluate later.

Earning Your Devotion

Earnings are a tricky thing. Historically, the price-to-earnings ratio was considered a reliable measure of a stock's value. Investors could evaluate a stock's merit based on its relationship to others in its industry: A P/E ratio higher than the industry average meant a stock was relatively overpriced, while a low P/E often signaled a good value. The meteoric rise of Internet stocks, however, flies in the face of all previous notions of buying companies with great earnings. Lots of these companies have no earnings; indeed, some regularly lose money, yet share prices stay in orbit around Jupiter!

The secret here is momentum, my boy; momentum. A stock that is in motion remains in motion—at least until it hits the wall. As Internet companies merge and consolidate, prices will remain volatile. If you like this sector of the market, remember that most of these shares trade not on earnings, but on the service's number of subscribers.

Will You Still Love It Tomorrow?

Sometimes you make an investment that just takes off. Maybe it's a popular new issue or the turnaround of an old favorite;

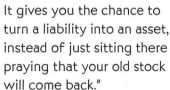

Trainer's Tip

"A small loss, when realized, becomes the opportunity for profit elsewhere. It gives you the chance to turn a liability into an asset, instead of just sitting there praying that your old stock will come back."

—Martin Zweig, manager, Zweig Mutual Funds

maybe it's just your turn (finally) to get lucky. Whatever the reason, you very quickly amass a 20 percent profit in a choppy market. How do you know when it's time to let go?

One strategy involves determining a price ceiling and selling when the stock reaches it. Since no one can accurately predict the bottom or the top of the market, sell when your stock reaches your target, unless there are specific circumstances—such as a takeover bid, sharp jump in earnings, or share buyback—that portend a higher stock price. Hanging on for "just one more point" is often not a good idea. Look at it this way: If you make a 20 percent profit on every trade you make, you will be one happy (and wealthy!) investor.

You can facilitate this strategy by entering a sell order at a specific price. This is called a *sell-limit order*, and it ensures your stock will sell at the designated price or higher. NASDAQ-traded stocks don't have the "or better" provision; when the share price hits your limit, it becomes a market order. This way you don't have to spend too much time making the same decision over and over. If you change your mind, you can always adjust your order.

Cut Your Losses

In stocks, as in relationships, it's not a good idea to hang onto a loser hoping things will change. If your stock is down 15 percent, it may hurt to sell it, but a 15 percent loss is easier to swallow than a 20 percent or 30 percent drop. It's better to get out with at least some of your money (and dignity) intact.

How to tell if your stock is a loser? Check the annual and quarterly reports. If quarterly earnings are less than last year's or lower than anticipated for two or three consecutive quarters, it's not a good sign. Many stock analysts subscribe to the cockroach theory of earnings: One quarter of bad earnings is bound to be followed by more, and poor earnings often translate into lower stock prices. Read the president's message for clues to the company's direction. An upbeat message filled with achievements and plans

Money Missteps

You've heard it many times: "You can't go broke taking a profit." In some cases, that's true, provided you're taking into account commission costs and tax consequences. Don't sell just for fun. If you enjoy trading things for the sake of trading them, consider baseball cards, not stocks.

beats a bunch of excuses for poor performance.

Check the buying and selling patterns
of company insiders. This public information often gives you helpful clues. While it
is possible that someone may be liquidating shares to pay for a son's braces or a
daughter's wedding, if sales overall far
outnumber purchases, perhaps you should
re-evaluate your position.

Healthy Habit

Review your
stop-loss orders fre-
quently. Setting
your stop-loss too
high can cause you to get
stopped out too early—you
may regret having sold your
stock because the market
fell just a little.

If you're worried about a stock taking a
sudden plunge, you can guard against
major downdrafts with a *stop-loss order*.
Traders use this technique to help safe-
guard their profits and limit their losses. Check your stock's trading patterns
and find out its support level (see Day 14 for a review of technical analysis)
and consider setting your limit at least 10 percent below this point. If the
price of the stock falls, your order becomes a market order, selling at the
next price available. Unfortunately, when markets trade rapidly and stocks
are dropping fast, your order may be activated at $50 but the next trade
might be $47. If the possibility of a free-fall terrifies you, consider a *stop-
limit order*. This locks in a particular price at which you're willing to sell; if
shares open below that price, you'll still own your stock.

Of course, if you decide to liquidate, you may lose the opportunity to
profit if stocks start to go back up. Ironically, bull markets have had the
greatest momentum in their early stages. This helps investors compensate for the time (and money) lost when stock performance lags behind
that of more conservative investments. If you've got all your assets in
cash or money-market accounts when the market goes back up, you may
miss out.

You'd Better Shop Around

While parting from a loser may not be such sweet sorrow, don't overlook the stock market when it holds a sale. Many investors wouldn't dream
of paying full price for a new suit but shy away when prices fall. Is it any
wonder they don't make money? Make a shopping list of companies'
stocks you'd like to own, and the next time the market corrects, pick your
shares at bargain prices. Don't think of it as a bear market; it's more like a
"blue light special."

Whatever else you decide to do with your portfolio, if appreciation is what you're after, some of your assets should be invested in equities. Before making any investment decision, consult your tax and financial advisors to review your overall situation, investment objectives and goals, and risk tolerance. Will you win or lose? Well, all's fair in love, war and investing.

DAY 19

Open And Shut Case

Investing in closed-end funds

> "One of the best rules anybody can learn about investing is to do nothing, absolutely nothing, unless there is something to do."
> —Jim Rogers

"Aunt" Mildred and "Uncle" Herman have been my clients for a long time; I inherited their accounts when other brokers left the firm. Lucky for me. In the never-ending search to secure enough income for these especially beloved clients (and about 100 other equally loved retired clients who depend on me to help make their golden years golden), we learned together about closed-end funds.

During the late 1980s and early 1990s, many new closed-end funds were issued. At first glance, they looked pretty good—low share price, good yield and no fee to the client. Wait a minute—how do you charge nothing to the client and still pay the broker? Turns out that while clients didn't pay a fee

Healthy Habit

Don't confuse closed-end funds with funds that are closed. The latter are open-end funds that have closed their doors to new investments. Some funds do this when their size makes them inefficient or when an influx of too much cash threatens the style of the fund.

on the initial offering of most of these funds, share prices dipped after a while about as much as the broker's concession (a.k.a. commission). Ah-ha. The key was to buy shares several months after the initial public offering. While clients paid commission at this time, often the share price was lower. Perfect. High income for my adopted aunts and uncles, commission that didn't sneak around, and a great way to diversify.

For the next six days, we'll change our focus and work out with mutual funds. We'll start today by broadening your horizons with closed-end funds.

There's an old Chinese saying, "May you live in interesting times." Certainly, the last several decades have provided their share of great and not-so-great markets. Some years it seems that just about all mutual funds end the year under water . . . at least those in your portfolio! It's enough to make you want to get off that investment treadmill and "invest" your money under your mattress. The problem is, a mattress filled with your savings won't help you reach your financial objectives—and it's mighty uncomfortable.

On the other hand, mutual funds, also known as open-end investment companies, offer many benefits for investors. They provide access to professional management, diversification and variety. For those with only a few thousand dollars to invest, mutual funds provide an assortment of choices that are otherwise unavailable.

Those searching for additional venues might consider another class of managed investments: closed-end funds. These investments provide the same benefits as their cousins, mutual funds—both are professionally managed, diversified investment pools. But unlike mutual funds, which continually issue new shares and redeem outstanding shares at net asset value (NAV), closed-end funds issue a fixed number of shares which are then traded on a stock exchange.

Think of a closed-end fund as you would a new issue of stock. Share prices fluctuate not only due to the merits of the underlying company, but also in response to investors' opinions of the company's future prospects. The same is true for shares of closed-end funds. When shares are selling for more than their NAV, they're selling at a premium; shares selling for less than NAV are said to sell at a discount.

Know Thyself—And Thy Investment

Which is better, an open-end or closed-end fund? That's like trying to decide whether a StairMaster or a Cybex Bike will help you shed more pounds. Often it's a matter of taste. Both instruments can play important roles in a portfolio. When investing in closed-end funds, here are some guidelines.

First, understand the fund's objectives, investment strategy and risks before you invest. Mutual funds are sold by prospectus. Closed-end funds, however, are only sold by prospectus when they are first issued. If you're buying at this stage, get a copy of the prospectus and read it before you invest. Once the fund's shares begin trading, information is available directly from the company. Most closed-end funds are only too happy to send information to you or to discuss their fund over the phone. Fund descriptions and phone numbers can be found in *Standard & Poor's Stock Reports*. *Morningstar's Closed-End Funds Report*, a research publication available in libraries and brokerage firms, includes basic information about funds, analysis and comparisons. There are also a variety of newsletters that deal with closed-end funds.

Secondhand Rose

New closed-end funds can be hot, often capitalizing on a new trend, an emerging market or a new twist on an old theme. But buyer beware—a too-hot fund can burn the unwary when it starts to cool. Even if new funds initially do as well as their managers expect, their share prices may fall during the first year anyway. Some funds, though properly managed, don't live up to all the hype, and although they perform adequately, investors are disappointed, running for the door as though someone had yelled "fat" in a crowded health club.

What's behind the great escape? Part of the problem is the way new funds are issued. Most closed-end funds are issued at prices greater than their NAV. For example, if you buy in at the offering,

Healthy Habit

Consider investing in a closed-end fund if it's trading at a fat discount to its net asset value and you have reason to think that it could become an open-end fund. If the fund goes open end, the discount will narrow or disappear, allowing closed-end shareholders the chance for profits.

you may be paying $10 per share for $8.75 worth of assets—and who pays more than retail? Even worse, if the market turns on your overpriced fund, your investment can go up in smoke when the share price sinks below NAV. Patience is often rewarded. You may be in for a great buy after the stampede is over.

Spread Your Wealth, But Not Too Thin

Overdiversification can be as bad for your financial health as underdiversifica-tion. If you want to try a closed-end fund, try buying half the total position you'd like to hold and wait to see what happens. If the fund takes off, you're participating. If the share price falls but you still think the fund fits your objec-tive, buy more at the lower price. You may not make a killing, but you won't get killed, either.

When buying funds, check the management style. Don't just go for those that had the best track record last year; often they become next year's losers. Make sure to invest in funds with companies of different sizes (small, medium and large capitalization) and with different management styles—both growth and value.

Variety Is The Spice Of Closed-End Funds

Think of closed-end funds as the Alice's Restaurant of investing: You can get anything you want, with equity fund options covering U.S., international and global funds and fixed-income funds of every descrip-tion. Look hard enough, and you can probably find funds that invest in countries you never heard of and blending every type of security under the sun.

By rushing in where mutual funds fear to tread (at least initially), closed-end funds sometimes provide the only professionally managed avenue for an investor interested in a thinly traded or relatively new market. Many single-country closed-end funds have no counterpart in mutual funds. Because of their professional management and diversification features, making an investment into uncharted financial territory is less risky with a closed-end fund than buying shares of individual securities.

Most mutual funds, whether open- or closed-end, are perpetual, meaning they have no specific maturity date and can theoretically go on for as long as there are investors. But for high current income and potential

Missing The Boat?

If you had invested a hypothetical $10,000 in the S&P 500 Index on June 30, 1994, by June 30, 1999, your $10,000 would have grown to $34,171, an average total return of 27.86 percent. But suppose during that five-year period there were times when you decided to get out of the market and, as a result, you missed the market's 10 best single-day performances. In that case, your 27.86 percent return would have fallen to 19.12 percent. If you had missed the market's best 20 days, that 27.86 percent return would have dropped to 13.60 percent. Of course, past performance cannot guarantee comparable future results.

Trying to time the market can be an inexact—and costly—exercise. The chart below (which tracks S&P Index for June 30, 1994 to June 30, 1999) shows the penalty for missing the market.

Period Of Investment	Average Annual Total Return	Growth Of $10,000
Fully invested	27.86%	$34,171
Miss the 10 best days	19.12	23,987
Miss the 20 best days	13.60	18,923
Miss the 30 best days	8.99	15,376
Miss the 40 best days	4.94	12,724
Miss the 60 best days	-1.92	9,078

The Standard & Poor's Composite Index of 500 stocks is an unmanaged group of securities widely regarded to be representative of large-company stocks. Results assume the reinvestment of dividends. An investment cannot be made directly in an index.

Sources: Aim Mutual Funds, Standard & Poor's and Bloomberg

appreciation, consider a closed-end fund with a termination date. And you may even find a bargain: When interest rates are high, many of these funds sell at a discount to their termination price. It's like buying a managed bond at a discount.

Cheaper By The Dozen

It's great to buy on sale, but don't buy a fund just because it's selling at a considerable discount to its NAV. There may be a good reason for that low price. To analyze a fund's history of premiums and discounts, check the charts in *Morningstar's Closed-End Funds Report*. In the best of all possible worlds, the funds you buy would be trading at a lower premium or higher discount than they have for the past year.

Before investing in a discounted fund (or any fund, for that matter) examine its past performance and what it is costing to run the fund, or its expense ratio. Though past performance is not a guarantee of future returns, expense ratios are certainties that last and last.

The dream of some closed-end fund investors is to buy shares at a steep discount and ride them to a premium. But don't spend all your time—and profits—trading. Although it's tempting to get in and out of the market whenever you've made a few dollars or experienced a few bad days, investors do better sticking with the program over the long haul. Being out of the market for just a few days can cost you, as the chart on page 119 illustrates. As they say on the Street of Dreams, it's not timing the market, but time in the market that counts.

Money Missteps

Things sometimes are not what they appear to be. If a fund has much higher returns than its siblings, check its annual report. To juice up returns, managers sometimes employ leverage, derivatives and option strategies. While these strategies can lead to higher returns, they can also increase a fund's volatility.

Another motivation to buy a closed-end fund is to get what everyone wants (but not everyone can have)—access to some of the best mutual fund managers, whose regular mutual funds may have temporarily closed their doors to new investors, impose too-high investment minimums or charge high initial fees to investors. Many of these sought-after managers run little-known closed-end funds that are remarkably similar to their open-end cousins. Even better, you may be able to buy in at a discount to what the shares are really worth (their NAV).

Whether you invest in open-end or closed-end funds, you'll profit most by remaining in the market through its ups and downs. If you can't decide if you're bullish or bearish, switch over to the Chinese calendar . . . and let the pigs or monkeys be your guide.

DAY 20

Get A Load Of This

How expensive is your fund?

> *"There's no such thing as a free lunch."*
> —Milton Friedman

Katie and Charles put a check on my desk—all the money they had. "We need this to live on," they said. "Everyone in our family lives a long time, and this money has got to last. Don't lose it for us." There's nothing like a little pressure. Before I could even take a breath, Katie added, "We've got to have some money out every month. What can you do?" The first response that came to mind was to jump through a window, but since my office was on the ground level, that wasn't much of a solution. I explained that to provide the amount of money they wanted every month, they'd have to put it in a mutual fund, then take a systematic withdrawal. Neither principal nor interest would be guaranteed, and some of the money they withdrew might come from principal. If they decided to liquidate it, they could get back more—or less—than they invested. In addition, the fund I had in mind had a high upfront sales charge.

Expecting them to run screaming from the room, I got a surprise: "Put the money there if you think it will work, and we'll try not to get too scared if it starts to go down," said Katie. "We're not planning to move it, so I guess it will be OK." Well, we didn't put all the money in there, but we put in a good bit. Fortunately, fate smiled on us and the fund performed even better than its hypothetical illustrations said it would. In the long run, it was worth every penny in sales fees that they paid. Since my office is now on the 15th floor, let's hope it keeps up the good work!

You can't get somethin' for nothin'. While you may know this in your heart of hearts, many investors still try . . . and they seek it from that bastion of capitalism, Wall Street. No matter how often you work out, sometimes you just feel like, well, taking a load off. Should you do the same thing when it comes to your mutual fund? Today you'll learn some of the secrets of mutual fund charges and how they should (or shouldn't) affect your investment decisions.

> **Healthy Habit**
>
> If you'll be picking funds on your own, pay close attention to fund costs. Low expenses make it easier for a fund to perform better. A good fund may command higher fees, but this will become a handicap in years when the portfolio lags. Some funds charge high upfront fees and very low carrying charges, making them a good alternative for those who want professional advice and low annual fees.

In the past 10 years, the number of investors has soared, along with the level of the stock market and the number and type of mutual funds. Where there were once just simple stock and bond funds, there are now funds investing in every conceivable type of security, using every kind of strategy: Some invest in particular sectors, others with specific styles, still others specializing in certain countries. At last count, there were more funds than companies listed on the New York Stock Exchange!

While funds have proliferated, so have the ways to invest in them, and many investors are more confused than ever. Let's make one thing perfectly clear: Although there may sometimes be a free lunch, there is no such thing as a free mutual fund. All funds charge for the expertise of their managers and/or for the trading of their securities . . . and that means your no-load fund, too. That said, here are some ways to decipher the payment options available.

Money Missteps

Fund fees aren't created solely to pay greedy financial advisors. Funds with high portfolio turnover have higher fees because fund managers, like any other investor, have to pay commissions when securities are bought and sold. Beware of funds that encourage frequent switching by shareholders. Too much switching can make a fund manager sell at inopportune times, and that can be a bad deal for the fund's long-term shareholders.

Fee For All

You will find everything you need to know about fees and sales charges, expenses and redemption fees in a fund's prospectus. Sales charges are sometimes called the "load"; the maximum load allowed is 8.5 percent of the assets invested. To suit the needs of various investors, many fund families have made different classes of funds available, allowing investors to pay either when buying or when selling shares. Here are the classes of fund shares:

- **Class A shares** charge what is known as a "front-end" sales load, which investors pay at the time of purchase of the assets. Fees can be as high as 8.5 percent of the assets, although most front-end fees are in the 3 percent to 6 percent range. Investors purchasing large amounts may reach a "break point" in sales charges—as sales increase over a specified dollar amount, the load decreases. To find the breakpoint for a fund family, read its prospectus. If you plan on making a large mutual fund purchase, this option may be of interest.

- **Class B shares** have a contingent deferred sales charge, sometimes called "rear-end" or "back-end" load. Some fund families provide this option to allow investors to invest without upfront fees. Fees in this class are highest for those who sell shares soon after purchasing them; they decline as time goes on. Most start at 5 percent and decline 1 percentage point annually. In most fund families, shares purchased through reinvestment of dividends and capital gains are exempt from rear-end fees and may be sold at any time without a charge. Investors may also switch from one fund in a family to another with little or no fee. (Switches made in taxable accounts may be taxable events, so consult your tax advisor.)

Class B funds include a "12b-1" fee paid to market the fund. This type of fund is often sold by stockbrokers and insurance agents; the 12b-1 fee is an annual fee that ranges from 0.5 percent to more than double that to compensate your financial advisor for monitoring your funds. These funds are often popular with investors who seek professional guidance in monitoring their investments.

- **Class C shares**, also sometimes called "level load," include a 1 percent contingent deferred sales charge on shares redeemed within approximately 1 year of purchase but not more than 13 months. These funds are often suitable for investors with short-term investment horizons (although mutual funds are long-term investments and are not designed for short-term trading). If you plan to hold a fund for a short period, this may be the least expensive way to go, but eventually, like the Merchant of Venice, the fund will have its pound of flesh. In many cases, over the long term, this class of shares becomes the most expensive.

- **No-load funds** are funds that charge no fee to buy or sell shares. Should you think at first glance that these funds are free, think again. All funds, even index funds, charge management and transaction fees. These fees are subtracted from the fund's share price, reducing the shares' net asset value. Fees charged by no-load funds may be higher or lower than those charged by load funds. Consult each fund's prospectus to find out. These funds have traditionally been offered directly to investors by the fund family. Today, investors can invest in these funds

Loaded Up

As the chart below shows, the effect of a sales load is mitigated over time.

	1 Year	3 Years	5 Years	10 Years	Load Adjusted Over 15 Years	Average Expense Ratio
Front	14.43	19.47	18.36	14.19	15.20	1.32
Deferred	13.97	19.01	17.46	12.90	14.18	2.04
No Load	15.52	20.12	18.92	13.53	14.88	1.08
Level	13.61	18.38	17.96	13.89	16.56	2.08

Front load: front load of 3 percent or greater
Deferred load: deferred load of 3 percent or greater (max.)
No load: no front or deferred load, 12b-1 of .25 percent or less
Level load: deferred load of less than 3 percent and higher 12b-1
(Although data is gathered from reliable sources, Morningstar cannot guarantee completeness and accuracy.)

Source: Morningstar Inc.

and those in the other classes through grouped accounts (more on this on Day 24).

I Can Get It For You Wholesale

What is a load, anyway? The dictionary defines a load as "something that weighs down or oppresses like a burden" or "a grievous weight." Although the load may not be grievous, when it comes to investing, why would anyone *pay* to invest in a fund when it appears they could get one for free? As noted, all funds have transaction fees when stocks are traded, and management fees to pay the person who does the selection and monitoring of the portfolio. Index funds are the least expensive, as very little trading and no management are involved. All other funds, load and no load, charge for their service, just as the gardener, dry cleaner or doctor does. The question is, under which type of charge do funds perform best?

As the chart on page 125 shows, after three years, the adverse effect of the sales charge is sharply diminished, and the load charged by a fund may not affect performance as radically as first thought on funds held for the long term; in this example, after 10 years.

Many investors have found that "no-load" may be translated as "no-advice." Although it is certainly possible to successfully invest in a selection of mutual funds and change them as your situation and that of the financial markets change, most investors are either too busy or too inexperienced to do so. What comes with a load is not only a fee, but usually the advice of a financial professional. If you're buying a shirt and you have the choice of paying the markup or not paying it, you'd probably choose not to pay it. After all, most shirts are not too expensive, can be replaced easily and don't need servicing. Investing your hard-earned money in mutual funds is a substantially more expensive and important endeavor.

Unfortunately, while loads are fixed, the value of the advice you're buying varies. Be sure that the financial advisor you select knows and understands your needs. A good financial advisor can monitor both your portfolio and your needs,

Money Missteps

You've heard that smart investors avoid loads at all costs. Well, that advice could be pretty expensive in the long run. The longer you hold a fund, the less impact an initial sales charge has on performance. If you plan to hold short term, though, sales charges can eat into your investment.

making sure that your investments continue to fill the bill. Ask what part the recommended fund will play in your portfolio, what makes it special and why it is recommended over other similar funds. If you are satisfied with the advice, it may be worth the price of admission.

Expense Account

Fees are only part of the story. Whether you pay when you buy, when you sell or while you're invested, management fees take a bite out of your performance. While it's reasonable to expect to pay some fees, if your fund is returning double digits, why worry about how high the fees are? Consider this: Assets in mutual funds have quadrupled in the 1990s, yet management fees have increased, not decreased. You don't have to have a Harvard MBA to see that that makes little sense. After all, running a $2 billion fund can't cost much more than one that invests $1 billion, can it?

Healthy Habit

Perusing a prospectus for your fund's fees as a percentage of assets? These are listed as the expense ratio. According to Morningstar, the average expense ratios for funds that buy stocks are: asset allocation, 1.46 percent; sector, 1.23 percent to 1.86 percent (depending on the sector); foreign, 1.64 percent; income, 1.23 percent; balanced, 1.28 percent; growth and income, 1.23 percent; small company, 1.40 percent; growth, 1.39 percent; and aggressive growth, 1.75 percent.

While some investors expect that their mutual fund will always return 18 percent annually, when they get a dose of reality and returns come back to earth, fund fees will become a lot more important. Bottom line: Even though some funds have outstanding results despite high management fees, it's harder to do so. Check the fees in the prospectus before you invest.

On Your Own

Investing with index funds

> "A fool and his money are soon parted. What I'd like to know is how they got together in the first place."
>
> —Cyril Fletcher

"Hello, Lorayne? This is David. I want to sell out of all those stupid mutual funds you put my father's money in. They've done a lousy job compared to the S&P 500 index fund in my company's retirement fund, and I'm transferring the money to that fund."

"But David," I replied, "That 'lousy return' amounts to 10 percent for the first six months of this year and 25 percent last year."

"Well," he answered, "that still doesn't beat the S&P 500—it did 34 percent last year, and I want this money to do something, not just sit there. So sell everything and send me a check."

Interestingly enough, David's strategy isn't news to me—lots of people want to make the returns they hear about on TV commercials, and investing all their money in a fund that mirrors the S&P 500 index seems like an easy, cheap way to do it . . . until the market corrects or changes direction. Don't get me wrong: Index funds can be a great way to diversify a portfolio, but only a fool (and I don't mean a motley one, either) would put their life savings in any one investment, no matter how well is has performed in the past!

To index or not to index? In today's financial markets, where some investors seem to think that double-digit returns are an inalienable right, many question not whether to invest in an index fund, but whether to invest in anything else. In search of the highest returns, fans of index funds would point out that figures don't lie: According to numbers generated by Kevin McDevitt, mutual fund analyst at mutual fund rating service Morningstar Inc., from 1995 to the end of June 1998, the performance of the Standard and Poor's 500 index would place it in the top 24 percent of all mutual funds that invest in large companies. If you consider just a few years an aberration, consider the index's trailing years' performance: for three years, the index landed in the top 7 percent of all large-company funds; for five years, the top 7 percent; 10 years, the top13 percent; and 15 years, the top 8 percent.

Although past performance is not an indication of future returns, don't think investors haven't noticed: Over the past five years, they have poured billions of dollars into index funds. While it's great fun to participate when stock prices are on the rise, in a falling market, will index funds drag you down or become the goose that lays the golden egg? These funds may have a place in your portfolio, but make sure you understand where your money is going. There's a lot more to index funds than meets the sharpened pencil.

Index In Your Pocket

Investing in an index funds seems like pure investing—just you and the index, right? Wrong. Contrary to popular belief, investors cannot invest directly in an index. An index fund, as defined by the *Dictionary of Finance and Investment Terms*, is "a mutual fund whose portfolio matches that of a broad-based index such as Standard & Poor's index and whose performance therefore mirrors the market as a whole."

What makes funds that track the S&P 500 so popular? Consider the positives:

- **It's virtually impossible to significantly lag the market.** Index funds either mirror their benchmark index or consist of a group of stocks that are close to the underlying index. Unlike their managed brethren, there's no chance that the manager will misread the market's cues and concentrate funds in a sector just as it unravels. On the other hand, index funds don't provide the opportunity for a savvy manager to over-weight a portfolio in an undervalued sector that might be the next to take off.

- **Low cost.** Index funds are notoriously cheap. Since portfolio turnover occurs only when stocks are added or dropped from the underlying index, trading costs are low. Investment management fees are generally lower than actively managed funds. Information about fees and management charges can be found in a fund's prospectus.

- **Lower taxes for some investors.** Low portfolio turnover may make index funds more tax efficient than some managed funds whose portfolios change more often. Check the prospectus and consult your tax advisor for more information.

Trainer's Tip

Are index funds that great, or are you comparing grapes to grape-fruit? Fund managers "are not as dumb as they appear," says Gus Sauter, managing director of index funds at mutual fund company Vanguard Group. "I don't think it's at all fair to compare the S&P 500 to the typical U.S. stock fund because the typical stock fund has a smaller cap bias"—and, according to *The Wall Street Journal,* many funds beat the comparable Russell 2000 index.

What's Behind Door Number One?

Like Monty Hall's famous doors, all is not as it seems with index funds. The index you may be interested in "owning" may not be what you think. My informal poll of 25 investors showed that every one of them thought an investment in the S&P 500 was an equal investment in the 500 largest companies in America. Actually, the S&P 500 index consists of 500 domestic stocks and is capitalization weighted, meaning that larger stocks are more highly represented than smaller equities. Because of this weighting, its movement reflects the movement of the largest issues. Included in the index at the time of this writing were the stocks of 400 industrial companies, 40 financial companies, 40 public companies and 20 transportation companies. Since mid-

---

Itsy-Bitsy SPDR

Looking for a way to trade the S&P 500? While index funds mirror the index, they are not the index. For a pure trading vehicle, SPDRs may be just the creatures you want.

Standard & Poor's Depository Receipts, also known as SPDRs (symbol: SPY), represent ownership in the SPDR trust, an investment that was established to hold a portfolio of common stocks intended to track the price performance of the S&P 500 composite index. Holders of SPDRs receive proportional quarterly distributions corresponding to the dividends that accrue in the S&P 500 stocks in the underlying portfolio, less expenses.

SPDRs trade like any listed stock. Each SPDR represents about one-tenth the value of the S&P 500. If, for example, the S&P was trading at $700, the SPDRs would trade at about $70 per share. The purchase of one round lot of 100 SPDRs would cost about $7,000, plus commission.

1989, this composition has been more flexible than in prior years, and the number of issues in each sector has varied.

In all, the S&P 500 represents only about 70 percent of the U.S. stock market, so its performance doesn't really reflect the entire stock market. What does its weighting do to its performance? Since larger companies are the ones that get a higher proportion of incoming investment, the increase in the value of the S&P 500 becomes a self-fulfilling prophecy: The higher the index goes, the more money it seems to attract, and the more money attracted, the larger the proportion going into the companies at the top. The higher these companies' stocks rise, the more inviting the index may seem, and the more money goes into it . . . you get the picture.

In some ways, investing in the S&P 500 becomes a momentum play, where investors buy highly priced stocks and continue buying as prices increase, a situation most value investors shun. Should some of the wind be knocked from the sails of the popular stocks at the top, the resulting fall in the S&P 500 could be sharper than many would have anticipated. For this reason alone, it generally makes sense to diversify beyond this index.

In addition to the S&P 500, many more indices exist, as do the funds that mirror them. One such index is the Russell 3000, consisting of various permutations on 3,000 large U.S. companies ranked by market capitalization. As of July 1, 1998, the average market cap of the Russell 3000 was $221.9 million to $271.6 billion; the Russell 2000, the 2000 smallest companies in the Russell 3000 index, represented approximately 11 percent of the Russell 3000 total market capitalization. The index's average market cap as of 7/1/98 was $500 million, and it is used as a benchmark with which to compare the performance of small-company investments.

Cash As King

Index funds provide investors with the opportunity to have all their investment invested all the time. They don't hold cash—a nice position to be in when the market is rising, but not a very comfortable perch when stocks are on the way down. Still, if you're a long-term investor and it's possible to garner high returns with low expenses through an index fund, why consider using a managed fund?

"You're looking backward vs. what can happen in the future," says Michael Lipper, president of Lipper Analytical, a firm that analyzes investment and brokerage companies. "At times, immediate past performance is mistaken in terms of turning points. The definition of a market at the top is everyone thinking that it's going higher and it doesn't. In theory, there is less volatility with managed funds because you have cash—this dampens the volatility in both directions, up as well as down."

Lipper also notes that some managed funds hold larger concentrations of certain industries considered undervalued by their mangers and/or positions in companies of varying sizes. If large companies stumble but small and medium firms outperform, the presence of the latter issues could balance the managed fund in a market downturn. Of course, small companies could also lower a portfolio's return should large-company stocks continue to outperform their smaller brethren.

Healthy Habit

Looking for something different from an index fund? Consider a focused fund. Here, fund managers limit their holdings to a few choice picks. Theoretically, a good stock picker can produce returns that are substantially better than an unmanaged index over time. But even the hottest stock picker can cool off, making this type of fund's return less predictable and more risky than that of a broadly diversified index, so they're not appropriate for everyone.

Who Could Ask For Anything More?

If you plan to look beyond the S&P 500 to diversify your holdings among stocks of different sizes, you may want to think twice before considering another index fund. Whether you read *The New York Times* or you're a fan of *Money* magazine, you've probably noticed funds that mirror the S&P 500 have recently been outrunning managed funds in the same sector (i.e., those invested in large-cap stocks). But the same is not true of all indices and their respective managed counterparts. McDevitt notes that when dealing with small- or medium-sized company indices, "the indices perform decently, but there are more small companies to cover, and more are illiquid. In these market sectors, active managers add value." He adds, "The S&P is not representative of the whole market. Investors there have no exposure to small-cap, mid-cap, overseas or bond markets. If all you have is the S&P 500, you'd have a very concentrated, undiversified portfolio."

What's a bewildered investor to do? Many investors feel comfortable with part of their portfolio invested in the S&P 500 index. How much is enough? While no one can give blanket advice and each situation is different, Michael Lipper believes that for even the most aggressive investor, no more than 25 percent of a portfolio should be allocated to funds that mirror the S&P 500. As for the rest, investors should consider diversifying their portfolios based on their age, temperament, financial goals and tolerance for risk.

DAY 22

A Perfect 10

How does your fund rate?

"Why do I have all these stupid funds that aren't on the recommended list of *The Charlotte Observer*?" a client whined. Strangely enough, I had not realized that particular list was considered the be-all and end-all of the investment world. Not to take anything away from that venerable paper or from the concerned client, but ratings are, well, just ratings, and while everyone from Jimmy the Greek to your Web-crawling grandmother would like to pick a winner, a portfolio of last year's stars does not guarantee investment success.

As for the aforementioned client, when showed the results of several other rating services, he tossed up his hands and decided to evaluate his funds based on their returns. Farewell whining . . . hello smiling.

No matter what kind of survey it is, there's nothing like being number one. Most fund managers and their funds can't claim the position that Jane Fonda did for years as the reigning doyenne of exercise videos. But whether you prefer Richard Simmons or Victoria Principal, how your mutual funds are rated can make you sweat a lot more than jumping around to the oldies.

So what's the deal with all these fund ratings? It seems like everybody is getting into the act. You expect it from publications like *Business Week*, *Forbes*, *Money*, *Barron's* and *The Wall Street Journal*. But when you start seeing a list in *Golf Digest*, you may decide to chuck the whole mess in the trash. Which list is best, and what service provides the best "service"? Here's how to evaluate these different approaches to selecting mutual funds.

Twist And Shout

Many of the fund rankings you see in popular magazines and newspapers use information compiled by Lipper Analytical Services. If it's ratings you want, though, you're in the wrong place. "We don't rate mutual funds; we rank them," says Melissa Daly of Lipper. "Rating is sometimes confused with an opinion. You can rate a restaurant or a movie, but in ranking something, you are placing it against its peers. Funds should be ranked with a number like one, two or 10 vs. other funds. You don't rate houses, spouses or investments."

How does Lipper rank its funds? Funds are classified into more than 20 different groups that reflect portfolio characteristics and performance attributes. Confusing or vague classifications like "growth" and "growth and income" are replaced by descriptions like "large-cap growth" and "large-cap value." Grouping funds this way makes it easier for investors to more accurately compare fund performance.

Lipper also ranks its funds on an A-B-C-D-E system. Daly notes that other mutual fund information services use a quartile system, which, in her opinion, just isn't as accurate. With a quartile system, one basis point difference in performance can move a fund from a bottom ranking to a top ranking. Lipper's ranking system, which breaks funds up into five quintiles, shows investors that managers whose funds fall in either the "A" category or the "E" category are doing something very different from those in the middle quintiles. Adds Daly, "It's a lot more difficult to figure this out if you're just dividing your funds into four parts."

Trainer's Tip

"Knowing how a fund is rated helps you understand what kind of fund is appropriate for what kind of investor. That way you won't be recommending a highly volatile small-company fund to Great-Aunt Irma."

—*Matthew Muchlbauer,*
Value Line
Investment Survey

No Stars For You

You may not be seeing stars when you look at your fund, but Amy Arnott, editor of *Morningstar Mutual Funds* and *Morningstar No Load Funds*, contends that her firm's evaluations are a good starting point for investors who want to order up the right fund.

Unlike Lipper's performance-based ranking system, Morningstar's recipes are based on risk-adjusted performance. The universe of open-end mutual funds is divided into four broad groups: domestic stock funds, international stock funds, taxable bond funds and municipal bond funds. Morningstar's ratings have two parts, the return component and the risk component. The return component is a measure of a fund's return relative to its rating group, adjusted for sales charges. Risk is calculated by judging performance against that of the 90-day Treasury bill, which is considered to be an almost risk-free investment.

While many other calculations go into this formula (we don't want to be responsible for giving away the recipe, but we have it on very good authority that you can find it on www.morningstar.net/InfoDesk/InvestFAQ.html), stars are assigned by subtracting a fund's risk score from its return score and then ranking it against funds in the same rating group. The top 10 percent of funds are awarded five stars, the next 22.5 percent receive four stars, the middle 35 percent get three stars, the next 22.5 percent receive two stars, and the bottom 10 percent receive a single star. Funds must have at least a three-year track record to be included.

According to Arnott, Morningstar offers more than stars in your eyes. Check out a fund's Morningstar rating sheet, and you'll find lots of impor-

Who Can You Turn To?

If you can't totally rely on the rating services, who can you trust? Why, yourself, of course! Rating services provide useful information that you, too, can interpret. While whole books could be written on ways to rate funds (yawn), here are a couple of shortcuts:

Looking for consistency? Check out the fund's standard deviation. A high standard means that annual returns will vary more.

A Sharpe ratio calculates how much performance a fund provides vs. its level of risk. A higher Sharpe ratio means that a fund delivers more for its level of risk.

tant information: written analysis that discusses how the fund is managed and what investors may be able to expect from management; charts that show fund performance over time and vs. an appropriate index; the "style box," a tool that represents the fund's characteristics in graphic form, showing at a glance whether a fund invests in large, medium or small stocks and if it's managed in a value, growth or blend style; and many other components that help investors get a sense of a fund's flavor.

All this information is great, but will it turn you on to the right fund? Arnott says, "When you're looking at straight total returns, there's no predictive value." But Morningstar's ratings, unlike rankings based solely on performance, give an idea of what to expect so you can match it with your goals and risk tolerance. "Risk," Arnott notes, "is more stable over time. Even though it's not predictive, what's high risk tends to stay high risk." Finding funds that have historically provided good returns relative to their levels of risk give you an idea of which funds might be worth investing in, she says.

Healthy Habit

Here are some points to remember when selecting a fund:

- Don't focus on short-term returns. Even a broken clock is right twice a day.

- Is the fund's current manager the one whose track record you admire? If not, consider looking elsewhere.

- Bond funds won't deliver the same performance as a stock fund; a growth and income fund most likely won't keep pace with an aggressive growth fund. Compare funds to similar competitors.

Instant Replay

Another source of information is the Value Line Mutual Fund Survey. Its research manager, Matthew Muchlbauer, contends that his company's ranking system is the most useful in helping investors find out what's investment-worthy and what isn't, compared to the competition. Value Line provides two rankings. An overall ranking divides funds into three universes: equity, taxable fixed income and municipal fixed income; a risk ranking divides funds into equity and bond categories. Funds are further divided according to the standard deviation of their returns for 36 months in a five-tier system. One is the least volatile, five the most. Unlike "that other rating service," Muchlbauer says that Value Line's service shows the fund's most recent developments over the past 22 weeks, plus a methodical analysis of the fund's management and, in many cases, a recommendation describing what kind of investor should consider the fund.

Let's Get Physical

Whether you're a "do it yourselfer" or you prefer to have help from outside sources, how do you know which fund service is the best? No one suggests their service can predict the future. Mark Hulbert, editor of the *Hulbert Financial Digest* (HFD), which has been tracking Morningstar's performance since the beginning of 1991, notes that over the subsequent seven years, Morningstar's top-ranked no-load equity funds have lagged the stock market by an average of nearly three percentage points per year. Unfortunately, according to Hulbert, Value Line hasn't fared any better: Since 1994, when HFD started tracking the service, its top-ranked no-load general equity funds have lagged the market by an average of nearly four percentage points a year.

You can only conclude there is no conclusive method that will ensure success in any kind of investing or give you an automatic upper hand. What rating services provide is a simpler way to sort through the immense amount of information to identify investments worthy of further investigation. By understanding the various methods used by these services and their shortcomings, investors can hopefully make more astute choices.

While some investors hungrily devour tomes of performance figures, analyses of management styles, star ratings, risk analyses and other technical and not-so-technical sources of information, others would rather let someone else's fingers do the walking. Financial advisors can provide insight into which funds are most suitable for specific situations (see Day 44). Even if professional recommendations just help narrow the field, they can save time, effort and money.

Whichever way you choose to go, before you invest, get a copy of the fund's prospectus and read it. Management style, fees, sales charges, investment policy and many other important facts can be gleaned from this essential document. Put this information together with your preferred type of analysis, remember that past performance is not an indication of future returns, and you'll increase your ability to make the right choices.

Change Your Diet

Calling it quits with your mutual fund

> "Don't try to buy at the bottom and sell at the top. This can't be done—except by liars."
> —Bernard Baruch, financier

Ralph attended one of my workshops and came up afterwards waving a copy of his statement. "I can't understand it," he cried, handing me the sheet with a copy of the prior year's top-rated funds, 'I bought all the ones that had the best ratings, but they're just not doing anything! What should I do?"

Ralph had done what many of us are tempted to do: He bought the funds with the best ratings and sat back to watch the fun. Unfortunately, most of the time the funds with the best one-year track records are also funds of similar style—and often even similar portfolios.

Fortunately, Ralph's selections were all part of large fund families and were invested through his IRA account, both of which made switching funds around a snap. While he ended up keeping several of the funds, by switching some into other market sectors, Ralph's portfolio had a better chance for long-term success. It pays to know when to quit.

There are few things as annoying as waiting for your mutual fund to make money. Perhaps that's because funds are diversified, long-term investments that take a while to increase in value . . . or is it because a watched pot takes forever to boil? Whatever the reason, how do you know when your mutual fund is, well, "done"? Today we'll find out when you should stick with your fund and when to serve it up and out.

It's not hard to decide to get out of funds that charge outrageous annual fees or consistently lose money in all kinds of markets. But what about that investment that's been solidly plugging along? Or the fund whose track record placed it at the top of the heap for its five- and 10-year performances . . . until, of course, you bought in?

"It's never a good idea to sell your mutual fund just because it hasn't done as well as you'd like in a short time," says Jon Teall of Lipper Analytical Services Inc., which tracks and analyzes more than 12,000 mutual funds. "Unfortunately, investing is not a straight-line thing. You don't just win, win, win."

Mutual funds are long-term investments and shouldn't be judged on short-term performance. And even if you put in all the right ingredients, you may never find the perfect investment recipe. While there are no hard-and-fast rules about when to bid farewell to your fund, here are a few suggestions for serving up the right investment menu.

Don't Get Basted

Popular funds, with big followings and large asset bases, are usually popular for good reason. But if you've noticed the size of your fund dwindling because investors are selling, don't be the last one out of the pool. A shrinking asset base can cause expenses to skyrocket, squelching the fund's return to its remaining investors.

Don't let popularity be your only guide. In 1989, high returns in international issues whetted the appetites of investors, and substantial purchases were made in foreign funds. Small-company issues were not so popular, with net sales of these funds dropping. But time reversed the trend, and from 1989 to 1994, the return on international stock funds declined, while return on small-company funds soared. Instead of the most popular funds, investors should have bought—you guessed it—the "turkeys."

If more people are selling out than buying in, it's probably not because the fund has a superlative track record. While mutual funds rarely disappear completely, sticking with a loser in hopes it will turn around is a waste of your time and money. On the other hand, poorly performing mutual funds are often merged with winners, sometimes changing the character of both investments. If this happens, be sure to read the prospectus of the new fund before deciding to stay in.

Cut The Fat

"The 10 Best New Funds"; "6 Best Funds to Buy Now"; "The Best Mutual Funds You've Never Heard Of" . . . tempting titles like these sell a lot of magazines, and, more to the point, quite a few mutual fund shares. But be careful not to get burned. "Hot" new funds like these are sometimes small and nimble, which may be a factor in their success. A huge influx of cash from new investors could change the character of such a fund and destroy its performance.

Funds that invest in emerging markets, health-care or utility stocks, or a limited geographic area may have fewer choices of where to place their money than larger balanced or growth and income funds, so be cautious when investing in sector funds.

If the sector you've chosen is gaining ground but the fund you've chosen is lagging behind, the fund's management might have made an error. Switching to cash or betting heavily on several positions that don't pan out can temporarily ruin a fund's performance. Before you switch, check your fund's performance against similar funds and indices composed of stocks that reflect your fund's composition.

Are you comparing your fund to

Smart Stretch

To find out more about a fund, check these Web sites:

● *S&P Personal Wealth*: www.personalwealth. com

● *Morningstar.Net*: www. morningstar.net

Healthy Habit

If you're considering a mutual fund switch, check to see what fees will be involved. Some wrap programs allow switches between fund families at low or no cost (see Day 24).

those touted by investment magazines? Be sure you're comparing apples to apples. Check your fund against funds of similar style and market capitalization. If that style of fund has performed poorly but your particular fund is not down sharply, you may want to hold on a bit longer. If your fund falls at the bottom of the heap, however, consider bailing.

Sales charges and annual fees can take a bite out of a fund's performance, but don't let an upfront fee or reasonable yearly expenses discourage you. Instead, be wary of rising or excessive management charges. Certain fund families charge up to 13 percent a year, making big profits hard to achieve—unless you're the fund's manager! One or two years of great performance doesn't justify a steep fee increase. If you like the style of investing but not the higher charges, vote with your feet: Find a similar fund at a more reasonable price. Remember, always read the fund's prospectus before you invest or send any money. It contains complete information on the investment, including all charges and expenses.

Beware A Galloping Gourmet

If a star manager is the reason you signed up with a fund and he or she moves on, should you do likewise? Before you switch, find out whether the new manager will follow his or her predecessor's style. Many funds have investment teams at the helm rather than a solo player. The team approach usually signals continuity, so don't leave until a few quarters of performance have been served up.

How do you know if your fund management has changed? Check annual and quarterly reports for more information. Managers don't usually change frequently, but reading proxy notices can help you keep abreast of what your fund will be dishing up in the future. If you don't want to wait for printed reports, call the company and get more information.

Oysters and caviar or hot dogs and beans? No, we're not investing in the Emeril Lagasse fund, but just as everyone has a different idea of what makes the meal, opinions on what makes the best fund mix vary widely. If you've been with the same fund for many years, it may still suit your needs—or it may have outgrown its place in your portfolio. Portfolios, like menus, need to be periodically updated. If your needs have changed, consider re-evaluating your fund selection, shifting to funds with different styles (from growth to value, from large company to small company, from domestic to foreign) or different objectives (growth to growth and income or growth to income). Reallocating your assets should balance your investment portfolio and improve performance over time.

Next Course, Please

If your mutual fund was up one year and down the next, you may be tempted to switch to something with a more consistent track record. Most of the time experts suggest you resist the temptation, but how long should you wait for a turnaround? While market cycles could run months or years, consider giving your fund six months to a year before ditching it. When weighing the possibility of selling a fund, don't lose sight of the goal behind your investment. For example, if you're saving for far-off objectives like retirement or a child's college education, fluctuations in performance are not as big a concern. Consider buying shares at monthly or quarterly intervals to help balance out long-term performance.

Before adding to a losing proposition, review the fund's one-, three- and five-year total return compared to that of its peers, and check its standard deviation, beta and Sharpe ratio. If these figures demonstrate your fund has more risk and less performance than other similar investments, consider a fond farewell.

If looking at your mutual fund statement makes you reach for the Maalox every time, you may have invested too aggressively. Reviewing your investment objectives might help. A switch to less volatile funds could do wonders for your heartburn, and in many cases, you can switch from one type to another within a family of funds for little or no cost. Keep

Joggin' Jargon

- A *Sharpe ratio* measures risk-adjusted returns; it should be above 1.

- *Standard deviation* measures the variability of a fund's returns. Funds with consistent performance have low standard deviations.

- A fund's *beta* is its volatility compared to the overall market. A beta of less than 1 means less up and down than the general market.

in mind that while switching funds may improve performance, changes always bring tax consequences. The rules are complex, so be sure to consult your tax advisor before selling.

In short, if expenses have risen, your objectives have shifted, the manager has changed, or the market is consistently knocking the stuffing out of your fund, get out. If not, stick with your fund through the tough times—it may yet serve up a tasty profit.

DAY 24

Wrap Sheet

The pros and cons of using professional money managers

Rodney, known to his friends as Pee Wee, has been managing a lot of money for a long time. Too bad none of it is his. Almost 12 years ago, Pee Wee's wife, Cissy, underwent some routine surgery that turned out to be anything but routine: She ended up in a coma, and he ended up with a stack of bills from here to eternity.

After winning a lawsuit against the offending hospital, Pee Wee faced a new problem: How would he make his $1,025,000 last and still pay more than $100,000 in ongoing medical bills every year? Cissy has a life expectancy of more than 50 years, and at the rate the bills were coming in, he figured he only had enough for about 12 years.

Enter some good luck (high interest rates on high-quality bonds) and some individually managed (wrap) stock accounts. It's been 10 years since Pee Wee started paying Cissy's bills, and he's paid out more than $1 mil-

I Want My IRA

IRAs can be ideal for an individually managed account. Since managed accounts trade securities on an individual basis, April 15th may bring quite a bit of paperwork. In an IRA account, however, capital gains or losses don't have to be declared on your 1040. And if you pay the manager's fees directly instead of having them deducted from your investment account, some of this payment may be tax deductible. Bear in mind that withdrawals of deductible assets and all earnings are taxed as ordinary income and may be subject to a 10 percent federal penalty if taken prior to age 59½.

lion. What's the total left in the accounts? $1,259,000. Now, that's a spicy meatball! For some people, wrap accounts can be the cat's meow!

All for one and one for all. When it comes to wrap fee investment programs, that about sums it up. The term "wrap fee program" usually describes a collection of investment services that have been wrapped together and are covered by a single fee, which includes trading and management costs as well as investment advisory services. Once the domain of only the wealthiest investors, even the non-Rockefellers of the world can now participate.

Why bother with such an account? If you have the time to follow capital markets at home and abroad, scrutinize annual reports, study analysts' findings, follow an asset allocation model and amass enough information on large, medium and small companies to make decisions that affect your financial future and that of your family, step right up and do it yourself! But if you'd like to know your money is working as hard as you do and still have time to attend your kid's soccer games, work to make your business a success and grab a bite to eat, perhaps a little help isn't a bad idea.

It's A Wrap

Is wrapping for you? That depends on the type of investor you are, your financial goals and how much money you wish to commit. Wrap fee programs are designed to address the needs of investors who seek professional management of their assets but don't meet the minimum account size associated with the industry's top investment managers, which, in many cases, is in excess of $1 million. A wrap program can invest assets in many types of securities, including but not limited to common stocks;

government, municipal or corporate bonds; convertible bonds; preferred stocks; and foreign investments.

In addition to giving you access to the financial industry's leading investment advisors at much lower minimum account sizes, many programs give you objective third-party monitoring of your manager's performance. To make the grade in national brokerage firms, managers must meet minimum standards on legal compliance, assets under management, organizational support, relative performance with a verifiable track record, and investment philosophy.

Your broker may give good advice on investments, but most retail brokers are registered representatives, not registered investment advisors. Registered investment advisors have passed an exam given by the Securities and Exchange Commission. Your broker can introduce an array of independent money managers to you and help create a personalized program. He or she then ensures that the manager selected is appropriate for your goals and oversees every aspect of the relationship, monitoring the manager's performance and your expectations. Brokers may also recommend firing a manager who is not serving your interest.

What's The Bottom Line?

Wrap accounts are established on an all-inclusive fee basis, often called—you guessed it—a "wrap fee." In many cases, fees decrease as the account's assets increase. The wrap fee usually ranges from less than 1 percent to 3 percent, depending on the size of the account, and covers the money manager's fee, commissions and transaction costs, ongoing oversight, reviews and performance monitoring. In most cases, there is no entrance or exit fee. If you decide to terminate the relationship, you can do so at any time without penalty, and any unused portion of the fee is returned on a pro-rata basis.

At first glance, these fees may be enough to give you vertigo, but think a bit more about it. Unless you're investing in an unmanaged index fund, most funds

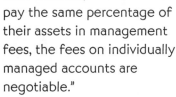

Trainer's Tip

"Unlike mutual funds, where all investors, regardless of the size of their account, pay the same percentage of their assets in management fees, the fees on individually managed accounts are negotiable."

—Stephen Kepes, managing director, 1838 Investment Advisors

have management fees and transaction fees that can average close to 2 percent annually. And if you buy a fund with a front- or back-end load, your total fees may exceed 3 percent.

Wrap accounts are designed to provide individual investors with diversification and professional management. Your managed portfolio is customized to fit your financial goals and objectives. It takes into account your individual investment style, risk tolerance, tax situation and needs for liquidity. Mutual funds also provide diversification and professional management, but with a big difference: In periods of stock market volatility, redemptions by panicky mutual fund investors may force portfolio managers to sell part of their holdings when prices are low. Individual portfolio managers, on the other hand, buy and sell stocks when they think the time is right. Proceeds from these sales can be held as cash or short-term instruments until prices are low enough to take new positions at more advantageous prices.

Little Big Account

If you're worried about putting all your eggs into a single manager's basket, there are many ways to diversify. Instead of using one portfolio manager, one style and one account, some mutual fund asset allocation programs offer a menu of different mutual funds. Minimums can be as low as $10,000, and the number of funds available to choose from can be up to several hundred.

In most cases, potential investors in these funds fill out a questionnaire profiling their investment objectives, time frame, risk tolerance and other issues (much like the one required by professional managers). Based on the results of your questionnaire, the fund then proposes a breakdown into bond and stock funds that suit your objectives. Stock funds are divided by market sectors (large-, medium- or small-company stock funds), style (value or growth), and origin (domestic or foreign). Bond funds are separated into corporate, government, foreign and other areas, depending on the program you choose and your investment objectives.

Healthy Habit

Some wrap programs offer a combination of individually managed and mutual fund wrap accounts—providing access to the best in both these worlds.

Many programs will reallocate funds on a quarterly or annual basis to keep your preferred allocation in line, selling shares that have performed well and buying those that have underperformed. They usually provide access to load and no-load funds and allow investors to switch not only between funds, but between families to avoid incurring a sales charge.

Fees for this type of wrap account begin in the 1.25 percent to 1.5 percent range and may decrease as assets under management increase. Before you get involved, get a copy of the offering statement and the prospectuses of the funds you'd like to use.

Professional money management may not be suitable for all investors, but if you've worked out to the max or are just in the mood to relax, a soothing wrap might be just what your portfolio ordered.

DAY 25

Gimme Shelter

Screen your portfolio from taxes with annuities

Harry and Elaine are two of the most endearing people you'd ever want to meet. They were politically correct long before the idea came into favor and are committed to helping other people, but they are clueless about investments. As a professor, Harry had an annuity contract through his employer for many years, and it represented a sizable portion of the family's assets. Sounds good—except that it was stuck in a fixed portfolio, and at a low rate at that. For a long time, Harry tried to get information from the company on how to make more money. Letters were written and calls were made, but nothing happened. While costs were low, so was performance, and service was nonexistent.

After several years of frustration, Harry finally switched his annuity to a company that offers more choices and better customer service. The results aren't in yet, but at least Harry and his financial advisor can take control, and that's half the battle.

If you're looking to take control over your investments and get tax deferral and some estate planning in the bargain, annuities are an option to explore. Along with retirement accounts, tax-free bonds and the roof over your head, annuities are among the few tax shelters left. An annuity is a type of tax-deferred savings plan contracted with a life insurance company. It has several participants: the annuitant, on whose life the contract is based; the owner, who controls the investment (the annuitant and owner are often one and the same); and the beneficiary, who receives the proceeds of the contract upon the death of the annuitant. Unlike life insurance, which is designed to pay a lump sum after you die, the purpose of annuities is to provide a series of payments while you're alive.

Is an annuity right for you? Before investing, take this test:

- Are you looking to invest long term (10 years or longer)? If not, you may want to consider a different investment.

- Will you be 59½ when you start to take distributions? If not, you'll pay 10 percent in penalties to the IRS in addition to regular income tax on any funds withdrawn.

- Have you exhausted all your tax-deductible alternatives? Be sure to max out your contributions to retirement plans and/or tax-deductible IRAs and Roth IRAs before starting or adding to an annuity.

If you answered yes to all of the above, read on.

Under The Umbrella

Everyone should wear sunscreen, but some people are more susceptible to burning than others. Consider the protection of an annuity if:

1. You're afraid of a lawsuit—most states protect at least some assets held in an annuity from creditors. If this describes your situation, consult an attorney.

2. You have little or no retirement savings and need a steady monthly check.

Slather It On

Although all annuities have elements in common, they are among the most varied and flexible of investments. And while there are about as many different annuities as summer has freckles, there are really two main varieties: immediate and deferred. *Immediate annuities* allow individuals to invest a lump sum, which is then paid out over a lifetime or for a specific period; payments begin immediately. In a *deferred annuity*, deposits accumulate interest that is tax-deferred until you decide to withdraw the funds.

The style of investment varies, too: A *fixed annuity* locks in an interest rate for a specific time period, while a *variable annuity* invests in various professionally managed stock, bond and balanced accounts.

Unlike certificates of deposit, which are guaranteed up to $100,000 by the FDIC, annuities are backed solely by the issuer, whether you invest through a bank, a broker or an insurance agent. This is of lesser importance in variable annuities because your money is usually invested in separate managed accounts and is therefore separate from the assets of the underlying insurer (although if the separate account becomes insolvent, the insurer's higher rating won't apply to that account). But if a fixed annuity is your preference, the safety of your money depends on the strength of your insurer.

Before investing, be sure you're buying through a strong insurance company whose claims-paying ability has been rated high by respected ratings agencies such as A.M. Best, Moody's Investor Service or Standard & Poor's. Your local library may have information from some of these sources; the insurer's home office may also provide this information over the phone.

Healthy Habit

If you're concerned about putting all your money in a variable annuity's different subaccounts at once, many policies have a dollar-cost averaging provision. Your initial investment is invested in a money-market or stable-value fund, and a percentage of the total is moved monthly into the funds you've selected. Minimum monthly investments range from $200 to $1,000, and you can stretch your investment as long as your money holds out.

Tan, Don't Burn

Before you decide on a particular fixed annuity, check the company's rate renewal history, surrender penalty schedules and length of rate guarantee. Some fixed annuities combine a long surrender penalty and a short guarantee period. Surrender penalties are lower than those for variable annuities but can still be substantial, starting as high as 7 percent if you withdraw right after investing; they then decline in increments annually, taking anywhere from one to five (or more) years to disappear completely. Rates can be locked in for variable time periods, but after the initial locked-in rate expires, most fixed-rate annuities guarantee a minimum interest rate. While some contracts offer a "bailout" provision that allows policyholders to surrender a contract without paying penalties if the renewal rate falls below the stated bailout rate, fixed annuities are usually not a good deal. Unless the rate is high and guaranteed for the life of the contract, most investors should avoid them.

Unlike their fixed counterparts, variable annuities allow investors to shift funds to different managed portfolios. If you don't like the way one portfolio performs or your needs change, you can switch to another fund without terminating the contract or paying taxes and penalties. The best way to select a variable annuity is to study the quality and quantity of its investment choices. Request and read the prospectus carefully before you invest any money. It can tell you all you need to know about fees, risks, investment choices, portfolio performance and how the investment works.

> **Smart Stretch**
> No-load and low-load variable annuities offer no or low surrender charges, and annual expenses are lower than annuities sold through agents. A partial list of companies that will provide information packets includes: Jack White, (800) 622-3699; T. Rowe Price, (800) 469-6587; Ameritas No-Load, (800) 552-3553; John Hancock, (888) 742-6262; Schwab Variable Annuity, (800) 838-0650; and USAA, (800) 531-6390. Some companies may not be licensed in your state. Read the prospectus before you invest.

Pealing Out

Although there are no fees upon investing, most variable annuities are not cheap. In addition to fees to manage your money—up to several percentage points annually—there are other annual charges, including mortality, expense and administration fees. And, of course, surrender penalties generally apply when you withdraw. Called a back-end load, these charges are heavy indeed. Some begin as high as 10 percent and decrease annually. While many contracts allow withdrawals of interest or a percentage of the original investment without a surrender penalty, income tax will be due on any portion of your withdrawal attributable to earnings unless you roll it to another annuity.

If you're under age 59½ when you make your withdrawal, you will incur an additional 10 percent penalty. The reason for the penalty is simple: Annuities, like traditional IRAs, are intended to help you save for retirement. They aren't designed to be short-term investments and are not appropriate for investors with short-term liquidity needs.

The ultimate way to withdraw from an annuity is, of course, to die. That's when the highly touted death benefit kicks in. Some variable annuities guarantee that in the case of the annuitant's death, beneficiaries receive at least what was invested, less any withdrawals. Other programs include a "step up" benefit, in which the minimum death benefit increases as the account's value rises. If you're investing in an annuity solely to provide for your beneficiaries, this is a great benefit. Most contracts charge a hefty annual fee for this death benefit, but in volatile market conditions, it could pay off.

Get Rid Of Those Tan Lines

What can you do if your fixed-rate annuity contract rate was just reset so that it's below market but not low enough for you to bail out without a fee? Or what about that variable annuity whose returns lagged behind similar investments? Fear not. Even though you signed a contract, unlike Faust, you may be able to get out with your soul *and* most of your investment intact.

One way out is through annual withdrawals. Whether you take distributions (and pay taxes and/or penalties as required) or switch to another annuity, most contracts allow a percentage of assets to be withdrawn annually without fees.

Although you still have to pay any applicable surrender charges, a tax-free transfer called a "1035 exchange," named

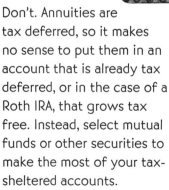

Money Missteps

Thinking of buying a variable annuity in an IRA account? Don't. Annuities are tax deferred, so it makes no sense to put them in an account that is already tax deferred, or in the case of a Roth IRA, that grows tax free. Instead, select mutual funds or other securities to make the most of your tax-sheltered accounts.

after that section of the Internal Revenue code, lets you move assets from one annuity contract to another, free from current tax penalties. Select an annuity, sign the paperwork required by your new company, and let it take care of the transfer.

With a 1035 exchange, investors in variable annuities can make the most of their guaranteed death benefit. If an appreciated contract is 1035-exchanged to a new company, the old contract's appreciated account value becomes the new contract's death-benefit guarantee.

If you've chosen a fixed annuity and are concerned about the company's claims-paying ability, a 1035 exchange may be worthwhile. But look before you switch to be certain the new annuity will provide everything you need. That way, you'll never have to say "The devil made me do it."

Healthy Habit

If your retirement income will be high enough to keep you in a top income tax bracket, remember that annuities convert long-term capital gains into short-term income, and you could end up paying more tax. Ask your accountant what's best for your situation.

Bon Voyage

Investing in foreign markets

Fred and Martha were adamant: No foreign "stuff" in their portfolio. "We don't travel outside the United States and we don't want our money going to any foreign countries," they said. "What's good enough for Uncle Sam is good enough for us." Their largest holdings? Philip Morris, Procter & Gamble and Coca-Cola—a global portfolio if there ever was one!

Even if the plane ride to Hong Kong is too long, you don't know who Fodor is and you don't care what they're wearing in Paris this season, there are lots of reasons to go abroad . . . with your money, that is.

With any number of record-breaking years for stateside markets under their money belts, few investors may be tempted to take their portfolios on a foreign trip. After all, why bother to roam when results have been so fine at home? A study of world markets between 1970 and 1992 done by research firm Ibbotson Associates concluded that a portfolio investing up to 35 percent in foreign stocks was *less* risky and earned 1.2 percent more each year than one invested exclusively in U.S. issues. Even though past performance is no guarantee of future returns, that's some pretty fancy footwork, considering that the aforementioned study included some of the finest years in U.S. market history.

Sometimes, just as U.S. markets are peaking, foreign markets are at the beginning of a turnaround. Several ongoing factors should keep foreign pots bubbling for a while: economic recovery and growth, the privatization of state-controlled companies to individual and corporate investors, the spread of democracy and the rise of capitalism. The removal of trade barriers and the increase in global communications has made the world a smaller place, with big opportunities for adventurous investors.

Foreign Territory

Of course, with any opportunity to profit comes the risk of potential losses. Few investments could rival the spectacular performance of emerging markets in 1993, with total returns higher than 67 percent . . . or the sucking sound as emerging markets *sub*merged in 1994 with the collapse of the Mexican peso. Just as a civilized traveler must be ready for anything, international investors must be prepared to take on a variety of risks:

- **Currency risk.** Foreign securities are denominated in foreign currencies. If the U.S. dollar rises in value, when profits and dividends are converted back into U.S. dollars, investment returns can be less than expected—and a great year can turn into a mediocre one.

- **Political and economic risk.** Sudden changes in government policies can wreak havoc on the most diversified portfolio. South American

---

Should You Stay, Or Should You Go?

Consistently timing any market properly is impossible. That goes double for international markets. There are so many variables that trying to decide which area, industries and companies of the world will be the next winners (or vice versa) is a full-time job, and one at which quite a few professional money managers haven't been too successful. To succeed in foreign investing, consider selecting a few areas, invest in them slowly, and adjust your allocation as time goes by. You'll avoid concentrating too much of your investment in any one country, style or industry, and it's a lot less time-consuming.

stocks, for example, at times highly profitable, can also fall sharply in sync with that region's economic woes. Hong Kong, now under Chinese rule, and China itself are other examples of potentially risky situations.

- **Differences in accounting practices.** Accounting and reporting procedures in foreign companies can differ from U.S. methods, and their annual reports may be difficult to understand—even if you can read the language.

- **Market risk.** U.S. markets are highly regulated, liquid and efficient, making it easy to judge objectively what shares are worth. But liquidity (how easily a stock is bought or sold) in individual foreign issues can be a problem, as can trading and accessing price information.

If this sounds like more effort than it's worth, keep in mind that potential rewards can be worth the extra effort. Twenty-five years ago, about two-thirds of the world's equity markets consisted of U.S. stocks. Today, by not investing internationally, you could miss out on seven of 10 of the largest automobile, financial services and insurance companies, and eight out of 10 of the world's largest electrical, chemical, machinery, engineering and utility companies. In fact, in a little over a decade, markets outside the U.S. have grown to represent almost two-thirds of world markets.

Investment in foreign stocks certainly diversifies your portfolio, but even better, as your dollars take a run for the border, they provide a stabilizing effect on your portfolio. Since foreign markets don't usually march in lock step with domestic markets, when one zigs, the other may zag. In the first 11 months of 1993, for example, the Morgan Stanley Europe, Australia, Far East (EAFE) stock index rose 24 percent, compared with a 9 percent gain for the Standard & Poor's 500. So if you're game for adventure, dust off your passport and join me on a tour of foreign investing, from the mundane to the exotic.

Joggin' Jargon

If you want to diversify with a pure play in foreign securities, don't leave home without knowing the difference between international and global. *International funds* invest exclusively outside the U.S. *Global funds*, on the other hand, can invest a percentage of their holdings stateside.

The Accidental Investor

Don't look now, but you may already be reaping the rewards of foreign investing—without leaving home! Many large

American companies are multinational, deriving more than one-quarter of earnings and profits from foreign businesses and subsidiaries. In most parts of the world, it's possible to FedEx a letter, sip a Coke, bite into a Big Mac, cruise in a Chevrolet and shave with a Gillette Sensor. International exposure provides new markets and new profits for companies willing to deal with diverse cultures. Not only is there a McDonald's in every American city, but growth overseas could keep Ronald McDonald flipping burgers in new cities until the *next* millennium and beyond!

Healthy Habit

Consider splitting your dollars between two types of funds: developed markets and developing markets. The former is considered by some to be more predictable than the latter but with less potential upside. By spreading your investment around, you can better cover your bases.

As a first foray into foreign markets, multinational corporations provide a foreign excursion . . . and you don't need a visa. The risk here is similar to that of investing in foreign securities. Profits earned in foreign currencies are subject to fluctuating currency values and may get lost in the translation, although profits and earnings from large multinationals are not as vulnerable to such ups and downs as are shares in individual foreign companies.

Europe On $100 A Month

If the idea of investing in foreign markets on your own makes you queasy, consider hiring a tour guide, familiar to most as a mutual fund manager. Many funds invest in overseas markets, but for the beginning traveler, a broad, well-established international portfolio could be a good starting point. By studying the prospectus of several funds, you should be able to get an idea of where in the world they invest.

Does the fund concentrate on large, established, mature economies like those of Western Europe, or does the manager prefer high-risk areas in what used to be called the Third World (now affectionately known as emerging markets)? While the best growth prospects are probably to be found in China, Chile, Mexico, and other South American and Pacific Rim countries, follow the same rules for investing as you would if eating in a foreign country . . . if you don't know what it is, don't take a big helping. Try a little bit; if you like it, there's always more. Find out the minimum initial investment, then add to your portfolio on a regular basis.

Be sure you understand the menu . . . I mean prospectus. Read it before you order, or what you thought was a dish of pasta could turn out to be piled high with eels. Although you may eventually develop a taste for seafood, in the meantime, your portfolio could suffer from a bad case of indigestion.

Abroad Alone

If you're still determined to travel solo, consider investing in individual stocks through American depository receipts, or ADRs. ADRs are securities issued by U.S. banks against actual shares of a foreign company. Dividends are paid in U.S. dollars and shares are bought and sold through stockbrokers and other financial institutions. ADRs are available for hundreds of stocks from a wide variety of countries. The benefits of ADRs include avoiding the red tape of purchasing shares of foreign companies, getting price quotes in U.S. dollars, receiving all shareholder communications in English, and owning stocks that are traded on U.S. markets just like those of any American corporation. Unlike actual shares of foreign stocks, companies that set up ADRs must go through extensive disclosure procedures before they are allowed to trade on U.S. markets. ADRs are available in a variety of forms, including common and preferred stock, bonds, and convertible securities.

Healthy Habit

A fund's return is more than the sum of its stock picks—asset allocation plays a part, too. If sending your money abroad to seek its fortune makes you nervous, consider funds that also allocate assets to foreign debt securities. These "multi-asset" funds are often less volatile than funds that invest exclusively in stocks.

Seasoned travelers know that next to knowing how to say hello and ask where the restroom is, the most important skill to master is converting your currency to that of the locals. Hong Kong clerks size up potential customers as they walk into the store: Calculators click and prices are immediately converted to dollars, pesos or marks, whichever they guess will suit you. The foreign exchange rate is the price of one currency in terms of another. If you have the time and a taste for risk, currency speculation allows sharp traders to capitalize on differences in the exchange rates of various currencies.

Planning A Trip

Take these tips from Mark Mobius, managing director at Templeton Funds:

"If you plan to invest in foreign markets, the key is to look before you leap. Find out all you can about the people who are running the company. Even if you're not in the country, you can find out a lot of information on the Internet. Talk to people in the country who know what is going on. Talk to a broker in that country and get more information. You can use chat rooms to talk to people who know people in various companies. This takes a lot of time, so if you don't have the time, the best vehicle to use is a fund: You get diversification, professional management and liquidity any time you need it."

Huge profits are possible, but large losses are more common among small investors. Perhaps you'd prefer a trip to the casinos of Monaco?

Even if you'd never want to visit some of the places your portfolio will travel, long-term returns from foreign investments could make the trip worthwhile. And you don't even need to get your shots up to date.

DAY 27

Location, Location, Location

Fitting real estate into your portfolio

They say that timing isn't everything, but when it comes to investing, it sure helps. In 1998, after three years of stellar performance, real estate investment trusts (REITs) were all the rage on Wall Street. New issues came out almost weekly, yields were high, and projections for prices were higher yet. Having held single issues of REITs in client portfolios through several of these boom years, the opportunity to introduce clients to a professionally managed portfolio of REITs proved irresistible.

But no sooner was the ink dry than the bottom dropped out of the REIT market. While dividends remained high, prices plummeted. Regular investors begged to sell and switch to technology stocks (not a bad idea), and REITs hit rock bottom. But the professionals took a different tactic: They began to recommend this down-and-out sector. Within six months, REITs were on the comeback trail, fortunate for those who saw the opportunity for high total return and bought while they were down. The moral for these REIT investors? Buy high, add low.

What can real estate investments do for your portfolio? Chicken Little and some of Wall Street's more panicky mavens are fond of telling their followers the sky is falling—whether it's inflation or deflation, a war in a far-off land or turmoil on Main Street. To reduce their exposure to such crises, many investors seek ways to hedge their equity exposure with investments in other asset categories, including hard assets like gold, collectibles and real estate. Whether these investments are right for you is a matter of taste, but we'll take a look at real estate as our exercise du jour.

Money Missteps

When investing in individual REITs, avoid aggressive projections of rental income, aging apartment complexes, older shopping centers, obsolete office buildings and towns with just one industry.

The Real World

What was true when Mark Twain's steamboats ruled the mighty Mississippi is just as true for investors today, with perhaps a few exceptions. Real estate ownership doesn't have to entail bricks and mortar, paying mortgages or collecting rent. Investors have the option of investing in real estate without the hassle of direct ownership, through REITs.

REITs are diversified instruments that invest in various kinds of commercial real estate. Think of it as owning shares in a mutual fund that invests in properties. Like mutual funds, your investment is divided among the various properties composing the particular REIT you've selected, which can include hotels, apartments, office buildings, hospitals, mobile homes, hotels, shopping centers—even gambling casinos. Some REITs purchase many types of real estate; others specialize in one area. Unlike other forms of real estate ownership, REITs don't require big down payments, and they're more liquid: Because they are sold as shares of stock, buying and selling is possible on major exchanges.

Smart Stretch

Looking for more general information on REITs? The National Association of Real Estate Investment Trusts, at (800) 3-NAREIT, offers a free brochure on the basics.

REITs are attractive because of their relatively high dividends, but they have proved to be fair-weather friends. Stellar returns, as measured by the NAREIT composite index, like 1996's 36 percent, were offset in 1998 when REITs lost 19 percent vs. the S&P 500's positive 27 percent return.

If this makes your feel cautious, you're not alone. While today's investors may be in for a wild ride, for diversification beyond stocks, bonds and cash, renting out space to a REIT might be a landlord's dream.

Park That Exercise Machine Here

First off, don't confuse today's REITs with earlier forms of real estate financing. Until the tax law changes in 1986, tax incentives drove real estate development. Financing by banks, savings and loans, limited partnerships, institutions and insurance companies was plentiful. Unfortunately for investors, so was leverage. The 1980s saw a drop in property values that exacerbated the effect of heavy borrowing, resulting in huge losses for some REITs—and their reputation as a rip-off.

Today, REITs are a house of a different color. Instead of using debt financing, many are now equity-financed. Formerly, REITs could be compared to bonds; now they are more comparable to stocks. (This also explains the term "equity REITs.") Financing through the public market has forced developers to secure the strong balance sheets that Wall Street demands: An average debt-to-capitalization ratio of 30 percent is a major improvement from the 80 percent levels of the 1980s. Careful scrutiny by institutional money managers and corporate and public pension funds has also improved portfolio composition, resulting in higher-quality holdings.

When it comes to buying property, any real estate agent will tell you the three essentials: location, location and location. With REITs, add management to that list. Unlike mutual fund managers, who need only specialize in buying and selling stocks and bonds, REIT operators must be proficient property managers. It's always good to put your money where the boss puts his or hers,

Trainer's Tip

"REITs do well following anemic economies. Because this is a lagging relationship, you have a factor that is a barometer of REIT performance. If the previous year's GDP growth is less than average (roughly 3 percent), then the following year is usually a good one for REITs."

—*Charles Babin and Venkat Chalasani, principals, State Street Global Advisors* so find an investment where the manager has put his money as well as his mouth, and you have a better chance of success.

Another driving force behind REITs is the diversification they add to portfolios. Investors disappointed with low payouts from fixed-income investments have turned to the higher returns available from REITs. Many REITs should continue to provide sound dividend growth, thanks to rent increases, new development and new acquisitions. Long-term investors could see even more growth through appreciation in property values.

In addition, REITs are tax efficient. Unlike limited partnerships, REITs do not distribute Form K-1 (and a migraine) at tax time. Instead, REITs issue 1099s for the dividends they have paid to investors, as do most other publicly traded securities. And since a portion of the company's dividends may be considered return of capital, which is taxed at lower long-term capital gains rates, there is some tax deferral. However, possible tax benefits should not be your motivation for making an investment.

Healthy Habit

REITs might trade like regular stocks, but they invest in property, so evaluating them is not the same as analyzing a company that manufactures pharmaceuticals. While most stocks can be compared by their price-to-earnings ratio, which includes a company's depreciation, REITs investors use funds from operations (FFO), which is earnings with depreciation added back in. Look for REITs with a steady history of increasing FFO.

Room To Maneuver

While REITs pay attractive dividends, don't buy them just for yield. Unlike insured investments that pay a secure dividend, the principal of a REIT is not insured or guaranteed. Instead, think of REITs as total return vehicles, and look for situations that can deliver growth as well as yield. For example, when it comes to choosing the type of properties, don't forget geography. Select investments in a region with demographics that can support its growth . . . location, location, etc.

Which sectors show the most potential for investors? Office buildings have been risky because of overbuilding in the 1980s, but as occupancy levels increase, risk may decrease. Increased travel from aging baby boomers could bode well for hotel and casino REITs. And teenagers aren't the only ones cruising the malls: Recreational shopping is an American

Beach Bums

As baby boomers enter their retirement phase, vacation home prices should increase along with increased demand. Consider buying a place where you'd like to retire and becoming a landlord until you're ready to move in.

If you rent it out for 14 days or less, you can keep the money, tax free. Beyond that, rental payments are taxable, but you can deduct expenses from rent income. Find out more from a tax advisor.

institution. Whether it's factory outlet centers, massive malls or strip shopping centers, retail REITs might also warrant some scrutiny.

It's Never Too Late

Have you missed the boat for buying into REITs? Many institutional investors don't think so. Investors in pension plans, as well as in balanced, growth, utility, and income and growth mutual funds, for instance, have become buyers in the real estate markets. Many experts agree that real estate follows a five-year cycle, so when investing, it pays to pay attention to where you are in that cycle.

Some analysts recommend shares in new issues because they are less expensive than older REITs. But before you invest, do your homework. Demand has increased the supply of offerings, with shares in new as well as established companies going for a song. When evaluating an investment, be sure to ask for a prospectus on a new issue or for the latest annual report and quarterly statements on an older one. Be sure cash flow is high enough to easily cover the dividend, or look for companies with a history of increasing dividends and earnings.

Investors can also participate in this market by buying shares in individual issues or in a mutual fund investing in real estate. And remember, like all investments, prices fluctuate. Even the best-managed REIT can lose value if the real estate market falters. Scarlett O'Hara may not have been exactly right; the land *isn't* the only thing that matters. On the other hand, smart investors might heed Mark Twain's advice: "Buy land— they're not making it anymore."

DAY 28

The Zen Of Investing

Socially conscious investing

> "I'm not against maximizing returns, but don't do it at the expense of my great-grandchildren."
> —Amy Domini, principal, Domini Social Investment Funds

Earth Day, 1989. I had nothing to do, so I trotted down to a celebration armed with every piece of socially responsible investment material I could find. At the time, I didn't care whether a company saved the whales or processed them, but all that would change. Enter Hope (no kidding, that's her real name)—and enter a glint of consciousness in my investment subconscious.

Hope appeared to be the quintessential leftover hippie, complete with her flowing hair, Birkenstocks, and tie-dyed madras skirt. When it comes to investing, Hope has proved to be no fool. She may not have known what a P/E ratio was when she started out, but she knew what she expected from a company that was worthy of her investment dollars. Through the years, she has shown me just how important women's intuition can be. We built a portfolio based on her specific requirements, selecting companies that did business in socially responsible ways, and in doing so, we avoided many corporate blow-ups and made money.

What Hope lacked in investment acumen she made up for in knowing and understanding people. The result? Her portfolio performed so well that it financed her entrance into retail with a store so unique (and socially conscious) that people are begging to franchise it. Saving the planet has never been so lucrative.

You don't have to wait for Earth Day to put your investment mettle to the test. Even if you were born on a lily pad, it isn't always easy being green. Recycling soda cans, detergent bottles and newspapers is basic stuff compared to conserving the wetlands or saving the whales. Some investors choose to take their personal vision into the realm of their portfolio.

Socially responsible investing (SRI) began as far back as the 1920s, when some church endowments avoided investment in "sin stocks," including liquor, tobacco and gambling issues. Social activism reached new heights during the Vietnam War, and this translated into increased vigilance on the part of investors in the 1960s. For the first time, many investors realized that the companies that provided them with washing machines and TV sets also made warheads and tanks. With the birth of the Council on Economic Priorities in 1969, companies were rated on the essential issues of the day, including military contracts, environmental pollution and minority hiring practices.

The politically correct climate of the 1990s has heightened public awareness to the possibilities of investor activism. More and more investors are considering the products and services of companies in which they invest with an eye to a double bottom line: Not only do they want to know if the company is a good investment, they want to know if the company meets their chosen social criteria. Over the past several years, some of the hottest issues to emerge in the field of social investing have included the environment and labor. But interest in the traditional social issues of alcohol, tobacco, gambling and weapons manufacture has not diminished. Some of today's hotbeds of activism include contraceptives, abortion, pornography, animal rights, nuclear power and the environment, to name a few.

You've spent the last 27 days pounding your body—now it's time to stretch your mental muscles and your investment perspective.

What's Your Mantra?

Before embarking on a mission to save the portfolio, don't jump at the first investment touted as socially responsible. Perhaps the most important criteria to keep in mind are your own. Individual social priorities vary widely, and it isn't enough to say "I want to invest only in good companies."

There are two general ways to screen a portfolio: positive and negative. A negative screen avoids particular companies or industries; no mining, oil or chemical manufacturers, for example. Positive screens look for companies with above-average records in a particular area, like workplace practice or the environment. The key is to define your own criteria, then build your portfolio as you like it. Do you care about cleaning up the environment, or do cigarette manufacturers burn you up? Would you prefer to avoid companies that make nuclear weapons, or do you actively seek out companies that are proactive in minority hiring and family-friendly policies?

To reach financial as well as social goals, investors should avoid becoming so restrictive that whole industry groups are eliminated. By picking your battles, it's possible to find companies that are acceptable on more than one level, building a profitable portfolio that has the potential to make money and doesn't tie you up in knots.

Hatha Investment Is Better Than None

No matter how "good," every company has some qualities that may be considered by somebody as socially

Smart Stretch

For more information, read *Investing From the Heart: The Guide to Socially Responsible Investments and Money Management* (Crown Publishers) by Jack A. Brill and Alan Reder.

Smart Stretch

Access the Domini Funds' Web site at www.domini.com for information on shareholder activism and socially conscious screening criteria. Access is free of charge.

*un*redeeming. Standards used for judging companies are as individual as investors themselves; what is considered socially responsible or irresponsible is subject to interpretation. When putting together your portfolio, consider the two general categories of ethical or socially responsible companies: Companies either provide a product or service that is considered inherently responsible, or they focus attention on doing their best for their employees, their communities and the environment. While few companies are stellar on both fronts, some come close.

Consider, if you will, Ben & Jerry's Homemade Inc., a company almost as well-known for their fair hiring practices as for their delicious products. At first glance, they seem to have it all . . . unless your screen eliminates companies whose products do harm: All that fat and sugar *can't* be good for you!

Socially conscious investors may avoid U.S. government-backed securities based on the government's conservative or liberal stances on various issues. On the other hand, money raised through the sale of these debt securities also funds AIDS and cancer research, supports the arts, pays for school lunches, and backs programs designed to help the poor and the elderly. For that matter, those who choose to be socially responsible in a strict sense, avoiding, for example, stocks of tobacco companies, may have to wrestle with the idea of using other products made by the same conglomerate. Many investors are surprised to learn that some tobacco companies produce widely used products ranging from candies to pickles. The same companies may also contribute to society by donating space, time and money to museums, ballet companies, struggling theater groups or public television stations.

Ask Your Yogi

If you're looking for a moral clearinghouse, look no further than your friendly financial advisor. Several firms provide research on SRI and can steer investors toward individual issues or mutual funds that match their goals. When it comes to funds, the varieties are as numerous as the opinions. There are funds that invest on Christian principles; funds designed just for Catholics or exclusively for Muslims; funds that seek out companies favorable to women, minorities or any number of specific issues . . . even funds that provide a screened version of the S&P 500.

But does using your heart mean leaving your head behind? Many fund-rating services would have you think so. Morningstar Inc. notes that of the 7,000 mutual funds they track, only 46 are socially screened. Certain financial publications assert that socially conscious investors can expect to do good, but that their investments rarely do well. These opinions come from the idea that it's difficult enough to make money in stocks, and checking whether a company meets particular socially responsible criteria consumes extra time and effort, which harms a fund's performance.

When looking at the performance of socially responsible funds, keep in mind that mutual fund performance is judged against a standard, usually that of the Standard & Poor's 500, for any given period. Comparing all socially responsible funds against this bellwether is like comparing organic apples with inorganic oranges: Funds may include cash, bonds, small- and medium-sized company stocks, and other securities in their portfolios, yet they are compared against a large-company stock index that is always fully invested in its 500 large-company issues. A more appropriate comparison would pit only the performance of SRI large-company equity and equity income funds against the S&P 500 index.

After leveling the playing field, it seems that most socially screened funds can't stand up to the comparison. According to Michael van Dorn of Morningstar, only four funds have track records longer than seven years, and in that time, many of them come up short. On the other hand, so do most relatively new funds. According to Morningstar, over the past five years, fewer than one-third of the nearly 500 standard growth and growth and income funds have matched the S&P 500 index's performance.

Anyone who knows anything about mutual funds will tell you (right after they admonish you to get and read the prospectus before investing) that a mutual fund is a long-term investment, that five years is nothing in the life of any fund, and that past performance is not an indication of future returns. So it would seem, as far as the relative performance of socially screened funds, the jury is still out. "There

Money Missteps

Know what you're investing in. Not all SRI investors lean to the left. Others are more "right-minded," investing against companies that promote abortions and pornography, but for companies that manufacture guns and tobacco.

are talented fund managers and some buffoons out there, and talented managers make money while others may not, no matter what kind of investing they do," says van Dorn. Remember, too, that all mutual funds screen the universe of stocks and bonds, so one screen may prove more efficacious than another, whether it involves socially responsible criteria or not.

The use of SRI criteria in building a portfolio has its positives. Companies that treat their employees well, preserve a clean environment, or produce products and services that better the lives of their customers often face fewer regulatory problems, lawsuits and strikes. It makes good sense (and dollars, too) to consider these factors when choosing investments.

Some investors may not want to consider their investments on more than a financial level, preferring to go for the best return possible without regard to their investments' social consequences. If that's the route you choose, you can still do your favorite organization a favor (and get a tax deduction) by donating a share of your riches.

Olympic Effort

Saving for your children's education

> *"A mind is a terrible thing to waste."*
> —Slogan of the United Negro College Fund

Anita and Barry had been saving for Nick's college education since he was a baby. While they didn't put a lot away, they invested aggressively—and their bets paid off. Now that Nick is starting his first year at the school of his choice, his parents are thrilled that it is well within their means. Of course, it helped that Nick is a smart kid and was recruited by several schools. Thanks to his parents' savings, his choice wasn't based solely on finances (although a sizable scholarship helped out). Says Anita: "We didn't want him to choose a school based on the kind of aid package that was available, so we were prepared to bite the bullet and take money out of savings if we needed to. We just wanted him to have a choice—we're so glad he did!"

Saving for college seems as difficult as winning a gold medal at the Olympics. Though most Olympians admit to training for their sport as tiny tots, many parents don't start saving for college in earnest until their children are much older. But whether you run a four-minute mile or prefer to cheer athletes from the sidelines, you, too, can discover award-winning ways to finance your children's higher education.

According to Kalman Chany, author of *Paying for College Without Going Broke*, with college costs escalating by 4 percent to 5 percent per year, a freshman in 2010 could face a tab of $312,955 for an Ivy League school, $208,750 for a private college, and $99,906 for a public school (for four years' tuition, room and board, and books). Fortunately, you don't have to go it alone. Today we'll work on what you can do to save for college; tomorrow we'll move into using other people's money—financial aid, scholarships, and loans.

Olympic Trials

No matter what college you select, early saving and investing make all the difference. Parents who start saving when their child is born will need to save approximately $3,100 per year (growing at 8 percent) to raise $125,383 by the time that child enters college. Should they wait until Junior enters high school, the tab rises to about $25,700 per year to reach $125,072.

Starting early not only decreases the amount you'll have to save, but allows more flexibility in your investments. By giving yourself a longer time horizon, you can invest in higher-return investments, such as common stock, to provide the best opportunity for keeping pace with rising college costs. But no matter what age the child, prudent investors don't put all their investment eggs in one basket. Asset allocation, or spreading investments across investment classes including cash, bonds and stocks, can improve overall returns while minimizing exposure to risk.

Healthy Habit

If you're an older parent whose children will attend college after you reach age 59½, consider saving for their education by fully funding your retirement accounts or through tax-deferred annuities. Savings here grow without current tax and won't be counted as part of your assets when schools look at your financial aid application. And, unlike UTMA and UGMA accounts, these assets are your property, not your child's.

Right On With The Roth

Despite what the experts suggest, many parents forgo saving for college until their kids are in their teens. By then, the panic is on. And if you had

Kids' Stuff

Trying to teach your kids that money doesn't grow on trees? Here are some sites that can help:

- www.kiplinger.com/kids/: designed to teach kids how to develop a budget, save for college and get the best college deals

- www.kidsbank.com: offers information about money, saving, checking and interest with the help of cartoon characters; calculators help kids analyze financial goals

- www.independentmeans.com: offers entrepreneurial information for females under 20 (An Income of Her Own, an online version of the group's game, is also available.)

- www.youngbiz.com: includes tips on credit cards, profiles on famous people who got their start at an early age, daily performance updates on three stock portfolios comprised of companies familiar to kids, and an investment calculator

- http://tqd.advanced.org/3096: designed by kids, teaches about different classes of investments, including stocks, bonds and mutual funds; includes a stock game, financial quiz and glossary of financial terms; can search the site as a beginner, intermediate or advanced investor (Maybe Mom and Dad could learn a few things here, too!)

your children later in life, you may be paying for college just when you had hoped to begin your retirement. So where do the limited funds available go—to your retirement or to Junior's college fund? The quick answer is to save for both. After all, you can get a loan to help offset college costs, but convincing someone to lend you money on which to retire may be a bit more difficult. While you may not be able to afford maximizing your 401(k) plan, try to contribute at least enough to earn any matching funds offered by your employer. Matching funds give additional leverage to these tax-deferred accounts, and you can always borrow from them to offset college costs if you have to.

If you're in this spot, there's still hope. If your child has at least $2,000 in earned income, they can contribute that much annually to a Roth IRA. Contributions grow tax free, and Junior can take out contributions (but not earnings) tax free to pay for college or living expenses. Five years of Roth IRAs could mean $10,000; not a bad sum to offset tuition or fees. If you are eligible (income levels of $150,000 to $160,000 per couple or $95,000 to $110,000 for individuals), consider a Roth IRA for yourself.

Trainer's Tip

"If you want to have any hope of getting financial aid, avoid Education IRAs, Roth IRAs or regular IRAs in your children's names, UGMA and UTMA accounts, and all pre-paid tuition plans. You're better off keeping the funds in your own name."

—Kalman Chany, author of Paying for College Without Going Broke

You can contribute $2,000 annually even if you're covered by a retirement plan at work, and you can pull out contributions (but not earnings) to help with your children's college costs. Earnings continue to grow in the account, helping you reach your retirement goals.

Educating IRA

Another option is to talk to Mr. Ed . . . not the horse, the Education IRA. Created in 1998, the Education IRA allows contributions of $500 per child per year. The child must be under age 18 and can't have contributions made on his or her behalf to a qualified state tuition program. Contributions grow tax-deferred and can be withdrawn tax free to offset education costs, including tuition, books, room and board. Provided you don't exceed the income limits of $95,000 for individuals or $150,000 for couples, the Education IRA is a gimme. If your income is too high, ask a grandparent, relative or friend whose income does qualify to make the contribution.

Seem like much ado about nothing? First, it's better than nothing, and the account can grow until its beneficiary reaches 30 years of age. If one child decides not to go to college or wins a giant scholarship and doesn't need the funds, they can be passed on to another member of the family.

Best of all, Education IRAs don't preclude contributions to Roth IRAs. If you meet the income levels, you, your spouse and your child can all contribute to a Roth in addition to your Education IRA. That's $6,500 you can save per year, tax deferred . . . now that's using your horse sense!

Playing By The Rules

Before you rush out to invest your baby's shower gifts in savings bonds or commodities, consider the tax consequences. While your child is learning the ABCs, learn a few new letters yourself: UGMA and UTMA. The Uniform Gift to Minors Act and the Uniform Transfer to Minors Act (only one applies in each state) are designed to make it easy to gift securities to minors. Each parent can gift as much as $10,000 per year to a UTMA or

UGMA. Under the acts' provisions, the minor is the owner of the securities, but a parent or legal guardian acts as custodian of the child's money, responsible for prudently investing assets until the child reaches maturity, either age 18 or 21, depending on your state.

Potential tax savings in these accounts can be substantial: The first $700 of unearned income in a minor's account is exempt from tax, regardless of his or her age. The second $700 of unearned income is taxed at the minor's rate. Amounts of more than $1,400 are taxed at the parent's highest marginal rate. At age 14, all income greater than $700 is taxed at the child's own rate; 15 percent for income, 10 percent for capital gains (figures may be indexed for inflation).

UTMA and UGMA accounts are a great idea for some investors, but assets in these accounts could interfere with your child's ability to qualify for financial aid. Aid qualifications are subject to change, but generally the amount of financial aid your child qualifies for depends on your family's expected contribution, your child's portion of which is 35 percent of his or her own assets and half his or her annual income over $2,400. The more assets in your child's name, the harder it will be to qualify for aid. Parents must contribute a maximum of 5.65 percent of their assets to tuition before the student qualifies for need-based financial aid. Assets in tax-deferred accounts, like 401(k) or other retirement plans; annuities; and cash values of insurance policies are generally excluded from these calculations of parents' expected contributions.

Taxing Matters

The "kiddie tax" was designed to keep Mom and Dad from shifting all of their income to their kids' names to avoid paying tax at their higher marginal tax rate. Depending on how you've invested Junior's money, you may reach this threshold sooner or later. Here are some ways to keep your savings away from the taxman:

- **Are you a frequent trader?** Avoid active trading in your kid's account. Choose investments to hold for the long term and sell them after your child has reached age 14, when his or her tax rate will be 10 percent instead of your 20 percent.

Money Missteps

Looking for financial aid? Common sense tells you it's best to keep money in your name so you don't disqualify your child, right? If you're in the top tax bracket, think again. Since you probably won't qualify for any need-based aid programs, you may as well put the money in your kids' names.

Smart Stretch

Need information on what rate applies to your bonds? Call (800) 4US-BOND (487-2663).

- **Are U.S. savings bonds a possibility?** While their returns are likely to be less than a stock fund, if you buy them in your kid's name and Social Security number and don't cash them in until after age 14, you'll avoid the kiddie tax and owe tax at your child's rate of 15 percent. Consult your tax advisor.

- **Thinking stock or stock funds?** Think low dividend. While dividends are delightful, they're also taxable. Consider low- or no-dividend stocks or funds to cut down on tax, so long as you can stomach their potentially higher volatility.

- **Close to your goal?** When your child reaches age 14, start selling off your high-flying growth stocks and funds, and opt for a more conservative strategy. You'll be beyond the kiddie tax years and have time to set aside liquid funds for your soon-to-be short-term needs.

Bond Boosters

Got some savings bonds that a favorite aunt or uncle awarded to your children (or to you)? Here are some ideas on how to make the most of them:

- A Series EE bond reaches face value no later than the end of the term for which it was issued. New Series EE bonds have an original maturity of 12 years.

- Bonds issued after November 1, 1982, and held for at least five years earn competitive interest rates with a guaranteed minimum on some bonds of 6 percent. The market-based rate is equal to 85 percent of the average yield on five-year Treasury marketable securities during the time the bond is held, compounded semi-annually.

- Bonds held less than five years earn interest on a fixed, graduated scale.

Playing To Win

Winning at the scholarship game

> "You can't win any game unless you are ready to win."
>
> —Connie Mack

John and Diane have one smart son. (Actually, they have two, but only one is applying to colleges at the moment.) Max graduated at the top of his class from a large public high school, got 1600 on his SAT and qualified for a National Merit Scholarship. Although his parents would be considered by most to be well off, David also qualified for several other scholarships and a small aid package from the college of his choice. How? By carefully scouring books and the Internet for information on programs that could provide assistance and by filling out numerous tedious financial aid forms. David is proud of his achievement—he found these scholarships on his own. While his parents still have a heavy burden to send him to the school of his choice, every little bit helps.

Whether your child is starting the first grade or already looking at college catalogs, one thing is certain: It will take more than an Olympic medal to keep those happy golden days on track. Paying the bill for a college education can prove a Sisyphean challenge. The cost of a private college education, including room and board, can reach hundreds of thousands of dollars.

But while many students are on the "study now, pay later" plan, primarily using loans to make up for savings shortfalls, many thousands of dollars in scholarships and financial aid are left unclaimed annually. Since 1992, when government student loans became available regardless of the recipient's income, millions of new borrowers entered the system. You don't have to depend solely on Uncle Sam's largess, however. There are many byways on the road to the gold, including financial aid, scholarships and a variety of loans.

Financial Aid: The Price Is Right

Before you skip this section, don't assume you won't qualify. While deciphering financial aid packages can be as difficult as the SAT, understanding the rules makes all the difference. Begin your in-depth study when your child starts 10th grade, and start by selecting schools not only on the basis of their price tags but also on their history of providing financial aid. It's often tougher to get aid from low-priced or midpriced schools than from expensive schools. Many high-priced colleges are "need-blind"—they accept qualified applicants without considering finances, then help parents figure out a package to cover costs. These packages may include scholarships, grants, work-study programs and low-interest loans.

Trainer's Tip

"The key to getting financial aid is understanding how eligibility is determined and planning your finances to maximize eligibility. To qualify for aid, you need to lower your EFC."

—Kalman Chany, author, Paying for College Without Going Broke

While Junior is front and center writing admission essays, you'll be in the bleachers filling out a daunting pile of paperwork. Schools like to target potential aid recipients early, so have your taxes done as soon as possible. Some schools have deadlines before you even get your 1099s; in these situations it's OK to estimate your earnings on the aid form.

Aid decisions for the first year of college are based on financial information starting January 1 of your child's junior year of high school. Your expected family contribution, or EFC, is the amount of money a family is expected to contribute per year toward the student's cost of attendance. Colleges use this figure to determine a student's eligibility to receive aid. The higher your earnings during the year in which you apply, the less aid you'll qualify for. If you plan to sell appreciated assets, do so before January 1 of your child's 11th-grade year so capital gains won't be counted as part of your bottom line.

Even if your earnings are too high, your child may still be eligible for financial aid in the form of merit scholarships, which are awarded regardless of need. As colleges compete for the best and the brightest, the number and size of these scholarships has risen.

Smart Stretch

Trying to decide which schools to apply to? Consider these bestsellers from Princeton Review, which categorize schools by size, location, selection criteria, and type of loan available:

- *The Best 331 Colleges*
- *Pocket Guide to Colleges*
- *The Complete Book of Colleges*

Wheel Of Fortune

Does the idea of poring over hundreds of thousands of pages of scholarship descriptions in your local library send you into a panic? Spend your time surfing instead . . . surfing the Web, that is. The Internet is an excellent source for information on scholarships and financial aid. Sallie Mae, the nation's largest source of funds for college, boasts an informative Web site at www.salliemae.com, with more than 350 pages of information on federal and private student aid programs.

FastWeb (www.fastweb.com), a site run by Student Services Inc., is the largest scholarship service to go online and can simplify your task. Mark Rothschild, director of scholarship services, notes that there are 180,000 scholarships on the FastWeb site. Of the more than $50 billion in annual financial aid, says Rothschild, $40 billion is from state and federal sources, $10 billion from universities, and $2 billion from private groups.

To start the FastWeb search, applicants provide a self-profile that matches them to appropriate scholarships. Intended major, hobbies, religious and other affiliations, ethnic and racial background, state and county of residence, and parents' employers are some of the requested facts. Seem a bit too personal? Says Rothschild, "You don't have to be Michael Jordan or have a sparkling GPA to qualify for a scholarship—to the contrary. So many

Smart Stretch

Paying for College Without Going Broke (Random House), by Kalman Chany dispels the myths about financial aid and tells you how to minimize costs by maximizing your child's eligibility for financial aid, how to negotiate for more aid, and what are the best loan programs available. It's the definitive guide on paying for college.

providers are looking for people with different kinds of characteristics." An interest in photography or a parent's membership in the Knights of Columbus could be qualifications for potential scholarships.

After the profile is completed, the student initiates the search. Results arrive in an electronic mailbox and include the application deadline, where to apply, criteria, number of scholarships available and the amount. Students select those of interest, and at the click of an icon, a form letter requesting more information is generated, ready to be signed, sealed and delivered. FastWeb is free; watch out for unscrupulous companies that require application fees, charge for otherwise free information or "guarantee" a scholarship.

Selecting potential scholarship opportunities is just the first lap of the competition. Don't enter the second heat without a copy of *The Princeton Review's The Scholarship Advisor* by Chris Vuturo. Since Vuturo won more than $885,000 in scholarships, you might want to check out his advice. This book guides you through the application process, from getting the required elements of an application together to writing the essay and preparing for the interview. Vuturo also provides sample forms. Don't miss the sections entitled "The Scholarship Locator" and "The Scholarships"—they'll help you make sure you don't leave any "free money" on the table.

Let's Play Jeopardy

The answer is: "Education loans sponsored by the federal government." If your question was: "What is the Federal Family Loan Education Program?" you've won the Daily Double! These low-cost loans provide money to about half of today's college students. The three low-interest loan programs are Perkins Loans, need-based loans with a 5 percent interest rate (available at most four-

Smart Stretch

For more information on federal borrowing programs, order the free brochure called *Borrowing for College* by calling (800) 891-4595.

year colleges); Stafford Loans, the most popular student loan, with a variable interest rate and an 8.25 percent cap (available to most students regardless of financial need); and PLUS Loans, loans for parents of undergraduate students, with a variable rate and a 9 percent interest rate. (Rates are subject to change.)

Healthy Habit

If you qualify for a need-based Stafford or Perkins loan, Uncle Sam will pick up the tab for the interest while your child is in school on at least a half-time basis.

Before you jump into the loan pool, you should know that most federal loan programs have strict borrowing limits ($2,625 for most freshmen, for example), so you'll have to muster other money elsewhere. To receive any of these federally sponsored loans or any other type of need-based financial aid, you must first prepare the Free Application for Federal Student Aid (FAFSA). Get one from your high school guidance counselor, library or call the U.S. Department of Education at (800) 4FED-AID. This form will help determine the types of aid for which your child may be eligible, including work-study, grants and public and private loans.

To Tell The Truth

Prepaid tuition plans and tuition savings accounts are all the rage, but are they worth the price of admission? Prepaid tuition plans, where parents pay in advance over many years for an education at a school in their state, are now portable, making these plans more attractive.

Tuition savings plans are state-sponsored savings plans, but you need not invest in your home state. Check with your state of residence and the state in which your college of choice is located. Funds are tax-deferred until used for college, but you can't withdraw early from these plans without a significant penalty. Each plan is managed differently, and while some states allow a deduction on your state taxes, these savings could be minor compared to what you might lose in appreciation in the value of your account. Taxes are due when funds are withdrawn from these plans, so be sure to take this into account.

The Winner's Platform

Even after scholarships, savings and financial aid have been factored in, education debt can mount quickly, and paying it off can take years, depending on the career at the end of the tunnel. Is it worth it? If these numbers from the College Board in Washington, DC, are any indication, it doesn't take a college degree to figure it out: In families with a working spouse, the lifetime earnings of a high school graduate are approximately $1.47 million, or $36,751 per year. Annual family income with a bachelor's degree comes to approximately $2.2 million, or $61,700 annually. A doctorate could mean lifetime earnings of $2.99 million, or $96,935 annually (professional degrees such as those earned by physicians and attorneys amount to approximately $106,000 annually). That makes winning your sheepskin worth its weight in gold.

DAY 31

A Matter Of Taste

Art as an investment

Picture this scenario: While on vacation, you wander into an upscale gallery, where you find a great buy. Having done plenty of prior research, you're sure that this Miro aquatint is the one you want. The dealer even provides a certificate of authenticity, so obviously it's the real thing. At home, it looks even better on the bedroom wall, and you admire it every night.

Sound like a dream? Well, this "astute" investor, yours truly, has now retitled the work "Fake Miro in Lovely Frame." Luckily, we still enjoy the piece, and until now, we were the only ones who knew it was a fake.

Stocks and bonds are nice, but pretty as the certificates are, you make more money trading them than you can from hanging them on the wall. If you have a yen for more artistic endeavors, collecting can be fun, interesting and a great way to diversify an investment portfolio. Although some people collect art solely for investment purposes, most experts agree that the best approach is to buy something you love. That way, whether it appreciates in value is immaterial; the pleasure of its company will be enough.

Of course, you can make a killing in the art market if you can predict what new artist will become the next Jackson Pollock or find a Dutch master at a country yard sale. While the chances of that are slim, and not all investors can afford to purchase a Monet or Mondrian, or place a Pissarro or Picasso on their living room wall, even if you don't have a few million to toss around, you can get a lot out of collecting.

Love At First Sight

The best collections are those put together by art lovers with a passion for their subject. Whether it's Venetian glass, Egyptian pottery or Chinese porcelains, before you go on a buying spree, do your homework. Experts suggest that your first purchase should be books on the subject that interests you. Select one area and focus on it. Spend time visiting museums, galleries, auction houses and dealers to get a feel for what's out there and how it's priced. Take note of what catches your eye and why. Join local museums and take advantage of any classes available to help you develop your eye.

Healthy Habit

To become an art collector rather than an art buyer, pick a genre, like 19th century American art, learn everything you can, and select pieces in that area exclusively. You can always change your mind, but you'll have a better chance of becoming a serious collector than if you buy a hodgepodge of styles and works.

When you're ready to purchase, think of it as you would any investment . . . you wouldn't buy a mutual fund without reading the prospectus (let's hope not after all my reminders!), checking up on its track record and determining if its style fits in your portfolio. Your art purchases should be no different. Experienced collectors develop a relationship with a dealer, and neophyte art investors should as well to be sure they're getting what they're paying for. Avoid buying damaged works or works whose origin is in doubt. An initial foray into collecting doesn't have to involve oil paintings; works on paper are usually less expensive and easier to resell.

"Appreciation potential has to do with the level of art you're purchasing," says Jerald Melberg, owner of the Jerald Melberg Gallery. Most dealers and serious collectors agree: If you spend less than $10,000, you may have a work of art, but you don't have a financial investment. Melberg notes that six figures is usually the beginning of investment-level art.

Buying art as an investment is like buying blue-chip stocks: There's a lot more chance that works of well-known artists will appreciate than will the work of an unknown artist . . . or the stock of an unknown company. Any honest dealer will tell you that appreciation is not guaranteed, and just because prices have risen in the past doesn't mean your purchase will become a masterpiece worth a fortune. This should sound familiar to you by now: Past performance is no guarantee of future returns.

Joggin' Jargon

When attending art shows, connect with these dots:

- A red dot means the piece is sold.

- A green or half-red dot means the piece is reserved or another buyer has the right of first refusal.

Ain't Nothing Like The Real Thing

Even the most knowledgeable can mistake an artful fake for the real thing. What can you learn from my error? Before buying, ask for the history of the work, including who owned it before you and where it was purchased. Unless you're buying directly from the artist or from a gallery that specializes in a particular artist's work, make the gallery agree to take it back if it turns out to be a fake. Many galleries will allow you several months to have a piece authenticated. Take it to a museum or an expert in the field to get a professional opinion. They usually charge a fee, but isn't it worth it?

Joggin' Jargon

A work sold for the first time is usually sold through a dealer, in the *primary* market.

Works resold in the *secondary* market are usually purchased through a gallery or an auction.

In some cases, you may end up with a fake even after expert certification, and you won't be alone. There's an old saying that Rembrandt painted 700 works . . . and at least 3,000 of them are in the United States. Next to Rembrandt, the most frequently "copied" artists include Salvador Dali and, you guessed it, Miro. Buying a fake can be a useful lesson, one that hopefully won't cost you a fortune.

After all, my "faux" Miro looks as good now as it did when I thought it was the real thing.

Beauty Is In The Pocketbook Of The Beholder

Unless you've been traveling in space for the past few years, you've undoubtedly heard of the greatest auction on earth, where buyers armed with more cash than brains paid more than seven times the estimated value of pieces from the estate of Jacqueline Kennedy Onassis. Buyers parted with a sweet $34.5 million, absolute proof that the market for collectibles is alive and well. But don't be teed off if Arnold Schwarzenegger carted off the golf clubs you craved; in a few years, he may be selling them for what used golf clubs *should* be sold for.

In collectibles and art, as in securities, demand sets the price. When the majority of investors want shares of the latest, hottest initial public offering, prices can go into orbit. Disappointing earnings can turn a high flier into a meteor, bound for a crash landing. At the peak of the art market in 1989, Japanese investors, flush with cash from profits taken in stocks and real estate, paid previously unheard of prices for works of Impressionist masters, including Degas, Monet, Gauguin and van Gogh. Paintings that had sold previously for hundreds of thousands of dollars were bringing bids in the millions.

But what price is too high for an object that is priceless? Stock shares can split; Monet can't paint another "Waterlilies," unless he can do it *very* long distance. Nevertheless, in buying and selling art as well as in trading securities, the best deals may come in areas that are not so hot at the moment. Smart investors might develop a taste for styles that have yet to become very hot—but that some experts think may be the next rage.

One area that can provide special profits—or spectacular losses—is contemporary art. Like penny stocks, collecting the work of little-known artists could lead you to the next Mondrian . . . or a lovely work to display over the dining room table. If you love the piece, you at least get the aesthetic pleasure of enjoying it. When your penny stock becomes worthless, all you have is a stock certificate . . . though I hear they make nice wallpaper.

How do you know what your acquisition is worth? Says Melberg, "You won't know until you try to sell it. And most people don't want to sell something they love." The question, then, is when do you sell? If you love a piece and have bought it for its aesthetic satisfaction, the answer is never. On the other hand, if the objet d'art you once adored has lost its charm to you but suddenly becomes more in demand, sell while the market is hot. Many collectors use this opportunity to upgrade their collections, selling several good but not great pieces and investing the proceeds into a major purchase.

Beautiful Figures

Most people can't afford a diversified art portfolio composed of works with price tags beginning in the six figures. And unlike your stock certificates that can reside in your brokerage account or safe deposit box, works of art may need additional care and insurance. Liquidity can also be a problem. You can sell 100 shares of IBM quickly at a price that can be as easily substantiated, but if no one likes your 20-foot-by-20-foot Andy Warhol, you could get less for it than you'd hoped . . . a lot less.

Michael Moses, an author on art and chairman of operations management for New York University's Stern School of Business, takes another view, asking, "How many stocks have been around since 1600? Or 1700? Or 1800? Many paintings that were important in those periods are still considered treasures today. You can't say that about too many stocks." Moses has completed several in-depth studies substantiating his theory

An Auction House In Your House

Coming soon to a computer terminal near you: art auctions online. For more information, consult these sites:

- www.christies.com
- www.sothebys.com
- www.auctionuniverse.com

Concerned about putting up five figures for something you've seen only on your screen? Be extremely cautious. Reliable galleries don't ask that you send a check, money order or cash until you've evaluated the work. Real collectors let their dealers bid for them. While this service isn't free (average commission is half the work's selling price), at higher prices, it beats getting faked out.

that over time, some classes of art, including important modern, Impressionist, and 19th-century European old master works, after taxes and not including reinvested dividends, have better returns than the S&P 500, Treasury bills and utility stocks for the five- and 10-year periods ending in 1994 (the latest year for which statistics are available).

Many experts agree that art still has a long way to appreciate, although recent prices rank art up with stocks in terms of short-term appreciation. The following chart, compiled by *Business Week* magazine, compares recent returns on several broad categories of art with those of the S&P 500—and shows that with art, as in stocks, it pays to be in the right place (i.e., modern European works vs. modern U.S. paintings).

Paintings vs. Stocks	Price Change, Year Ending March 31, 1999
Modern European painting	28.1%
Contemporary masters	14.3%
Modern U.S. painting	-12.2%
Art 100 Index*	10%
S&P 500 Index**	18.5%
*Based on sales prices from 600 galleries **Including capital gains and dividends	

Source: Art Market Research, Bloomberg Financial Markets

Why you invest and what you should do with your money are questions more ancient than any security or work of art. Indeed, if the perfect answer existed, think of the fun you'd miss out on . . . after all, all that glitters isn't gold.

Gym Buddies

Writing a prenuptial agreement

> "What's mine is mine, and what's his is mine."
> —Lucille Fiorillo

Maryanne was an attractive 30-something small-business owner about to marry a wealthy older man. As he was the one with all the assets and she a relatively poor soul with a new business and lots of debts, he demanded a prenuptial agreement. It was a pretty standard document, in which his lawyers were careful to state that what's his would remain his and what's hers would remain hers, while anything purchased together would be jointly owned. Maryanne's attorney asked why she didn't mind signing such a one-sided document. "Oh," she replied, "I'm my mamma's only heir and she has a few little businesses that she wants to give me, so I'm not really worried about any of his money." The few little businesses? The town's gas utility, taxicab company and newspaper, to name just three.

"Love me, love my dog" may sound fine when you've just fallen in love and your beloved's every trait (and most of his or her possessions) seem endlessly endearing. But as you move from beloved to betrothed, things sometimes take on a whole new light: Your fiancée admits to an allergy to Fido and you notice that your significant other's credit card bills

Smart Stretch

If you're a non-working spouse, it's between difficult and impossible to establish your own credit. But it's also vital. Apply for credit in your own name (as Jane Doe, not Mrs. John Doe). Ask your credit card issuers to report your credit separately from your spouse's.

are, well, significant. If you're attached to your dog and believe credit card bills should be resolved every month, you may be in for an adjustment period. You might come to an agreement on where Fido lays his furry head every night, but changing a lifetime of spending habits is a lot more difficult. When it comes to money, property and financial goals, love can be less than a many-splendored thing.

With more marriages ending in divorce and couples remarrying or marrying later in life, prenuptial agreements have become a hot topic. Not every marriage starts out with vast inequities, and many continue for years without the hint of a hoodwink on either side. Still, after the bloom is off the rose, having it all on paper sometimes turns out to be a not-so-bad idea. Besides protecting assets, prenuptial agreements can help establish a marriage's priorities, expectations and goals. So if you're planning on exercising with your spouse, before you sign up at a gym, make sure you both like to work out—and don't skip this chapter!

The "Rights" Stuff

In its most common form, the prenuptial, or antenuptial, agreement involves the bride and groom and outlines the property rights of each in the case of death or divorce (and may even supersede a will in certain situations). In a prenuptial agreement, each partner waives some or all of his or her rights to the other partner's property. This creates two classes of property: *marital*, or that which is acquired during the marriage with marital time, effort and energy; and *separate*, which belongs solely to the individual. Only marital property gets divvied up in a divorce, but as a marriage progresses, lines of demarcation blur. That's where the prenuptial agreement comes in handy.

Prenuptial agreements aren't just for the Donalds and Ivanas of the world. Many people bring into marriage careers, children, trust accounts, vested retirement plans, businesses of which they are sole or part owner, or other property. If the marriage doesn't work out, keeping their financial lives intact is a high priority. In cases where there is inequity between spouses, an agreement can answer a plethora of questions.

While most agreements outline disposition of property, some also seek to define the character and goals of the marriage, such as who will stay home and care for the children, who will manage the money, and even who will take out the garbage and do the food shopping. Most attorneys recommend limiting such items to substantive expectations, including waiver of alimony, lost spousal support, property distribution and inheritance rights. Avoid adding nasty provisions, like a penalty for every pound the wife gains after marriage. If the agreement is ever disputed, a judge could see this and throw the whole thing out.

Often the prenuptial agreement is sought by the wealthier partner, but it can protect both. If the bride and groom are young and just starting out on equal financial footing, it's probably not worth the lawyers' fees to have an agreement drawn up. On the other hand, if you're both just starting out but you're going to put her through medical school or he stands to inherit substantial wealth—prithee, get thee to the lawyer's office!

State Of The Union

My mother always taught me that what's mine is mine . . . and what's his is mine. Unfortunately, when I got divorced, the state of North

Sign Here

Your word is your bond, but when it comes to legal issues, it's your signature that really counts. Keep these tips in mind:

- Don't ever forge your spouse's name or let your name be forged on any document—in some cases, the only signature a financial institution may accept may be the forged one.

- Never sign anything unless you know what you're signing. That goes for any contract—and double for your income tax return. If the full tax debt is not paid, both parties are liable for it, plus possible interest and penalties. The "innocent spouse" defense is rarely successful.

- Sign up for at least one major credit card and one department store card, and keep at least one bank account and a brokerage account (no matter how small) in your own name.

- If your spouse is rolling money from a retirement plan to an IRA, you'll be asked to sign a waiver of benefits. It's OK to do so, but be sure you're the beneficiary on the new account.

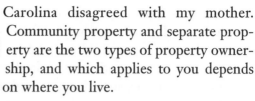

Smart Stretch

To learn your rights in your state, check the Family Law Advisor Web site at www.divorcenet.com.

Carolina disagreed with my mother. Community property and separate property are the two types of property ownership, and which applies to you depends on where you live.

In the nine community property states—Arizona, California, Idaho, Louisiana, Nevada, New Mexico, Texas, Washington and Wisconsin—any property earned during the marriage is usually split down the middle. The remaining states dictate a fair, though not always equal, division of assets. In both systems, gifts received by the married couple belong to both parties. States grant judges who preside over such cases varying degrees of freedom in deciding who gets what.

Once the prenuptial agreement is in place, be careful about how assets are titled; consult with an attorney before adding your spouse's name to your brokerage account or the deed of your house. Mingling premarital assets with those earned or acquired after marriage can become a tangled mess if you need to separate them—it's tough to prove who's entitled to what. Think you'll remember? When my first marriage dissolved, my former spouse noted despondently that we knew whose record albums were whose because I would never allow them to be combined. Too bad I didn't do that with our brokerage account!

The focus always seems to be on who gets what assets, but don't forget to divvy up debts as well. Before you sign any agreement, make sure this is in your contract. Avoiding being saddled with a debt that's not yours could be worth a lot more than assets!

The Not-So-Brady Bunch

Unlike property, no prenuptial agreement can assign custody of children. The court retains jurisdiction over children whether or not they exist at the time of the agreement. But what a prenuptial agreement can do is protect your assets for the support or use of your children.

If your spouse does not choose to or cannot adopt your children, be sure to ask your attorney how to protect their rights to the property you intend for their support. The prenuptial agreement is often part of the estate plan, but if your spouse will be your children's guardian in case of your death, you should also be sure to set the guardianship up properly.

If you're a business owner, you may feel almost as strongly about your company—and the employees for whom you're responsible—as you do about your kids. Unless you are sure your spouse can run your business as well as you can, a prenuptial agreement is a must. You don't have to be Bill Gates to need this kind of protection: In a community property state, half your business's ownership could go to your spouse. If not for yourself, protect it for the sake of your employees and partners.

Truth Or Consequences

OK, you've agreed to a prenuptial agreement, but do you have to tell her that the Renoir in the bedroom is the real thing? Does he have to know about the collection of Krugerrands you have hidden under the bed? If you're considering leaving out a few details, one word of advice: Don't. In most states, a valid agreement requires full disclosure on both sides. A failure by one or both parties to provide adequate information could challenge the validity of the agreement. Most states don't require that you list all possessions; often a statement of minimum asset value will suffice.

Although some states may allow full disclosure to be waived, both parties must explicitly agree to waive these rights. But consider this: Putting aside the legalese for a moment, recall the reason for getting together in the first place: You're about to promise to "love, honor and cherish" . . . doesn't telling the truth come in there somewhere?

Whatever else you do, make sure your spouse inherits some assets if you die first. If you have money in a 401(k), IRA or Roth IRA, your spouse is the only one who can roll it over without substantial penalties. It's tough enough to make a go of a marriage of two people . . . you don't need the IRS in there, too. Some experts recommend a life insurance policy on which the wealthier spouse pays the premiums (although that may backfire if the spouse who's the beneficiary gets *really* mad).

Be assertive, but be as generous as you can. If you're too concerned about what you'll have to give away, your spouse may get the idea that money is more important than he or she is—and that's no way to start a journey to happily ever after.

Smart Stretch

Did you know that gifts given to the couple before the wedding are the property of the bride and those given after the wedding are property of the couple?

Trainer's Tip

"Consider a time limit on the prenuptial agreement, making it null and void after seven, 10, 12 or whatever years of marriage. This can take some of the sting out of it for the spouse who may not be eager to sign."

—*Sharon Murdock, attorney at law*

As Time Goes By

Today's prenuptial agreements hark back to ancient times. Back then, a marriage was arranged and parents agreed on a dowry. Now you select your spouse, discuss transfer of property and replace the matchmaker with an attorney. Ah, tradition!

Both parties should retain separate counsel and begin the process well in advance of the wedding date to allow time for negotiations. Agreements signed at the eleventh hour may get you to the church on time but may be called into question later. Finalize agreements no less than 30 days before the wedding, although experts recommend three months. Some attorneys videotape the signing as proof that both sides accepted and understood all aspects of the contract.

A final suggestion: When writing your prenuptial agreement, consider making it advantageous to stick it out. One client got so mad at her spouse that she wanted to leave him immediately, but her prenup stated that the longer she stayed, the larger her alimony payments. Since her income could potentially increase by $15,000 for every year she hung in there, I asked her if she couldn't manage one more year with Mr. Imperfect. She did—and is still married 10 years later (happily, I might add).

Are prenuptial agreements for you? Not everyone—even those with substantial assets, businesses or inheritances—finds them appropriate. Listen to your attorney's recommendations, weigh the alternatives and decide what's best for you.

Top Dogs

Making the Dow Dividend Strategy part of your routine

Some people just don't like mutual funds. Joe is one of them. "If I can't see what those guys are buying and selling, I don't want to have any part of it," he said. So we tried professionally managed individual accounts, where Joe was privy to every thought running through his manager's head—who sometimes sold five shares of a stock one day at a loss and bought it back 10 days later for more than he paid for it originally. But that wouldn't do, either. "No, no, no—these people are crazy, too," said Joe. "Doesn't anybody have a normal, logical way of buying and selling this stuff? I mean, doesn't anybody buy low and sell high anymore?" Enter the Dow Dividend Strategy (DDS), where you know what you have, why you have it, and when it's time to get rid of it. "Ah," said Joe, "finally."

This strategy—which can provide consistent, and occasionally outstanding, returns with minimal research and even less second-guessing—begins the third part of our regime. For the next six days, you'll start putting together all the information you've learned so far, starting with today's workout: investing in select stocks that have been in the doghouse.

The Dogs Of The Dow

As stock indices vault effortlessly through record after record, investors in search of a bargain have begun to wonder if there is *anything* left to buy low that can later be sold high. They say every dog has its day, and for value-oriented investors, the solution can be found as close as the nearest pound . . . investing in some "dogs," of course.

Now we're not talking about adding just any old mongrel to your portfolio. To briefly explain, the idea is to buy equal amounts of the 10 stocks that currently sport the highest yields in the Dow Jones industrial average (DJIA). Considered the "Dogs of the Dow," prepare to hold them for a year, reinvesting all dividends. After 12 months and one day, the lowest yielding stocks are replaced by the current year's dogs . . . in essence, buying low and selling high. And since DDS investors hold positions for more than a year, capital gains receive long-term treatment and are taxed at the lower rate.

Investors have poured hundreds of thousands of dollars into this investment approach. By emphasizing the 10 highest yielding stocks (usually familiar household-name companies with long histories) rather than the 10 DJIA stocks with the highest dividends, the DDS's disciplined approach to equity investing aims for enhanced total return from both capital gains and dividends.

The Dog Breeder

Thinking of adopting a pet? Before you invest in a leash and collar, make sure you know how to take care of your new dog. While you may wish to buy shares in individual issues and rebalance positions annually yourself, you may also opt to leave the breeding to someone else. Mutual funds are available to manage this type of investment.

Care And Feeding

What's behind this theory? First, consider yield as an inverse indication of a stock's popularity. The more popular the stock and the higher its price, the lower the yield. Yield is a reflection of a stock's annual dividend and stock price (yield = annual dividend ÷ stock price). So if ABC Corporation pays a $10-per-share annual dividend and the share price is $50, ABC's yield is $10 ÷ $50, or 20 percent. If the share price of ABC rises to $100 while the dividend remains the same ($10), the new yield is 10 percent. At first glance, the drop in yield seems negative, but what has actually happened is a bonanza when you sell . . . capital gains *and* income, a pedigree worth having!

With a variation on the theme, the Low-5 DDS, investors limit their choices to the five lowest priced stocks of the DDS on the day the portfolio is established. Again, all dividends are reinvested and the portfolio held for a year. In both the Top-10 and Low-5 DDSs, investors should ideally stick with it, adjusting positions annually, for at least one complete market cycle of three to five years.

Champion Bloodlines

Both the Top-10 and Low-5 DDSs have historically rewarded investors, as the chart on page 200 illustrates. While past performance is no guarantee of future returns, in the 20 years between January 1979 and the last trading day of 1998, assuming total return proceeds were reinvested at the beginning of each calendar year, the DDS was ahead of the DJIA with an average compounded annual total return of 19.48 percent vs. 17.13 percent.

Surprisingly, the Low-5 has provided an even higher average compounded annual return of 21.58 percent for the same 20-year period. To see it more clearly, say an investor put $10,000 in the Low-5 DDS at the start of 1979 and continued the plan annually. The investment would have grown to more than $504,000 in 20 years, compared to $351,800 for the Top-10 DDS portfolio and $242,600 for

Healthy Habit

Although these dogs don't need a big yard or lots of exercise, often the best place to put them is in a tax-deferred account, such as an IRA or a retirement plan. That way, when the portfolios change, capital gains and dividends won't be taxable.

How Does It Work?

The data below compares the total annual return of the Dow Dividend Strategy (DDS) against the Dow Jones industrial average (DJIA).

Year	DJIA Total Return %	DDS Top-10 Total Return %	DDS Low-5 Total Return %
1979	10.52	12.99	9.91
1980	21.41	27.23	40.52
1981	-3.40	7.52	3.63
1982	25.79	26.04	41.88
1983	25.68	38.91	36.11
1984	1.06	6.43	10.88
1985	32.78	29.44	37.84
1986	26.91	34.79	30.32
1987	6.02	6.07	11.06
1988	15.95	24.54	21.64
1989	31.71	26.45	10.49
1990	0.57	-7.57	-15.27
1991	23.93	35.09	61.80
1992	7.35	7.85	23.01
1993	16.71	26.92	33.85
1994	4.93	4.15	8.56
1995	36.20	36.48	30.25
1996	28.57	28.06	25.96
1997	24.78	21.62	19.95
1998	18.14	10.63	12.34
20 years	**17.13**	**19.48**	**21.58**

The Dow Jones industrial average is the property of Dow Jones & Co. Inc., which does not participate in the creation or sale of the DDS and has not approved any information contained herein. Total return is the sum of the change in market value of each stock between the first trading day of a period and the last trading day of a period, and the dividends paid during the period divided by the opening market value of each stock.

Past performance is no guarantee of future results. The above results are hypothetical and do not take into account any commissions, taxes or expenses. The withdrawal of dividends or capital for current income may result in performance lower than that of the DDS.

the full DJIA portfolio. (Results exclude the effects of state and federal taxes, commissions and sales charges.)

While past performance is never a guarantee of future results, two forces are behind these returns. The first is the effect of yield. Dividends paid by the companies in the DJIA have increased in 60 of the past 68 years, and this accounts for about 40 percent of overall return. Second, compounding these dividends accounts for 10 percent of the improved total return, giving further credence to the idea that time *in* the market is more efficient than tim*ing* the market.

Currently, neither strategy is matching the return of the S&P 500. As a value-oriented investment (by forcing you to buy low and sell high), this style has recently been out of favor. Some experts believe that success has taken its toll on these strategies; the more people who use them, the lower the strategy's return. Nonetheless, these numbers are something to bark about.

Money Missteps

The total return of the dogs has dragged behind that of bellwether indices like the S&P 500 and the DJIA, and some experts think these dogs should head for the pound. Before you give up, remember that every dog has its day. When it comes to long-term investing, slow and steady still wins the race.

Race To
The Finish

Understanding

risk

Curtis, Bud and Tom are very different people with one thing in common—they're not afraid to take a risk. Bud is a retired physician with almost all his money in the stock market. Why so heavily invested in equities? Since he's not depending on these funds to live on, he feels comfortable investing in companies that he believes are solid. Tom recently sold his business and enjoys researching and trading stocks. He knows what he wants, sets a sell price when he buys, and sets a buy price when he sells. Curtis likes the idea of making a big hit. He trades one part of his money heavily, and is a good sport whether he wins or loses, knowing that the rest of his investments are in less volatile, more conservative securities.

What would you like your money to do? Come on, tell the truth—in your pocketbook of pocketbooks, wouldn't you like to earn a very high return in a very short time, 100 percent guaranteed? Stories abound of people retiring at age 35 with millions of dollars from an Internet company started out of their college frat house, and TV ads would have you believe that successful money management is as easy as washing your boat. Recent trends in stocks have added fuel to the fire, making money look easy and risky ventures seem secure. But in the financial world, the race doesn't always go to the strong or the quick—sometimes it's the tortoise that beats the hare. The difference between winning and losing is more than luck—it includes an investor's willingness to assume an appropriate level of risk.

What is risk? Risk is uncertainty, and in uncertainty lies opportunity. Without uncertainty, there's little chance to profit. But without some certainty, all you have is risk, and that's like starting a race with a sprained ankle. Risk means different things to different people, but how you deal with risk can affect your ability to finance your children's education, buy the house of your dreams, or retire comfortably. For most investors, the true nature of risk remains obscure. Understanding your relationship to risk can help you maximize your returns, minimize your losses and reach your financial goals.

You've been running at top form for the past 33 days . . . now it's time to work on your pace. Whether you're a sprinter or a jogger, there are investment strategies that will take you where you want to go.

On Your Mark, Get Set, Go!

There are as many kinds of risk as there are styles of running shoes. To some, risk is the chance of losing all or part of an investment. Without that possibility, the choice between one investment that offers a 5 percent return and another that offers 20 percent seems easy: Take the one that makes the most. The complications begin when risk pokes in its head and warns that all or part of the original investment could be lost. But investing doesn't have to be like a race where there's only one winner. Smart participants spread their investments to reduce the chance of loss and increase the opportunity for making money.

Like betting on the favorite, investments with very low risk probably won't make you rich. Take a look at the Fortune 500. When you consider how the wealthy got that way, you may see real estate, business ventures, stock portfolios and even inheritances, but you never hear that they invested in CDs and Treasuries. On the other hand, if you place some assets in secure investments, you probably won't be the last one to cross the finish line. Experts agree that the best strategy may be to allocate portions of your assets to high-, low- and moderate-risk investments to take advantage of all opportunities.

One manifestation of risk is volatility, also known as market risk. Anyone who has invested in equities and witnessed the stock market's undulations knows that some share prices move more wildly than others. Consider utility stock ABC, for example. Its price has fluctuated from 25 to 35 this year, while the price of technology stock XYZ has moved from 10 to 50. Stock XYZ, having moved five times as much, is thus roughly five times more volatile than stock ABC and has a higher perceived risk.

The result of market risk? You may receive less than you paid for your investment when you try to sell. But should fluctuations disqualify an investment from your portfolio? Not if you're a long-term investor. If your goals are at least three to five years away, don't let the daily, monthly or even quarterly vicissitudes of your investments sway you. Instead, consider investing in more than one stock, in more than one mutual fund, with more than one investment advisor. Risk can be controlled by placing funds in investments that do not move in tandem.

If You Can't Beat 'Em, Fake 'Em Out

Here are some tips to keep the taxman at bay:

- If you must trade like mad, do it in your retirement account—any short-term capital gains made in that account are nontaxable. Losses here aren't deductible, so trade carefully.

- If you're in the 28 percent federal tax bracket or higher, consider municipal bonds in your regular account to make up the bond section of your asset allocation. You'll cut down on taxes and diversify your portfolio.

- Use low-turnover, index or tax-advantaged mutual funds in your regular accounts.

- Use high-turnover or high-yielding strategies in your retirement account where dividends won't increase your taxes.

Company risk is the danger that the stock of a particular company will not increase or may even decrease in value. Credit risk is the chance that the issuer of a security, usually a bond, will not live up to its financial obligations, causing the issuer to default on interest or principal payments. Diversifying among types of stocks or spreading your investment over several different bond issuers or types of fixed-income securities helps minimize these kinds of risks.

Fixed-income investments are also subject to reinvestment risk. If interest rates fall or your bond is called just as it matures, you may not be able to reinvest your assets at the same rate of return you had been earning. This could mean less income or the necessity of taking more risk to retain your level of return. Mitigate this risk by laddering the maturities of your fixed-income investments.

Money Missteps

Even if you can't control the markets, you can control investment costs. Trading costs, account maintenance fees, management costs, and annual expenses on mutual funds all add up. They may seem insignificant when the markets are earning 20 percent or better, but when they go back to 10 percent, you'll notice them a lot more. Consolidating accounts, asking your broker for a discount and choosing funds with low annual fees can help.

Liquidity risk is another problem investors run into when they invest in real estate, collectibles, art, or thinly traded stocks or bonds. You may be forced to hold onto your investment until you find a buyer . . . not a bad idea if you like the Picasso on your wall, but no fun if you're stuck with a stock you can't sell.

Ending up short of your financial goals is one of the most feared manifestations of risk. You've felt it . . . your friends are bragging about the score they made on an IPO or how well their 401(k) plan is doing, and while you're happy for them, you're saying to yourself, "What about me?" Maybe the real question should be "What do I need?" It's nice to make 25 percent on your money, but is that kind of return necessary to reach your goals? Do you enjoy spending your free time checking your stock picks? Is managing your retirement account taking over your life? Take a moment now to catch your breath and remember, as we discussed in Day 1, that you probably don't need a villa on the Riviera and an aerie in the Alps to be happy . . . even if your neighbor is willing to drive himself crazy to get them.

Pace Yourself

Is there such a thing as a risk free investment? "Not on this planet," says Dan Taylor, managing partner of asset management and consulting firm The Taylor Group. "Some things are just more risky than others." Be wary of investments that promise a high return with little or no risk.

Even investments that seem risk free carry some chance that, if sold before maturity, you could receive less than originally invested. This type of risk, known as business or financial risk, is low in investments guaranteed by government agencies or ranked high by rating services. Such stable investments are great for those seeking income or for those who are saving for short-term goals like buying a house or a car. If you're investing for the long term, though, these investments may not allow your money to keep up with inflation or may be worth less than you paid if you sell them before they come due.

Inflation can have a very negative effect on your investments: A dollar invested may not buy the same amount in the future as it does today. Say an investment yields 6 percent. Factor in an inflation rate of 4 percent, and that return is down to 2 percent. If you figure in federal income taxes on the money earned in the 28 percent bracket, lop off about another percentage point. Suddenly you're not on your way to the winner's circle—you're back at the starting line. Avoiding this type of risk is one reason that all investors should consider investing in both stocks and bonds.

Crossing The Finish Line

So how much risk do you have to take to reach your goals? If your goals are moderate and far away and you sock away a good deal of money, it may be possible to attain them with a low level

---

Trainer's Tip

"A risk that people discount is consumerism. Someone will buy a car for $25,000 and when they drive it off the lot it's suddenly worth $17,000—they call that an investment. They will put $25,000 in a mutual fund that may go up 15 percent in a good year and down 5 percent in a bad year and call that risky. What's really risky is not being there, not participating, not diversifying to minimize the possibility of losing big, and sitting on the sidelines waiting for a better opportunity."

—Dan Taylor, managing partner of The Taylor Group

of risk. On the other hand, if your goals are ambitious, not far in the future, and you prefer to spend rather than save, you'd better be prepared to take more risk or change your habits. It all depends on your temperament, financial circumstances and age.

Many advisors give these general guidelines: Investors in their 20s are just getting started, and while income may be good, outgo is usually higher. Paying off educational loans, saving for a house or getting a family started are all expensive propositions. Although the time horizon is long, if you are in this group, you are probably not in the financial position to make high-risk investments. Instead, consider short-term, low-risk investments for most of your funds, and take more risk in long-term investments like retirement plans. The key here is to invest as much as possible while you're young. The compounding effect of time can make your financial goals easier to achieve.

Healthy Habit

Whether you're fully invested in your retirement plan or most of your money is on the sidelines, don't panic. Successful investing has a long-term focus. If you have 10 or more years until retirement, it won't matter if your portfolio is up or down on a given day or for a given month or even for a given year. Relax, take a deep breath, and be prepared to ride out the market's ups and downs.

Investors in their 30s are usually more financially set, but still on track to their peak earnings years. Saddled with the needs of a growing family, low- and moderate-risk investments are usually the best bet.

In their peak earnings years, the 40s and 50s, investors often have more disposable income and fewer obligations. Many families have finished their children's college financing (or passed the remaining costs on with the sheepskin) and are now faced with saving for retirement. At this point you really need to know yourself to make decisions that you are comfortable with. If you've never ventured into anything but shares of the local utility and can't stomach the slightest fluctuation, don't put your peace of mind at risk (to say nothing of your money) by taking a hot tip from a cold caller.

Tomorrow you'll learn how to diversify your investments and reallocate your portfolio as your financial situation changes. Thankfully, you don't have to win the Boston Marathon to reach your financial goals. Just a little common sense—and some smart diversification—should keep you in the race.

Body Beautiful

Using asset allocation to shape your ideal portfolio

> *"Investors jump ship on a good strategy just because it hasn't worked so well lately and, almost invariably, abandon it at precisely the wrong time."*
> —David Dreman

John and Peggy frowned as they looked at their statements. "I don't like how my money is performing," John said angrily. "Every time I get a statement, the amount is going down. When I looked at it in January, it was at $611,000, and now it's at $594,000. In January, the Dow Jones industrial average was at 10000, and now it's almost 11000. Why is my account performing so badly?" A look at their account revealed a few mitigating factors. For one thing, John had withdrawn $47,000 from his account in the first six months of the year. In fact, John spent more than 12 percent of his portfolio's value annually. Also, since John didn't like fluctuation, his was a diversified portfolio—unlike the Dow Jones industrial average. A quick calculation showed that after withdrawals, John's portfolio was actually *up* 6 percent. It was a miracle that his portfolio was down only $17,000—when all circumstances were taken into account, it was not only keeping up with the market, but beating it. What was the secret behind this much rosier view of John and Peggy's account? Allocation, my dear Watson, allocation.

Asset allocation is one of the buzzwords of the 21st century, but the concept has been around as long as there have been assets to allocate. In its simplest terms, asset allocation is the process of spreading your money around into different investments—otherwise known as diversification. Unfortunately for advocates of diversification, several great years of stock market returns have made it look like di*worse*ification. If you had done the unthinkable and put all of your eggs into one Internet basket when companies like AOL and Microsoft were new, you might be sipping a refreshing frozen beverage on your own tropical island right now instead of reading this book. Had your stock selections gone awry, though, you might not have even been able to afford this book. If you can accurately predict the future, you don't need asset allocation. But for the rest of us mortals, how we divide our money is a fundamental part of what makes a portfolio sink or swim.

Breaking Up Is Hard To Do

A study in *Financial Analysts Journal* demonstrated that the single most important factor for determining the performance of an investment portfolio is how its assets are divided among different classes. According to the study, asset allocation accounts for more than 91 percent of performance, with the rest attributable to security selection (5 percent), market timing (2 percent) and other factors (2 percent). It helps if you pick the investments that have the best potential for appreciation (which, of course, by now you can do with aplomb), but deciding how to divide your money is tougher than you think.

The first step in asset allocation is to assess your feelings about risk and apply them to your investment approach. If the stock market's daily fluctuations make you crazy with anxiety, consider investing in stock only with a portion of your assets earmarked for long-term appreciation. Worried about the effect of inflation on your savings? Allocate less money to long-term bonds. Remember, though, that you can't have it all—double-digit returns and no risk.

Healthy Habit

If you have a large amount of money to allocate at once, like a retirement plan rollover, figure out what general percentages you want in each market sector, then invest about 10 percent of your total. Before you add to your positions, wait and see if you like how things are going. Remember, you can always move your money around, so don't let fluctuations be a daily concern.

Second, consider your age. You may be young of heart or old before your time, but your chronological age is an important factor in how you manage your money. Some experts use a simple formula for allocating money to stocks and other investment classes: Subtract your age from 100, and you'll have the percentage of your assets that should be devoted to stocks. While this is a handy tool, it's only a starting place. Every investor is different, and asset allocation, like medicine, is as much art as science. As you gain investing experience, you'll learn what types of investments are appropriate for you.

Third, before you get too deep into deciding what to put where, consider divvying up your pile into short-, medium- and long-term financial goals (remember Day 1?). For example, invest your short-term money, what you'll need to pay Junior's tuition next year or use for a down payment on a house in six months, in something with little or no fluctuation, like a CD or money-market account. Longer-term goals (like your IRA, your 6-year-old's college savings, etc.) can tolerate more risk because fluctuations in the value of those accounts will probably work themselves out over time.

Divide And Conquer

If you want to get the most from your money, in addition to a broad range of individual investments, consider dividing your funds among different asset classes, including stocks, bonds, cash and real estate. In his book, *Get Rich Slowly*, William T. Spitz, treasurer of Vanderbilt University, notes that over the 20-year period from 1971 to 1990, the annual return of stocks as measured by the S&P 500 averaged 11.4 percent, with two years of fairly substantial losses, 1973 (14.8 percent) and 1974 (26.4 percent). If all your assets had been in the stock market during that time, your 10 percent average annual payoff would have been achieved, but with a fairly bumpy ride. Had you invested one-third each in stocks, bonds and real estate and rebalanced annually to keep the investment percentages the

Spread The Wealth

The following chart shows average annual returns for the 20-year period 1979 to 1998. The bolded results indicate the best performer for the year.

Year	Large-Company Stocks	Small-Company Stocks	Real Estate Stocks	Foreign Stocks	U.S. Treasury Bonds
1979	18.60%	43.07%	35.86%	4.75%	1.93%
1980	32.50	38.60	24.37	22.58	2.71
1981	-4.92	2.03	6.00	-2.28	6.25
1982	21.55	24.95	21.60	-1.86	32.62
1983	22.56	29.13	30.64	23.69	8.36
1984	6.27	-7.30	20.93	7.38	15.15
1985	31.73	31.05	19.10	56.16	22.10
1986	18.66	5.68	19.16	69.44	15.26
1987	5.25	-8.80	-3.64	24.63	2.76
1988	16.56	25.02	13.49	28.27	7.89
1989	31.63	16.26	8.84	10.54	14.53
1990	-3.11	-19.48	-15.35	-23.45	8.96
1991	30.40	46.04	35.70	12.13	16.00
1992	7.61	18.41	14.59	-12.17	7.40
1993	10.06	18.88	19.65	32.56	9.75
1994	1.31	-1.82	3.17	7.78	-2.92
1995	37.53	28.45	15.27	11.21	18.47
1996	22.95	16.50	35.27	6.05	3.63
1997	33.35	22.36	20.26	1.78	9.65
1998	28.60	-2.55	-17.50	20.00	8.69

Past performance cannot guarantee comparable future results. Results shown do not necessarily represent the performance of any specific investment. The five benchmarks are the Standard & Poor's Composite Index of 500 stocks (S&P 500), which is widely regarded to be representative of large-company stocks; the Russell 2000 NAREIT (National Association of Real Estate Investment Trusts) Equity Index, a widely recognized index for real estate investment trusts; the EAFE (Europe, Australasia, Far East) Index, representative of foreign stocks; and the Lehman Brothers Aggregate Bond Index, representative of U.S. government and corporate bonds. Results are based on total returns and include reinvestment of dividends. An investment cannot be made directly in an index. Standard deviation is a measure of the amount of risk an investment exposes itself to in order to achieve its return.

Source: Lipper Inc.

same, your return for the same 20-year period would have been 10.3 percent—with a much smoother ride. Perhaps it's better to be good than lucky.

The idea here is to invest in asset classes that move in opposite directions so that some of the time some investments will be up and others down. You probably won't get the spellbinding returns of someone who invests everything in a hot market sector, but your portfolio won't get creamed when a hot sector cools off, either. (The chart on page 211 shows how different kinds of investments have performed over time.)

While past performance cannot guarantee future results, investing in a variety of asset classes may lower your portfolio's overall level of risk while improving your opportunity for higher returns over time.

One Picture Is Worth 10,000 Words

The following chart is one I draw with clients:

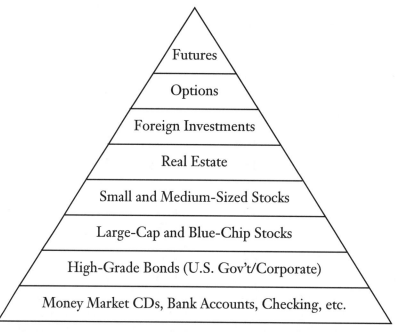

It contains a sample of some of the asset classes available and the relative risks associated with them. The least risky investments are on the bottom—things like money-market accounts and savings accounts don't have much risk, and they don't have much return either. Bonds are considered a bit more risky because they are subject to interest rate and default risk; we're talking about high-grade corporate and municipal and U.S. government-backed securities here.

Next come blue-chip stocks, those large-cap entities with reliable earnings and, often, dividends. A section is then devoted to mid-cap and small-cap stocks, whose returns can be greater than those of large-cap stocks, but whose risk is also higher. As you approach the upper regions of the pyramid, you see high-yield bonds and foreign securities, as well as two asset classes not discussed in this book: options and futures. While the latter two have the highest potential returns, they also involve the greatest levels of risk. Options and futures are often considered speculation, and many successful investors have never ventured into these specialties. To get good at them, you'll need another 45 days!

The investment pyramid is used to illustrate the varying levels of risk inherent in different classes of securities—but your pyramid may look very different. If you're a conservative investor over age 50, for example, your investment structure may look more like a trapezoid, with lots of money invested at the bottom levels and a very small portion in small-company stocks or foreign investments.

How your pyramid is allocated will also depend on how you feel about the markets at any particular time, how secure your sources of income, and other individual factors. Even younger investors may not have the desire or need to reach up to the higher pyramid levels. Remember that the pyramids were built as tombs for the Pharaohs—they're designed to provide eternal rest, not eternal anxiety.

Rebalancing Act

While there are computer programs and questionnaires (see today's workbook exercise) aplenty to help investors make general allocation decisions, asset allocation should be an ongoing process. Most experts focus on how spreading your investments through different asset classes can lower your portfolio's level of risk, but few point out that by figuring out what percentage of your money you want in each sector and then periodically rebalancing to maintain these percentages, you may actually be able to improve performance over time.

Money Missteps

Before you rush over to your portfolio and start to move things about, consider the effect of taxes on your maneuvers. In most cases, the most efficient place to use proactive asset allocation is in tax-deferred or tax-free accounts, like IRAs, Roth IRAs and 401(k) plans.

Healthy Habit

If most of your investable assets are outside tax-deferred or tax-free accounts, you can still actively allocate your money. Use dividends from one fund to buy shares in a different sector and invest new money into under-weighted sectors. Buying and selling in after-tax accounts can incur tax penalties, so before you trade one position for another, check with your tax advisor.

In a study done by mutual fund company T. Rowe Price Associates, an investment divided equally between the Wiltshire 5000 index of the most regularly traded U.S. stocks and Morgan Stanley's Europe, Australia and Far East (EAFE) index returned 13.7 percent per year from December 1970 through December 1998. But if an investment had been divided 70 percent in the Wiltshire 5000 and 30 percent in the EAFE stocks and rebalanced at the end of each year, the return would have been 14 percent. Don't think 1 percent amounts to much? According to T. Rowe Price, if you had invested $10,000 at year-end in 1970 and rebalanced annually, your money would have grown to $390,000. Without rebalancing, it would have been worth about $30,000 less. Not bad for a little fiddling around, eh?

Mutual fund companies and brokerage firms also provide easy platforms for asset allocation. Some fund companies offer aggregations of their top funds with specific allocations based on whether investors' risk tolerance levels are aggressive, moderate or conservative. The more aggressive the investor, the more money allocated to aggressive portfolios. These portfolios automatically reallocate periodically, so you can just sit back and let the pros do it.

Don't be fooled into complacency, though—you still need to be sure that this type of account meets your needs. Portfolio shifts can be great, or they can cause problems. If you're close to retirement and the portfolio manager decides to shift some money into gold or becomes bearish on bonds and the decision is wrong, it may not bode well for your money. Be sure to read the prospectus so you're familiar with how these funds work, and ask the funds for a list of their largest tactical moves over the past five years. You can also look for a fund with a certain allocation mix that will move only among certain asset classes.

No matter how you decide to split your money, remember that no allocation is written in stone: It's the privilege of every investor to change his or her mind.

DAY 36

Catch Some Z's

Limiting your portfolio's ups and downs

During my early years as a broker, I frequently urged my clients to make periodic investments instead of putting all their money to work at once. Having not done it myself, however, one day I decided to put my money where my mouth was, and so I began dollar-cost averaging, which calls for putting the same amount of money in an investment at designated intervals over a long period of time. The idea is that over time, even though you are buying shares at both high and low prices, you beat the performance of people who try to get into the market at the low (impossible) and out at the high (equally impossible).

I began by placing my entire savings of $4,000 at the mercy of the market, in the most volatile fund I could find, and committed to adding $1,000 per month. During this period, the market was all over the place, but I was undeterred. I didn't even look at my statements. Unfortunately, my former husband did. After six months went by, he asked me how much I had invested in the fund. "$10,000," I replied. "You'd better sell it right away," he exclaimed. "It's only worth $6,000!" I assured him we were dollar-cost averaging, but he insisted we were throwing good money after bad.

We decided to let it go a few more months. The following July, one year into the investment, I came home to find him again perusing the fund statement. When he asked how much we had invested, I timidly replied, "about $16,000." To my surprise, he said, "Then we'd better buy some more—it's worth $32,000!"

Whether markets move up or down in the short term, long-term investors need to stay the course. But that's easier said than done when your life's savings seems to evaporate before your eyes. If your portfolio is keeping you up at night, today we'll look at some ideas to give you a good night's rest. We'll start with the easiest strategies and work up to some pretty sophisticated ones. You may not use them all, but it's nice to know that you have options.

Trainer's Tip

"Stocks have outperformed all other classes of investments over the past 50 years, including Treasury bills and gold. [Investors should] stick with large-cap stocks of well-known companies with solid earnings and dividends. [Based on returns] over the past 10 years, you really can't lose."

—Joseph Tigue, managing editor of Standard & Poor's newsletter The Outlook and co-author of The Dividend Rich Investor

Slim And Trim

One way to feel a little more comfortable about your investments is to take some profits. Although stocks have pulled back, many are still selling at or near record prices. In fact, some IPOs that have gone through the roof may be on their way back into orbit. Before they come back down to earth, consider getting out while the getting is good. If you hold onto a company that makes something you've never heard of and don't understand, has no track record, or hinges on the success of one product, taking a profit now could save you headaches later on. Remember, few investors get in at the bottom or get out at the top. Set a price target or a percentage increase that will satisfy your goals, and when your stock hits that target, sell part or all of your position.

Before getting into the selling mode, however, keep in mind that unless you're trading in a tax-deferred account, Uncle Sam wants you—or at least a part of your profits in the form of capital gains. When the market is pitching and rolling, you may be tempted to cut and run, selling everything and heading for the mattress. But money doesn't make a soft cushion, and if you sell and make a profit, you may have to pay capital gains taxes on your winnings. If you plan to take profits, consider selling losers, too, so you can balance profits with losses. The best way to avoid tax problems? Keep good records, and consult your tax advisor.

Once you've sold, don't look back . . . look for someplace else to invest. If you've accumulated cash from selling positions at a profit and/or taking losses, think of the market's dips as potential buying opportunities. When top-quality stocks have fallen on hard times, it could be your chance to upgrade your portfolio.

A Little Here, A Little There

Dollar-cost averaging is a useful, simple, practical idea. It keeps you from doing something stupid (throwing too much money at the market when things are going up) and keeps you doing something smart (continuing to add to your investments when things are going down). It's the famous no-brainer of the investment world.

This is not to say that your results will mirror those mentioned above, but it can be sort of like a snowball in your portfolio that gathers momentum on its downhill course. Best of all, after you fill out the fund or stock program's investment form, you don't have to think about it again. There's no worrying about whether today is the day to buy XYZ stock or fund—your automatic investment just does its thing. It's the easiest and best way to get some sleep when the market is making all those day traders seasick.

Become A Convert

If you like the stock, you'll love the convertible, or so the thinking goes. Convertible securities come with some safety enhancers: They share the upside of stocks, but their coupon often limits their downside.

In 1998, for example, a very miserable year for many stocks, convertibles appeared to sink right along with stocks. Not so, says Russell Diamond, managing director of GEM Capital Management, a firm that manages convertible securities portfolios. "When the underlying stock of mid-cap companies got slammed," he says, "many of the corresponding convertibles dropped only two-thirds as much in price. But when the income from the bonds was added in, the portfolio of securities avoided a loss."

For investors intent on maintaining the overall value of their portfolios, a foray into convertibles makes sense not only because of their relative buoyancy in down stock markets, but also because of their low correlation to stocks and bonds. Their presence in a portfolio can improve diversification. (For a review of convertible securities, take a ride back to Day 13.)

I Dream Of Zeros

Over the past 50 years, stocks have consistently outperformed other types of investments, but not without cost: Investors seeking outstanding returns of equities have had to put up with quite a few fluctuations. For long-term investors, it's possible to have your stock and your beauty rest, too, by combining stocks with zero-coupon bonds. Here's how it could work.

Joe Sandman has $100,000 to roll over from his former employer's retirement plan. He invests $50,000 in zero-coupon bonds with a maturity value of $100,000. The other $50,000 is invested in individual stocks and mutual funds, or a series of mutual funds.

If Mr. Sandman invests in bonds yielding at least 7.2 percent, in 10 years he'll have his original $100,000 investment back. If rates are not so high, Sandman may have to devote more of his capital to bonds; if rates are higher, fewer dollars would have to be placed in this safe harbor. Should equities perform as they have since 1945, they could more than double in that period of time.

Whatever happens, Mr. Sandman can sleep at night, knowing that if he stays the course, his bonds will at the very least return his original investment at maturity. Life could be a dream. . . .

Healthy Habit

Owners of any type of zero coupon bond or other security issued at a discount will owe tax each year on the phantom income accrued. Keep good records of your tax payments and add them to your cost basis. Without these records, you could pay tax twice when you sell or redeem the bonds.

Saving On Your Savings Bonds

Savings bonds sound great as gifts, but they're not such great investments. Available in denominations of as low as $50, they are popular gifts for births, graduations and weddings. Interest rates are set at about 90 percent of a five-year Treasury bond.

If you like the idea of these securities but want more for your money, take a look at the new inflation-indexed savings bonds, or "I" bonds. Issued by the Treasury in 1998, they allow investors who are worried about the effects of inflation to rest easier.

Bonds can be bought in six denominations, with face values ranging from $50 to $5,000, and returns are protected from inflation for 30 years. Rates are adjusted twice annually, in May and November. Taxes on "I" bonds, like those levied on other savings bonds, are owed when the bonds mature. "I" bonds can be bought at banks or other financial institutions or through some employee savings programs.

While "I" bonds have a lot of good points, they may not be appropriate for all investors. Falling interest rates could eat into "I" bonds' inflation-linked interest rates: Deflation could cause a bond's interest rate to disappear (although principal is guaranteed). Purchases are limited to $30,000 per year, and those who cash in the bonds within the first five years forfeit five months of interest.

Cash Is King

If you still can't find that perfect sleeping position, consider placing some of your assets in short-term Treasury bills or certificates of deposit. You may not become rich overnight, but it could bring some rest at last. Because they are backed by the U.S. government and the FDIC, respectively, T-bills and CDs are considered very low risk. Keeping some of your assets in cash or cash equivalents gives you the chance to take advantage of opportunities that arise (or fall). If nothing else, you can spend some on a bottle or two of Maalox . . . for your high-flying friends, that is.

Using any or all of these strategies won't guarantee that you'll never lose any money or that you'll never worry about your money. What they can do is empower you to take action. As a result, you can plan for long-term goals and, like Mr. Sandman, count dollars instead of sheep. Pleasant dreams.

Losing Interest

Dealing with rising interest rates

> *"Your success in investing will depend in part on your character and guts and in part on your ability to realize, at the height of ebullience and the depth of despair alike, that this, too, shall pass."*
>
> —John Bogle, founder, Vanguard Mutual Funds

I t's 1994, and Bobby Joe is not at all pleased with what is going on in his retirement portfolio. "I'm going to sell all of this junk and put my money in CDs," he said. "At least then I'll have some money left." True, I assured him, but that money wouldn't grow at all, so after a few years, he'd be back at work. "But what can I do?" he lamented. "This is all I've got, and it's just going down the tubes. Can't we put it somewhere safer?"

Fortunately, the higher rates at the time made bonds more attractive, so some of Bobby Joe's cash went into government-backed zero-coupon bonds. He felt more comfortable because he could predict what he'd make, and I felt better because I knew that if he held on through the high times, eventually when rates fell, we could sell his zeros for a profit. That's exactly what happened, and now Bobby Joe and I can laugh about that little rough spot . . . and we're ready for another bout of higher rates when it inevitably comes our way.

Rising interest rates are like expanding waistlines—in most cases, not your friend. They often wreak havoc on income and growth portfolios, and for many investors, the fluctuations on their statements feel like more than paper losses. Falling interest rates have been the engine driving stock and bond markets to record profits. But what do you do when the rates reverse and your profits evaporate? Try broadening your horizons (instead of your waistline), and you'll see that rising rates don't have to be the enemy.

Fed Up

The Federal Reserve allows the economy to grow at the fastest rate possible without creating excessive inflation. The economic growth rate is measured by the gross domestic product (GDP), the value of goods and services produced in the United States. The difference between the potential growth rate and actual growth as measured by the GDP is an indicator of potential future inflation. As the economy reaches its maximum potential growth rate, many economists believe that inflation could take off. The highest rate at which the economy can grow without excessive inflation is estimated by the Fed to be 2.8 percent annually. When the GDP rises above this level, the Fed often steps in and tightens the money supply.

The Fed does this in several ways, including increasing the discount rate (the rate at which banks borrow from the Fed), raising the federal funds' rate and increasing the required level of banks' reserves. These actions can have several effects, one of which is an increase in short-term interest rates.

Healthy Habit

Hate the idea of holding your bonds to maturity? Some bonds have a special feature called a "death put," that allows them to be redeemed early at face value in case of the bondholder's death. Although you can't take them with you, your heirs can get a bond's full value instead of taking a possible loss when liquidating your estate. For more information, consult your financial advisor or the bond's issuer.

Healthy Habit

While CDs really do earn interest, the way the interest is calculated is important to your return. If interest is calculated as "simple interest per year," that means it is paid at the end of the year. Say you invest $1 at 5 percent simple interest. At the end of the year, you'd have $1.05; at the end of two years, $1.10. If, on the other hand, that 5 percent interest is compounded daily on your $1, at the end of the first year, you'd have $1.11; at the end of year two, $1.65.

So where does that leave your investments? Rising rates are viewed negatively by stock and bond traders because they add volatility and subtract profits from portfolios. But if you find yourself in a climate of rising rates and your instinct is to liquidate everything to rescue what's left of your investments, don't just do something—sit there. Following are several suggestions to make the most of your sagging stocks and battered bonds.

CDs Are Back

Remember your old friends, the trusty certificates of deposit? Like the platform shoes you saved in the back of your closet, hoping for their return to the fashion runways, when interest rates are high, CDs come back in style. High interest rates mean high yields on CDs, allowing savers to lock in some attractive rates. Remember, CDs are guaranteed up to $100,000 in interest and principal by the FDIC.

If you're deciding between a CD and a money market, you'll probably find CD rates are higher than money-market rates. The reason for the disparity? The bank knows how long they'll have the use of your money when you buy a CD, whereas money-market accounts are more liquid, so their tenure is less certain. If you decide to go the CD route, make sure you're prepared to wait for the CD to mature. Most banks charge an interest penalty on early withdrawals that could wipe out some or all of your earnings. However, unlike other investments, you always get your initial investment back from a CD.

Up The Ladder To The Roof

As rates begin to rise, investors may feel hopeful about earning more on their savings, but what if rates continue to increase? Should you lock your money up now or wait to see how high rates will go? Just as it's

Climbing The Ladder

Investing in a laddered portfolio can preserve principal, maintain liquidity and minimize exposure to interest rate swings. Here's how it works with $10,000 to invest:

?	$2,000	2005
6%	2,000	2004
5.75%	2,000	2003
5.50%	2,000	2002
5.25%	2,000	2001
5%	2,000	2000

impossible to predict the best time to sell or buy a stock, knowing when interest rates have peaked is a lost cause—except, of course, in hindsight.

If you think rates might rise but would still like to benefit from current interest levels, a laddered portfolio of corporate bonds can be an ideal strategy. This type of fixed-income portfolio allows investors to spread the total dollar amount of their investment among securities with increasing maturities. The strategy is suitable in an environment of rising interest rates, and it's flexible enough to keep pace with future market changes.

To employ this strategy, spread your investments equally over a five-year period. If interest rates move up, you can take the 20 percent of the portfolio that matures the first year and reinvest it at a higher rate of return. If rates drop, only that 20 percent will have to be invested at a lower interest rate; the rest is still protected. Better yet, that newly liquid 20 percent can be repositioned in a more timely investment.

This laddered-maturity strategy can position your portfolio to handle any move in interest rates. Different types of fixed-income investments can be used, including CDs or Treasury, corporate, municipal or zero-coupon bonds.

I Want Your ARMs Around Me

If you're looking for an investment to provide slightly better yields than your run-of-the-mill money-market fund, funds that invest in adjustable rate mortgages (ARMs) may be a good idea. These funds invest in mortgage pools; when mortgage rates rise, so does potential income from the funds. Some financial advisors recommend using them to replace lower-yielding short-term investments of one to three years.

Is this a replacement for money-market funds? Absolutely not. Unlike money-market funds, ARM fund shares fluctuate more widely in price. While the interest paid increases with rising rates, a sharp hike in rates could cause an equally sharp drop in share price. Many ARM funds are relatively new and have not been tested during periods of rapidly rising interest rates, so before you invest, carefully read the fund's prospectus.

Prime Time

Most bond portfolios get clobbered by rising interest rates, but holders of prime-rate income funds are usually spared. Since the prime rate peaked in 1989 at more than 11 percent, it has been drifting downward. But major banks have since raised the rate charged to their most favored borrowers, helping prime-rate income funds become prime investments.

Prime-rate income funds attempt to achieve a return equivalent to the prime rate. Shareholders benefit from a higher prime rate because it translates into a higher dividend, so holders of these funds should be pleased with the possibility of higher interest rates. On the downside, to earn these high yields, some prime-rate funds invest in instruments that are decidedly less than prime, leading to more volatility than the average investor can tolerate. Once again, before investing, request and read the fund's prospectus. A little extra work ahead of time can save a great deal of trouble later.

A floating-rate security is another option if you believe that interest rates will climb. These securities come in several species, including floating-rate preferred stocks, which are preferred stocks with coupons that reset as interest rates change. Most floating-rate preferreds have a minimum and maximum yield, but since every issue is different, check on the specifics of those you are considering.

Charge It—Not!

Rising rates may be a boon for savers, but they can be a burden for borrowers. If you've charged your credit cards to the limit, you may get an unwelcome surprise when you open your statement. Finance charges on many credit cards reset with interest rates, and many are dependent on short-term rates—the very ones that usually rise first. Consumer interest is not tax deductible, so if you've been stowing money in your savings account for a rainy day and charging like the light brigade while rates were low, pay off all you can before rates rise.

To see just what an impact credit-card rates have, consider that in the 31 percent tax bracket, you'd have to earn more than 15 percent on your investments to offset the 11 percent interest on a credit-card balance. Paying off that debt is like paying yourself 11 percent—risk free! Not a bad return. If you can't afford to pay everything off at once, consider consolidating your debts. For more information, review Day 4.

There's no denying it: Market conditions often become more volatile than most investors would like, but that doesn't mean it's time to panic. Before you liquidate anything, talk to your financial and tax advisors. If you hold on in a difficult market, invest in solid strategies and lower your debt, you may be in a better position when things go your way again.

Sweet And Low

Profit from declining interest rates

> "Money can't buy happiness, but it doesn't discourage it."
> —Anonymous

Charlotte retired from her job at a busy law firm and vowed she'd never work again. "I never want to have to go back," she exclaimed. "I'm having fun for the first time. You've got to make me enough money to keep me retired." Easier said than done. As interest rates fell, we had to get a lot more creative about where to invest the money from bonds that were called. Fortunately, we used this opportunity to refinance her mortgage and introduce new types of securities to her portfolio. That's all it took . . . and Charlotte remains gainfully unemployed.

Remember that old party game where revelers took turns ducking under an ever-lowering bar? You may not have the knees to be a limbo star, but when interest rates start to tumble, you may ask yourself, How low can they go? To keep playing when rates are low, you need to know where to go—and where to avoid. Here are some rules to help you come out a winner.

Home Sweet Home

Low interest rates make home refinancing a sweet deal. If you're about to skip this section because rates haven't reached two percentage points below your current loan rate or because you've recently refinanced, wait! As previously mentioned, the 2 percent rule isn't always the best benchmark. The reason for the 2 percent rule is to cover the refinancing costs, but during periods of sustained low interest rates, lenders often offer competitive packages.

To cut the best deal, be skeptical of offers that tout no out-of-pocket costs. These loans often include their fees in the total amount borrowed, so you end up paying not only the fees, but interest on them as well, over the life of the loan. When looking at the cost of the loan, you'll have to decide between a higher interest rate and no upfront costs or a lower rate and upfront costs. This is where the decision on whether to pay points comes in.

Consider this hypothetical illustration: Say the amount you want to borrow is $250,000, and you can get a 15-year mortgage at a 7 percent rate with no points. Your monthly payment is $1,663. With one point, the rate drops to 6.75 percent, for a monthly payment of $1,621. The difference in payments is $42 per month, but you're paying an extra $2,500 up front for that point (each point is 1 percent of the loan amount).

How long will it take to recap that additional payment? Divide the cost of the point by the difference between the loan amounts; the answer is the number of months it will take to make up the cost of the point. In this case, you're looking at about 60 months. Thinking about paying more than one point to get an even lower rate? Many experts advise that it will still take about five years to make up the difference, but after the 60th month, your savings will double.

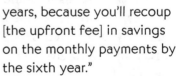

Trainer's Tip

"Points should be considered if you're going to live in your home more than five years, because you'll recoup [the upfront fee] in savings on the monthly payments by the sixth year."

—Suzanne Bach, vice president of mortgage brokerage firm IPT Financial Services

> ### Healthy Habit
>
> Getting the lowest rate possible may mean staying with your current lender. Your current mortgage holder may not require a credit check, land survey or title search, and this can save you money on closing costs.

When to pay your points is often flexible; you can pay out of your pocket at closing or include them in the loan amount and pay them off as you go. Points paid at closing may be tax deductible, so ask your tax advisor for more information.

Just A Spoonful Of Sugar

Once you've decided on points, there's also the term of the loan to consider. If you think rates are as low as they're likely to go and plan to stay in your home for an extended period, most experts suggest a 15-, 20- or 30-year loan.

If you're comparing a 30-year loan at 8 percent to a 15-year loan at 6 percent, the shorter loan increases your payments not by half, as you might expect, but by about one-third, while splitting the length of your mortgage in half. But if the idea of a big fixed monthly expense scares you silly, a longer-term mortgage makes sense, if not dollars. After all, you can always make additional payments to the principal to shorten the length of your 30-year loan, but you can't stretch out payments on a 15-year mortgage.

A short-term variable loan may seem like a good idea because you plan to move in a few years, but experts suggest caution. Rates are low now, but if they rise and you stay longer than you'd planned, you could be in for a shock when your mortgage rate resets or when you have to find permanent financing.

Recently refinanced and don't think it's worth the hassle of doing all that paperwork again? Before you discard the idea completely, consider this: If you invested $200,000 in an institution and the one across the street offered to give you 1 percent more interest, would you move your money? It all depends on what the move would cost—you just might decide it's worth it. Figure out how long it would take to recoup the costs of the loan before you decide that refinancing is definitely not for you. Lenders are competing for qualified buyers, so when rates are low, take advantage of their largess . . . and lock in a low rate. Still not sure if you should refinance? Use today's work sheet to find out.

Sweetening The Pot

Congratulations. You've refinanced your home and have some extra money each month. Before you start dreaming of the shoes you're going to buy or new Internet services you're going to order, take a look at your credit card balance. If you have one, now is as good a time as any to get rid of it. While rates on just about everything drop, credit card companies rarely cut back on their pound of flesh. Think of it as the only place you can get a guaranteed return of 15 percent or more without any risk.

It's not glamorous and it's not fun, but paying off your credit-card debt, like eating your oatmeal, is the right thing to do. If you're a poor credit risk, many card issuers may charge penalties and special *really* high rates (20 percent and higher) to those who don't keep their balances current. So take that extra money and apply it where it counts the most. When your cards are paid off, reward yourself . . . just don't put those Ferragamos on your Visa.

Cut Back On Your Intake

Low interest rates are great for homeowners, but bad for people who seek safe havens for their money. Rates on CDs are nothing to write home about, so many income-oriented investors are looking for other ideas. While some pundits recommend long-term Treasury bonds with maturities of 30 years, investors might want to take a shorter-term view.

To get the most out of fixed-income investing, consider bonds with maturities of no longer than seven to 10 years. For these maturities, you'll have the opportunity to get a high yield without taking the risk of an additional 20 or more years' maturity. Keep in mind, CDs are FDIC insured up to $100,000, offer a fixed rate of return, and generally may not be withdrawn prior to maturity. Other types of fixed-income securities are more liquid, but their return and principal value will fluctuate.

If investing in securities that are not backed by Uncle Sam is OK with you, look into the various types of floating-rate securities available. These securities have adjustable interest rates that change when interest rates move. They can follow the yields of many types of securities, but many adjust based on the highest yield of the three-month, 10-year or 30-year Treasury bond. Rates are effective for one quarter or more, and there is a minimum and maximum yield to which the dividend can be reset. If interest rates rise, this type of security can protect part of your investment.

Another way to exercise your options during periods of falling rates is the dumbbell strategy. Split your fixed-income dollars evenly between very short-term and much longer-term securities, and get one higher-interest payment and one that is lower. Don't limit your thinking to just one type of security, either. Mix and match corporate and government bonds . . . whatever provides the best potential return for your comfort level.

With any of these strategies, low interest rates can prove to be a great opportunity for investors, savers and spenders.

One Singular Sensation

Exercise your IRA options

> *"I don't want to be a millionaire; I just want to live like one."*
> —Toots Shor

Who says financial advisors don't have any fun? April 15th isn't just the year's busiest day for accountants, IRS agents and the U.S. Postal Service. Here are a few snatches from conversations I have had on and about this most auspicious of days:

- "I'm sending in my IRA contributions today, one for me and one for my wife. I think we might be getting divorced, so can you put them both in my name?"

- "I already put in my contribution to an IRA, but I want to change it to a Roth. What's a Roth?"

- On April 18th: "What do you mean it's too late to make a contribution to my IRA? I have an envelope right here postmarked the 15th—I did it myself this morning."

Smart Stretch

Still confused? Check your library for *The Roth IRA Book, An Investor's Guide* (Pricewater-houseCoopers) by Gobind Daryanani, Ph.D. It will clear up any questions you may have and answer questions you probably never thought to ask.

Hum a few bars, and you can fake it. That's the way most people feel about that old standby, the individual retirement account (IRA) . . . until now, that is. Major tax law revisions have given investors something to really sing about. Not since IRA contributions were first allowed in the early 1980s have changes been so sweeping . . . and so positive. Is your IRA doing all it can to help you reach your retirement goal? To find out, check out these eight IRA facts—they may have you singing a whole new song.

- **Not the same old song.** New and tax-efficient, the Roth IRA has revolutionized retirement savings. The most endearing aspect of the Roth is its federal-tax-free growth. For investors who expect their tax bracket to remain high during retirement, eliminating a major benefit of traditional IRAs, Roth IRAs are a welcome solution. Traditional IRAs have the potential to provide a higher total return than comparable taxable accounts, but the tax-free status of Roth accounts potentially makes them even more wonderful.

You may contribute to a Roth or convert your traditional IRA to a Roth at any age. (70½ is the maximum age for contributions to a traditional IRA.) You are not required to take distributions from a Roth, whereas minimum distribution requirements begin at age 70½ for traditional IRAs. If set up properly, Roth IRAs can grow federal tax free forever, my love.

- **A perfect duet.** Like the song says, traditional IRAs are for "just the two of us." Married couples who file a joint return may make a tax-deductible contribution of up to $4,000, with the maximum of $2,000 going to each spouse's traditional IRA, even if only one of them has earned income. (Note: Contributions may not be tax-deductible, depending on income levels, if either or both spouses participate in an employer-sponsored retirement plan.) A spousal IRA can be established if the individual is married at the end of the year, the spouse is under age 70 at the end of the year, and the working and nonworking spouses file a joint return. (Of course, the amount contributed can't exceed the couple's total earned income.) This new provision allows nonworking spouses to accumulate retirement nest eggs of their own.

- **One singular sensation.** Thinking about making an IRA contribution? You may be able to save time in a bottle, but don't put off your IRA con-

Hello, IRA!	
Traditional IRA	**Roth IRA**
Advantages	
Tax-deferred compounding, tax-deductible contributions (subject to limitations)	Tax-deferred compounding, tax-free qualified distributions (contributions are not tax deductible)
Eligibility For Contribution	
Under age 70½ with earned income; nonworking spouse also eligible	Anyone with earned income below the limit of $95,000 (single filers), $150,000 (joint filers); contributions are phased out for individuals with an adjusted gross income between $95,000 and $110,000, and for married couples between $150,000 and $160,000; nonworking spouses also eligible
Contributions	
$2,000 per person, per year, or 100 percent of earnings up to $2,000, whichever is less	
Deductibility	
Deductible if not covered by an employer plan. If you or your spouse is covered by an employer plan, you still may be entitled to a partial decuction depending on who is covered and your adjusted gross income level.	Nondeductible
Withdrawals	
Must begin withdrawals at age 70½ or by April 1 following the calendar year in which the owner reaches age 70½	No age 70½ mandatory distributions required

Continued on next page

Continued from previous page

Hello, IRA!

Traditional IRA	Roth IRA
Penalty-Free Withdrawals	
Withdrawals prior to age 59½ may be subject to a 10 percent penalty tax unless one of the following exceptions apply: • qualified first-time home purchase (up to $10,000 lifetime limit) • qualified higher education expenses • medical expenses that exceed 7.5 percent of adjusted gross income • ccertain health insurance premiums while unemployed • a series of substantially equal periodic payments that meets special requirements • distributions related to divorce proceedings • disability • death	Same
Taxes On Withdrawals	
Earnings and deductible contributions are tased upon withdrawal.	None, if the account owner holds the Roth IRA for five taxable years and: • is age 59½ • is a qualified first-time home buyer (subject to limitations • becomes disabled or dies

tribution. You have until the due date for filing your tax return, not counting extensions, to establish and fund your account for a given year. A contribution is considered on time if it is mailed and postmarked by the due date of the tax return, even if the IRA custodian or trustee has not received the contribution until after the due date. You can claim an IRA deduction on your return before you make the contribution, but you must make the contribution before the deadline. If your tax year is the calendar year, your deadline is April 15, so don't delay . . . do it today.

If you're in the mood to contribute early, contributions to IRAs can be made as early as January 1 of your tax year, which gives your money more time to compound and grow . . . it's one way of getting the most bang from your buck.

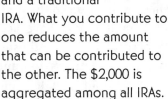

Money Missteps

You cannot contribute $2,000 annually to both a Roth and a traditional IRA. What you contribute to one reduces the amount that can be contributed to the other. The $2,000 is aggregated among all IRAs.

- **They're playing your song.** The new rules about IRAs may be music to your ears, but you can't make a contribution unless you have earned compensation. For IRA purposes, this includes wages, tips, salaries, professional fees, bonuses and commissions. For a sole proprietor or partner in a company, compensation is the net earnings from the trade or business reduced by his or her deductions for contributions to other retirement plans and the deduction allowed for one-half of his or her self-employment taxes.

  You cannot make an IRA contribution based on earnings from the sale of property, dividends from securities, rental income, pension or annuity income, or severance, unemployment benefits or disability pay. Earned income must be just that: earned.

- **Money makes the world go 'round.** Should you put money away that you can't access until you're 59½? The answer, most emphatically, is yes! The younger you are when you start saving, the less you'll have to save and the more you could have when you retire. Assuming a 10 percent rate of return, someone who starts contributing at age 25 and faithfully tucks $2,000 away every year until she's 64 will have contributed just $80,000. But compounding at 10 percent annually, that investment would be worth $973,704.

  No one can guarantee a 10 percent return, but compounding works—and the sooner you start, the better. In fact, why not set up an IRA for your children, too? Consider this: At a 10 percent rate of return, a person who contributes $2,000 annually from the ages of 18 to 24—a total of $14,000—would accumulate $944,651 by the age of 65. And someone who saved $2,000 for just five years from ages 14 through 18 (a total of $10,000) could have more than $1 million by age 65.

  IRA contributions are allowed for children, provided they have earned income (love that paper route, and baby-sitting, too) and their contribution does not exceed their earnings. The child's parent or guardian must sign the application. Getting started on your IRA early is a great way to save, especially because while your money is compounding, taxes, if any, on those earnings are deferred (or in the case of a Roth IRA, generally tax free) until you withdraw them at retirement.

- **Bang the drum slowly.** Individuals under the age of $59\frac{1}{2}$ may take penalty-free IRA withdrawals from traditional IRAs to pay for medical expenses that exceed the itemized deduction limitation. You qualify for this benefit if you have accumulated medical expenses in excess of 7.5 percent of your adjusted gross income. Money paid for health insurance premiums for unemployed individuals may also be withdrawn without penalty under certain circumstances. If you have received unemployment compensation for 12 consecutive weeks under any federal or state employment compensation program, provided that the withdrawal is made in the same year or the following year, and provided it doesn't exceed the cost of the health insurance premiums for you and your spouse, it may be withdrawn without penalty; consult your tax advisor.

- **We are family.** Thinking of making a child your beneficiary on a traditional IRA so you can take out the least possible amount in your required annual distribution? This can be a great idea, but if your spouse is still alive, you may want to make him or her your primary beneficiary instead. When you die, the funds accumulated in your IRA can be rolled directly from your IRA to that of your spouse. If your beneficiary is a child, the funds must be distributed and taxes paid if your child is under age $59\frac{1}{2}$. Before you make your decision, consult your tax and legal advisors.

Deciding on a beneficiary for your Roth IRA is a different tune altogether. Owners of Roth IRAs are not required to take distributions. Here, a beneficiary designation could allow the assets stored in your Roth to pass to the next generation free of income taxes (although these amounts will be

Healthy Habit

Whether your beneficiary is living or nonliving, selecting the right one is almost as important as the IRA itself. Living beneficiaries include spouses, children, friends, etc. Nonliving beneficiaries may be trusts, the estate of the account holder, charitable organizations and the like. In addition to the primary beneficiary, you may choose a contingent beneficiary who will receive the account assets if the primary beneficiary is not living.

considered part of your estate). Hypothetically, Roth IRA assets could continue to compound income tax free forever if beneficiaries and successor beneficiaries are chosen correctly. Consult an estate attorney for more information.

- **Deductibility is a many-splendored thing.** If you're interested in making a tax-deductible traditional IRA contribution and neither you nor your spouse is considered an active participant in a qualified retirement plan, you may do so regardless of your income level. However, if you or your spouse are active participants in a plan, the amount you can deduct for your contribution is determined by your tax-filing status and your adjusted gross income. The table below shows at what income level your deductible contributions will phase out.

Tax law changes have been music to IRA devotees' ears. If you haven't thought about your IRA in years, now is a good time to take another look. And we're not just whistling Dixie.

Year	Married Couple Filing Jointly	Single Filer
2000	$52,000–$62,000	$32,000–$42,000
2001	$53,000–$63,000	$33,000–$43,000
2002	$54,000–$64,000	$34,000–$44,000
2003	$60,000–$70,000	$40,000–$50,000
2004	$65,000–$75,000	$45,000–$55,000
2005	$70,000–$80,000	$50,000–$60,000
2006	$75,000–$85,000	$50,000–$60,000
2007	$80,000–$100,000	$50,000–$60,000

Roth IRA contributions are not tax deductible. As a single wage earner, you may contribute the full $2,000 maximum amount to a Roth if your adjusted gross income is less than $95,000 (joint filers, $150,000), indexed for inflation.

DAY 40

All 4 You

Making the most of your 401(k)

> *"I found myself shortening my anticipated life to make it all balance out."*
>
> —A fiftyish executive, on how he adjusted the variables in his retirement plan so it would appear that he was saving enough money

When Art retired from the company where he had worked for 30 years, he got a lot more than a gold watch. The $800,000 that had accumulated in his 401(k) plan was the ticket to his family's comfortable retirement. The problem: How was he to invest the largest amount of money he had ever seen? The solution: Diversify and conquer. Over the next three years, Art slowly learned about his risk tolerance (moderate), income needs (large) and how these factors make a difference in investment strategy. He and his financial advisor met monthly, and they gradually put his money to work.

Through up markets and down, Art stuck with it, learning more and spending more. After eight years, he and his advisor are proud of their accomplishments. Their conservative strategy has paid off: While Art has spent more than $900,000, his accounts are valued at more than $925,000. Now that's maintenance!

Not everyone retires with a golden nest egg, but many of today's workers will find that by the time they retire, their 401(k) plans will have become their largest asset. Currently more than $1 trillion is invested in 401(k) plans, yet some people pay little attention to them. Getting the most from your 401(k) plan doesn't have to be a full-time job, but an occasional tweak could make the difference between a great retirement and an average one. Here's your simple guide to investing smart. Happy savings!

Can I Retire 10 Years Early?

It's on the cover of every investment magazine: "You can retire 10 years early!" But do you want to live the lifestyle of a Tibetan monk, or would you prefer to proceed in the lifestyle to which you've become accustomed? Maybe the question should be, "At this stage of my life, have I saved enough to retire?" While this is certainly a loaded question and almost impossible to answer without specific information on your needs, desires, spending and savings habits, let's have a go at it anyway.

We're basing our assumptions on the following: You'll be replacing 75 percent of your pretax income at retirement, and this amount increases at

The Top 10 401(k) Bloopers

10. Not evaluating your plan's investment options—and not speaking up if they leave something to be desired

9. Trying to second-guess the stock market

8. Not watching your investments' progress

7. Parking all of your contributions in a "guaranteed" (GIC) fund

6. Not taking all the help your plan offers

5. Not learning about all your options

4. Not understanding that you are investing, not saving

3. Not contributing as much as you can

2. Not starting as early as you can

1. Not joining your plan

Source: Richard Sasanow, author of The 401(k) Book

the rate of inflation each year. You'll be saving 8 percent of your annual income between now and retirement, and this amount also increases with inflation each year. You'll be retired 25 years, and at the end, the account is exhausted. We're not making any adjustment for taxes, so all distributions are pretax. We'll express what you should have saved as a multiple of your current income.

Depending on what kind of investor you are, here are three different strategies:

● **Aggressive:** 80 percent stocks/20 percent bonds before retirement; 63/35 after retirement

● **Moderate:** 65/35 before retirement; 50/50 after retirement

● **Conservative:** 50/50 before retirement; 35/65 after retirement

Using the chart below, let's see how this whole thing works. The chart shows how much of your current salary you should have saved for retirement by now.

Say you're a 40-year-old who feels comfortable with moderate risk. To retire at age 65, you would need to have saved 172 percent of your current annual income. With a salary of $40,000 a year, you would have to have saved $68,000 (40,000 x 1.72) by now and keep up the pace until retirement. To retire at age 55 instead, you'd need 40,000 x 3.93, or $157,200. At age 35, assuming a salary of $35,000, you would need to have saved only $34,300 (35,000 x .98) to retire at age 65. Of course, should you want to retire sooner, you can use a more aggressive portfolio or save more money.

Nest Egg Know-How								
Investment Strategy	**Years To Retirement**							
	0	**5**	**10**	**15**	**20**	**25**	**30**	**35**
Aggressive	957%	675%	463%	307%	193%	109%	48%	3%
Moderate	1,046	773	558	393	268	172	98	42
Conservative	1,148	890	676	505	369	261	174	105

Returns and inflation assumptions are based on Ibbotson Associates' data for the S&P 500, intermediate Treasury bonds and inflation from December 31, 1946 to December 31, 1996. Note, however, that since we are projecting returns in the future, historical returns were calculated using the arithmetic mean, which is equal to or less than the average annual compounded return. So the arithmetic mean for the S&P 500 over this period was 11.92 percent, compared with 12.59 percent for the average annual total return. For intermediate Treasuries, it was 5.74 percent compared with 5.89 percent, and for inflation, it was 4.01 percent vs. 4.08 percent.

Source: T. Rowe Price & Associates

Up The Ante

Unless you're willing to bet on the solvency of Social Security to fund your retirement, your 401(k) plan is a great way to help you save for that goal. Not only are your contributions deductible from current income (thus saving on taxes now), but assets grow tax deferred until you take them out at retirement. Before you seek to invest elsewhere, make sure you've done all you can to make the most of your employer-sponsored plan. Many plan participants contribute only as much as the employer matches. If you can afford to save more, do so—the maximum annual contribution is $10,000, adjusted for inflation.

Contributing the max to your 401(k) plan may be considered the greatest thing since sliced bread, but what do you do if you're just barely squeaking by? Even if your contribution is small, the money still adds up. To use an illustration that is not representative of any particular investment, let's say a hypothetical single investor's annual salary is $25,000, putting her in the 15 percent federal tax bracket. If she contributes 2 percent of her salary, her total annual contributions will be $500, her tax savings $75, and the amount out of her weekly paycheck a mere $9.62. Why bother, you ask? Well, if our aforementioned investor's savings achieve an 8 percent rate of return for 30 years, they could be worth $56,641 . . . and that's a lot to get bothered about!

Should our hypothetical employee feel inspired by these numbers and decide to up her contribution to, say, 9 percent (perhaps forgoing eating lunch out and saving some pounds along with those dollars), annual contributions would total $2,250, federal tax savings $337.60, and a paycheck reduction every week of $43.27. The same money growing at an 8 percent rate would be worth $254,887 in 30 years. Now we're cooking with gas! So give yourself a raise: Bring your lunch, skip a few department store sales, and sock the extra dollars away for your retirement. You'll be glad you did.

Eeny, Meeny, Miney, Mo . . .

Today's 401(k) plans have plenty of options—seemingly too many, in some cases. Where can you go for help? Ask your employee benefits person for a contact at whatever company is doing the investing for your firm's retirement plan. While your company can't make decisions for you on things like asset allocation, they are responsible for helping you get information on the options available. (For a quick review on what kinds of funds are out there, go back to Day 9.)

The best way to learn about your retirement plan's options is to request and read the prospectus for the funds available. There's almost no end to the information available on specific funds and fund families, from in-depth analysis (consult Morningstar reports available in the library or online) to rankings of funds' performance in relation to their peers (check the special issue of your favorite financial magazine, newspaper or newsletter). For plans that offer privately managed investment pools, all information must come from your company.

Healthy Habit

Allocating your assets among the different types of funds is almost as important as putting money into the plan in the first place. One of the biggest and most frequently made mistakes of retirement plan participants is keeping too much money in something guaranteed. Unless you're fewer than five years from retirement, your 401(k) is meant for growth, so take another look at the exercise for Day 35—and re-evaluate your allocations.

Before you make your selection, consider how your other money is invested. As you learned on Day 35, it's not necessarily the particular investment but the asset allocation that makes the difference in long-term returns. Look at the big picture: If you need to save money on taxes, for example, consider municipal bonds for part of your investment outside your retirement plan. A word of caution: Record equity returns over the past several years have made some investors overly confident. Don't allocate all your money to high-risk sectors. Instead, after learning all you can about your plan's options, spread your savings through the various categories available.

Making Up For Lost Time?

If you've been less than loyal to your 401(k) plan, you might be tempted to go for broke—taking big risks and throwing caution to the wind. In a bullish market, your fellow employees may cheer your resolve. But hold on . . . and heed the advice from a little-known but unusually smart philosopher (my husband): "Don't just do something—sit there." You may mean well, but as your mother probably asked you many times, "If all your friends were going to jump off a bridge, would you jump, too?" If the answer is no, get some prospectuses, and turn to your financial advisor for help.

No financial advisor? Consider dollar-cost averaging, making equal periodic investments into the different funds available (see Day 36). This strategy neither ensures a profit nor protects against a loss should the market decline, and you need to make sure that you will be financially able to continue the process through periods of price declines. But that having been said, after a while you'll know what investments you prefer and you can make the necessary changes with your accumulated balance.

Money Missteps

If you like your company and believe in it, why not put a lot of company stock in your 401(k) account? Because too much of your future fortunes will be tied to the performance of one company. That's great if things are going well, but potentially devastating if fortunes turn. Consider diversifying your assets. Some plans match employee contributions with company stock, but many allow recipients to switch into other assets.

Lend Yourself A Hand—Not!

Your car's broken down, your kid needs braces and you're sick of your kitchen cabinets. Suddenly a bright idea—a loan on your 401(k) plan! It seems to make more sense to borrow from yourself and pay yourself interest, doesn't it? Nonsense.

While you may be borrowing from your account and paying yourself interest to do so, the problem is the potential returns you are missing out on. Most plans don't charge interest rates as high as what the investment opportunities within their accounts could return. If you're looking for a loan with tax-deductible interest, talk to your tax advisor about home-equity loans.

Parting Is Such Sweet Sorrow

Leaving your current employer? When you change jobs, you *can* take it with you. While some plans allow former employees to leave their

Healthy Habit

It may take anywhere from several weeks to several months for your former employer to send the proceeds from your retirement account to its next destination. Make sure that the check is written directly to the trustee of the new plan—not to you. A mistake could cost you 20 percent of the balance.

accounts where they are, you often have more control if you either roll it over to a plan at your new employer or to an IRA.

If you like the options offered at your new employer and rollovers are accepted, roll on over. On the other hand, if you prefer to manage the funds yourself, consider a "conduit IRA," where only funds that come from retirement plans are placed. If you keep these monies separate from your other IRAs, you may be able to roll them into another 401(k) plan down the road or receive special tax treatment on distributions when you retire. Consult a tax advisor before making any decisions.

These options probably sound easy and logical. Then why do more than half the workers who change jobs withdraw the money and spend it? Unless you have a dire emergency, don't even *think* about touching that money. If you do, you'll face a mandatory 20 percent withholding tax, state and local taxes, and a 10 percent penalty if you're under age 59½. Plus, you'll give up all the lovely tax-deferred money you could have made if you had rolled the money over.

Most people don't expect Social Security to pick up the tab for their retirement, but if there is some money left when you get there, won't it be nice to know that it will only serve to bolster your already sufficient savings? Making the most of your 401(k) plan can help you spend your happy golden years relaxing on Golden Pond—not working under the golden arches.

Healthy Habit

When you leave your employer, if the value of your 401(k) account is less than $5,000, you must decide where you want it to go or an employer has the right to send it to you—making you liable for taxes and penalties.

Will Power

The ins and outs of estate planning

A local bar was so sure that its bartender was the strongest man around that they offered a standing $1,000 bet. The bartender would squeeze a lemon until all the juice ran into a glass and then hand the fruit to a patron. Anyone who could squeeze one more drop of juice from the lemon would win the money. Many people tried, but no one could do it. One day, a small, thin man came into the bar, wearing thick glasses and a polyester suit. He said in a shrill voice, "I'd like to try the bet." After the laughter died down, the bartender squeezed the lemon and handed the remains to the man. To everyone's amazement, the man wrung six drops of juice from the lemon. As the patrons cheered, the bartender handed over the $1,000. "What do you do for a living?" he asked the winner. "Are you a weight lifter? A wrestler?" The man replied, "I'm an IRS agent."

No one escapes the sting of taxes, but with estates, it seems particularly harsh. It's bad enough to lose someone you love, and making the acquaintance of the IRS only adds insult to injury. Why must beneficiaries share so much of their inheritances with Uncle Sam? In many cases, although a will was in place, the decedent's estate planning was less than adequate. Even though you won't be around to reap its benefits, estate planning is one of the most important parts of financial planning—and often the most neglected.

Will You Or Won't You?

You've heard it a million times, but it probably hasn't sunk in yet: You need a will. Even if you're certain you don't have enough money to leave to anyone; even if you're young and healthy; even if you're too single, too busy, too "lawyerless" to bother, rest assured: You need a will.

If you own property and you die without a will, your property may be distributed according to the laws of the state in which you are a resident. How would you feel if the wealth you struggled a lifetime to accumulate were suddenly reduced by half and distributed in a manner you never intended? Let's say it again: You need a will.

Some people believe a will is a waste of time. A trust, they insist, is a better way to go. While trusts are marvelous instruments and useful in many cases, even if you have a trust, you still need a will to make sure that any odds and ends (like personal property) that didn't or couldn't make it into the trust will be scooped up and distributed properly.

Once your will is in place, an estate plan is the next step. It can spell out who should care for young children or older parents, manage your business and make decisions on your behalf if you become incompetent. When you've done as much preparation as you can by yourself, sit down with an estate-planning attorney and get the help you need. Our workbook section includes a form to help you prepare for that meeting.

Properly preparing your estate can cost several hundred dollars in a simple case and several thousand dollars if your estate is large or your finances or family situation are complicated, but it's money well-spent. Without good professional advice, all your planning can be undone by a simple mistake.

Assets, Assets, Where Are Your Assets?

To get started preparing your estate plan, first make a list of everything you own, both assets and liabilities.

Assets include the following:

- real estate, including your home, rental property and land

- investments

- cash, including savings and checking accounts, certificates of deposit, and money-market and credit union balances

- personal property, including cars, clothes, collections, artwork, jewelry, furnishings and books

- retirement accounts, including IRAs, Keogh plans and SEPs (note who the beneficiary is on each account)

- employee benefits, including stock options; group life insurance plans; profit-sharing, 401(k) and defined-benefit plans; and company pensions

- accounts receivable (list anyone who owes you money and the amount owed, including mortgages or ongoing professional fees)

- business interests, noting the names of partners, if any

- life insurance policies, including second-to-die policies and business succession programs, as well as whole life and term policies (list the beneficiaries and any loans taken from the policies)

- interests in trusts created for your benefit by others

Liabilities include:

- taxes
- money owed, including bills, mortgages, loans and margin accounts
- credit card balances

Healthy Habit

A letter of instruction is an important tool that many people overlook. Put down on paper the key actions your loved ones need to take, including the kind of funeral and burial you'd prefer, where your documents are located, who to call, and steps to eliminate immediate financial problems. You don't need a lawyer to do this, and it will make handling your affairs much easier for your loved ones.

Once you've got it all on paper, here's something else to consider. There are two types of property, probate and nonprobate. Probate property includes any asset that is passed on according to an individual's will. It is subject to the supervision of the probate court and hence to probate costs, the most substantial of which is the executor's commission. This ranges from 5 percent of probate assets in a small estate to about 2 percent in larger estates.

Nonprobate property is any property that passes outside of a will. Such property is not subject to the supervision of a court, nor is it subject to an executor's commission. Examples of nonprobate property include assets owned jointly with a right of survivorship, such as property owned by husband and wife, where the assets pass directly to the surviving joint owner; assets held in trust, which pass in accordance with a trust agreement; life insurance proceeds, which are paid directly to beneficiaries; pension plans, including IRAs, which pass directly to named beneficiaries; and annuities, which also pass directly to named beneficiaries.

True Value

What exactly are these taxes that everyone tries so hard to mitigate? Federal estate tax is imposed on the transfer of property resulting from an individual's death. Before you can figure out how to reduce it, you need to see how it is determined. A person's taxable estate includes the fair market value of all property in which he or she had an interest at the time of death. This includes but is not limited to insurance proceeds of a life insurance policy owned by the decedent, whether or not it is payable to the estate; retirement accounts; joint accounts; and property over which the decedent has control.

The fair market value of the estate is usually determined at the time of death. However, the estate's executor may elect to value the entire estate

It's Better To Give

Take some tips from estate-planning attorney Amy Birmingham: "Consider any gifts made during your life. If you paid gift taxes on gifts made within three years of your death, the gift taxes and the gift are added to your taxable estate as a kind of 'phantom' asset. This penalizes people for making deathbed taxable gifts.

"Other gifts made during your life are also taken into account in calculating your estate tax bill. The aggregate gifts made during your life are added back for the purpose of determining your estate tax bracket. For example, if you gave $2 million in gifts during your life and died with a $1 million estate, instead of using the 41 percent rate applicable to the $1 million estate, you would use the 55 percent rate applicable to $3 million estates, and your tax bill would be $550,000 instead of $410,000."

Money Missteps

One of the most common mistakes in estate planning is relying exclusively on the marital deduction. By leaving all your assets to the surviving spouse, you lose the opportunity to use the $675,000 exclusion at the death of the first partner. The solution? Use the unified credit for both spouses. This allows up to $1.6 million to be passed on to heirs without estate taxation.

on an alternative valuation date, usually six months after the decedent's death. The later valuation is used if the value of the overall estate has decreased during the six-month period, making the tax bill lower. If no estate tax is due or there is no decrease in the tax bill using the later valuation, the date of death is used to value the estate.

The next step in estimating an estate's value is to subtract deductions. Include executor's commissions, attorney's fees, probate court fees and any other administration expenses. Also include all funeral expenses, debts of the decedent and uncompensated losses from casualty or theft. Charitable bequests and marital bequests are also deductible.

Finally, add taxable gifts back into the estate. On any transfers within three years of death, the gift and the corresponding gift tax are added back to the estate. The tax is later subtracted as a credit to avoid double taxation.

Death And Taxes

Two things are certain: death and taxes. You can't avoid the first, but you can reduce the second—at least when it comes to your estate. Here's how:

- Gift giving allows you to transfer up to $10,000 each year to an unlimited number of individuals, whether family or not, free of gift taxes. For married couples, gifts of $20,000 ($10,000 from each spouse) can be made annually to an individual without incurring gift taxes. For example, if a single parent gave each of his seven grandchildren $10,000 per year for 10 years (a total of $700,000), none of that money would be subject to gift tax, nor would it reduce the lifetime exclusion amount (see page 250).

Healthy Habit

If you're giving gifts to reduce the value of your estate, give just under the maximum $10,000 per person limit. A picky auditor could question whether you actually gave more than the limit.

- Each individual may leave a sum, called a unified credit, free of any federal estate tax, to a named beneficiary. By January 1, 2006, this unified credit will be $1 million per person, less any gifts you made during your life of more than $10,000 per year. The level of this exclusion is shown in the following chart:

Unified Exclusion Increase	
Year	**Exclusion Amount**
2000	$675,000
2001	$675,000
2002	$700,000
2003	$700,000
2004	$850,000
2005	$950,000
2006	$1 million

- For married individuals, an unlimited marital deduction allows you to transfer any amount to your spouse (or to a qualified trust for his or her benefit) free of estate tax.

- Gifts to qualified charities are tax deductible to the estate.

- Transfers to an educational institution or health-care provider on behalf of another person are exempt from gift tax without limit.

- Payments of school tuition and medical bills, if made directly to the school or service provider, are not treated as gifts. A grandparent, for example, can pay his or her grandchild's tuition in addition to making a $10,000 gift each year.

Stretch Out With A Roth

A Roth IRA can be very useful in planning your estate. Say, for example, that Alice is 75 years old, has a traditional IRA worth $300,000, and has assets of more than $3 million. Her income level is such that she is allowed to convert her IRA to a Roth IRA. Should she do it? If her objective is to reduce estate taxes and provide an inheritance for her family, the answer is a qualified yes. By converting her IRA, Alice provides a vehicle that can grow tax free for many years. Taxes resulting from the conversion will reduce the size of her taxable estate. Finally, although her heirs will owe estate tax on the value of the Roth, they won't have to pay income taxes on its proceeds as they would on traditional IRAs, 401(k) plans or pension benefits.

Before you get too excited about this, however, keep in mind that these issues become very complicated, and you should seek help from an estate attorney. While mandatory distributions are not required by Roth IRA owners while they are alive, they may apply after their death. It is vital, therefore, to structure your beneficiary designation so that your heirs can continue to receive tax-free growth on their inheritance as long as possible.

Many experts suggest making your spouse the primary beneficiary to avoid estate taxes when you die. Children or grandchildren are then usually named as secondary beneficiaries. Upon the death of the Roth IRA owner, the surviving spouse may take the Roth IRA as their own, postponing distributions until their death. The children, as contingent beneficiaries, may then choose to begin distributions as of December 31 of the year of their second parent's death, based on the life expectancy of the eldest nonspousal beneficiary or within five years of the second death. If you want each child to be able to remove funds based on his or her own life expectancy, open separate Roth IRAs with each child as the beneficiary. Once again, before you take any steps, consult an attorney. A sharp CPA could also be helpful in sorting out these issues.

Executor, Executrix

No, you're not back in Latin class, but choosing someone to administer your estate can be an even more difficult endeavor. Settling an estate can mean a year or more of wrestling with paperwork, tracking down assets and filing tax returns. At first it may seem a great honor, but it's really a great headache. Choose someone who isn't daunted by the legal system and who has a good rapport with your attorney or another legal professional.

If your estate is large, your executor will need to file an estate tax return. The attorney who handles the estate should prepare the return. It is not usually necessary to involve an accountant. However, should the estate contain stocks, bonds and other investments, a financial advisor can help to liquidate it. In this area of financial planning, an experienced professional can make all the difference.

Who Can You Trust

Using trusts in estate planning

> "Death is not the end; there remains the litigation."
> —Ambrose Bierce

Virginia and her parents were setting up their estate and sought legal counsel. Unfortunately, the folks who did their estate planning should have been doing something else—anything else—other than estate planning. The family was intent on saving estate tax, but in the end did quite the opposite. The estate planners (not attorneys, I might mention, but members of a "professional legal planning" group), made a little mistake: Instead of making the trusts irrevocable, they made them revocable. What's a few letters between friends? About $400,000.

They say you can never be too rich or too thin, but when it comes to estate planning, many of us may be richer than we think. If you're a self-made millionaire (or on the way to becoming one), you probably know all too well the value of a dollar. But what happens to the money you've worked so hard to earn when you die? Does Uncle Sam have to take a huge chunk of it? Even more frightening to consider, after your will is read and the money is safely in your heirs' hands, will your still-tender-aged kids spend their inheritance on fast cars and high living? Will your spouse get hoodwinked by a con artist or a gold digger?

Although you can't take it with you, there is a way you can rest in peace: Consider a trust. For generations, trusts have been a standard estate-planning tool for the likes of the Rockefellers and Gettys. But trusts aren't just for millionaires: According to recent U.S. government statistics, 68 percent of trusts have less than $1 million in assets.

A trust does not take the place of a will, but certain types of trusts can help you save on estate and income taxes, avoid probate, keep others from knowing what you have while you're alive and to whom you plan to leave it when you die, and protect the rights of your intended heirs. Today you'll learn the basics of this valuable tool.

Trusty Terms

What is a trust? The *American College Dictionary* defines trust as "that on which a person relies; the condition of being confided to another person's care or guard." In financial terms, a trust is an arrangement that separates the legal ownership of an asset from the entity or person benefiting from that asset. A trust allows the grantor to transfer property to the trustee for the benefit of the beneficiary in keeping with the trust agreement.

Not quite clear yet? Here are the basics of trust terminology:

- The *grantor* is the person who establishes the trust and transfers property to it via the trust agreement.

- *Trust property* is the property that will be transferred to the trust. It can be transferred while the grantor is alive or after death, either under the terms of the grantor's will or as a pour-over from the grantor's will. The trust property can include cash, a life insurance policy, stocks, securities, real estate or anything else the grantor wishes to include.

- The *trustee* is the person or institution responsible for managing the assets or property of the trust. The trustee may be the grantor (under certain limited circumstances); a family member or trusted friend; a financial, tax or legal advisor; an institution such as a bank trust department; or any combination of the above.

  The primary legal requirement for serving as a trustee is the ability to accept legal title (ownership) of the trust property (eliminating minors from consideration). Legal title means the assets are owned in the name of the trustee, who is responsible for performing specific actions laid out in the trust document concerning the management and disposition of the trust's property; beneficial title is the right the beneficiary has to the trust property.

- *Beneficiaries* are the persons or entities who will receive the trust property. Beneficiaries should be spelled out specifically to prevent problems.

- The *trust agreement* explains all matters of the trust, names all participants, and delineates the handling and disposition of assets.

Dead Or Alive

There are almost as many variations of trusts as there are individuals who set them up. In general, however, there are two categories of trusts: those set up while the grantor is living, called *inter vivos trusts*, and those that become effective after the grantor's death, called *testamentary trusts*.

There are two types of living trusts: revocable and irrevocable. A *revocable trust* can be established, controlled and revoked by the grantor at any time up until his or her death. Since the grantor retained control over the trust's assets, these assets would be included in his or her estate upon death. An *irrevocable trust* cannot be changed once it is set up. While this is a fairly substantial drawback, the benefit of such a trust is that it is not

---

Revoke Your Revocable Trust

"People assume that they're accomplishing great savings when they establish a revocable living trust," says estate-planning attorney Amy Birmingham. "Avoiding probate is not a big deal—the maximum probate fee in most states is a few thousand dollars. The other costs typically associated with probate, such as attorney's fees and executor's commissions, can (and should) be negotiated during life, or in the case of attorney's fees, by your executor after your death.

"In many states, a revocable living trust doesn't protect your privacy, either. The real issue with estate planning is how to save on estate taxes, and revocable living trusts do nothing to save on estate tax."

included in the descendant's estate. The transferred assets and all future growth on their value are passed to the next generation outside of the estate as long as they remain in the trust.

Within these two basic categories of trusts, there are several types, including bypass, or unified credit, trusts; charitable remainder trusts (CRTs); and life insurance trusts.

The *bypass trust* is probably the most frequently used trust. It can be living or testamentary, revocable or irrevocable, but to obtain favorable tax treatment, it

Healthy Habit

Gay partners may be particularly well-served by a living trust. Since this relationship is often not legally recognized, a will could be challenged, while a trust is much more difficult to dispute.

must be irrevocable. Married couples most commonly include this trust in their wills to leave the full amount of the unified credit (up to $2 million in 2006; see Day 41) to their heirs free of estate tax. Jointly owned property must be divided before death to provide at least the unified credit amount in each spouse's name. When the first spouse dies, the designated assets go into the trust, but the surviving spouse is entitled to income and principal from it at the trustee's discretion. When the second spouse dies, the heirs receive the proceeds of the trust free of estate tax. Voila! $2 million is sheltered from estate tax.

The *charitable remainder trust (CRT)* is an effective instrument for a grantor who wants to benefit a charity by donating assets that have appreciated sharply during his or her lifetime. For example, suppose your grandfather, Sam Saver, has accumulated a large stock portfolio—he started buying right after the stock market crashed in 1929 and hasn't sold a share. Stock splits over the years have made him so wealthy, not even a cut in the capital gains tax would help.

Grandpa Sam wants to leave some of his money to his alma mater but also wants to be sure he'll have enough income to pay his bills until he dies. The CRT could be a solution. Once the trust is set up and funded with some of Grandpa's appreciated stocks, Grandpa or his designated beneficiary retains an income interest in the trust while the remaining interest goes to Grandpa's charity. The trustee sells the stock, and with the proceeds, purchases income-producing assets without paying the substantial capital gains tax that he would have paid had Grandpa sold them himself. Although the charity, as the beneficiary, owns the principal (but cannot cash it in until the trust terminates), the CRT would allow Grandpa Sam to receive income from the stocks for life.

On the other hand, if Grandpa Sam does not want to limit his income to that earned by the trust, he can insist on a fixed payment from the trust each year. In the year in which the trust is established, Grandpa Sam receives an income tax deduction equal to the present value of the future gift to the charity. When the trust terminates, the remaining assets pass to the charity. Variations on the CRT achieve similar but different ends. Discuss this with your estate attorney.

A *life insurance trust* is another type of irrevocable trust that may be advisable if the taxable value of your estate, including life insurance policies, is more than the exclusion amount. Life insurance proceeds are not usually subject to income taxes, but they could be treated as part of the taxable estate and thus increase the estate taxes due. A properly drafted irrevocable life insurance trust removes the proceeds from the taxable estate by making the trust the owner and beneficiary of the life insurance policy. Proceeds of the policy are paid into the trust at the grantor's death. Ownership of an existing policy can be transferred to a life insurance trust; however, if the grantor dies within three years of the transfer, the proceeds may be included in the gross estate.

Details, Details

Trainer's Tip

"With the exception of the CRT, it does not make sense to fund a trust with your highly appreciated assets. Hold on to them until death. At that time, your built-in capital gains disappear: Your estate assets are 'marked to the market' by virtue of the automatic step up in cost basis to fair market value."

—Amy Birmingham, estate-planning attorney

An individual can make annual gifts to living trusts, subject to annual gift tax limitations. In the case of a life insurance trust, the trustee uses this money to pay premiums on a policy insuring the grantor's life. Gift taxes on money contributed to a trust may be eliminated or reduced if the grantor uses the annual gift tax exclusion of $10,000 per person ($20,000 for married couples). You can give $10,000 per beneficiary per year, which could purchase a substantial amount of life insurance. Be sure to ask your attorney about "Crummey" withdrawal powers with type of trust.

As in the previous example of Grandpa Sam, you can also fund a trust with appreciated property or shares of securities. For the tax ramifications of this type of transfer, be sure to consult your tax advisor.

One of the most important decisions a grantor makes is the selection of a trustee and successor trustee. Trustees should agree to become trustees, have the ability to manage the trust's assets, have no conflict of interest and get along with the beneficiaries and be able to adequately assess their needs. Don't worry about insulting your spendthrift Uncle George or your partner Harry, who doesn't know the first thing about investing. The reason you're setting up the trust is to safeguard your heirs' futures, not to avoid hurting someone's feelings.

Smart Stretch

Estate Planning for Middle and Large Income Earners (JC Publishing; 800-808-2112) by Joy Casey, provides solutions to five of the biggest estate-planning problems.

Where an irrevocable trust can be a powerful ally in cutting estate taxes, a revocable trust does not decrease the taxes on your estate one penny. Nonetheless, this tool is very popular because in some states it allows assets to avoid probate, ensuring that your affairs are kept private. Both instruments are complicated and inconvenient to set up. The title on all assets must be changed to show that the trust is now the owner, and this is a lot more expensive and complicated than you can imagine.

Before you decide on any type of estate plan, see a reputable estate-planning attorney. Mistakes can invalidate a trust, so if you are going to go through the time and expense of setting one up, be sure to get your legal, financial and tax professionals' advice. Your heirs will be glad you did.

Members Only

The scoop on investment clubs

> "No man is an island."
> –John Donne

Tuckaway Investors is an investment club that has been around for more than 20 years. Its 20 members have learned a lot over the years, and earned a lot, too. How do they do it? Laura Starnes, the club's longtime treasurer, recounts the story behind one of the club's biggest coups: the purchase of Cisco Systems. It was long before the term "Internet" was the first word spoken by infants whose parents traded freely on the Web. Starnes says, "In 1995, my neighbor gave me a hot tip to buy Cisco. I did my research and brought the idea to the club. We were kind of scared to get into it because at $85 per share, it was pretty expensive. Nonetheless, we bought 100 shares, and now, after selling several hundred shares, we have 750 shares, valued at over $75,000!" And that's not the best part: When Starnes told her neighbor about the success of his stock pick, he laughed—he had recommended SYSCO, not Cisco.

If you're tired of sweating out the stock market on your own, take a cue from the Tuckaway members, and vary your exercise routine with a refreshing dip—into the world of investment clubs. You won't be alone. Since the first investment club was founded in 1940, the number of clubs has grown to more than 23,000. And with average annual returns of up to 12.7 percent, they sure beat an afternoon under an umbrella.

The beauty of investment clubs isn't exclusively in their ability to generate a profit, however. By combining your investment of time and money with that of your friends, you can come away with a better understanding of how to find and interpret information to become a better investor—and you can have a lot of fun doing it. Best of all, by pooling your money with that of other members, you don't have to risk as much of your own funds to learn. With that in mind, here's how to get started.

Everybody Into The Pool

Although there are many clubs out there, locating them isn't always easy. Some clubs advertise their meetings in local papers, but most are private affairs. To find one, ask around. Some clubs have been so successful, they have a waiting list for members. But don't let that scare you off. When in doubt, start your own.

Getting started is as easy as getting a group of friends or associates together. According to Barry Murphy, director of marketing for the National Association of Investors Corporation (NAIC), finding potential members is easy. Successful groups have been started among church choirs, people living in the same apartment building, bowling leagues, softball teams, bridge clubs or groups of co-workers.

"Most clubs have some affiliation before they get started," says Murphy. "The social aspect of investment clubs is important, but so is diversity." Clubs comprised solely of doctors, lawyers, nurses or engineers have the same limitations as portfolios consisting of only one type of stock. Diversification is what makes a portfolio—and a club—successful over time, so don't select members from the same industry.

If you're starting a club, how many members should you have? You can start

Money Missteps

You're all friends, so why get the advice of professionals? Make the Chinese proverb "the palest ink is better than the best memory" a bylaw of your club. In today's litigious society, professional advice is important. Whether your club is a partnership or a corporation, make sure that its contract is written properly and its taxes are paid correctly (unless, of course, your members look great in horizontal stripes . . .).

Smart Stretch

Looking for more information on investment clubs? Check out these sources:

- American Association of Individual Investors, (800) 428-2244

- The National Association of Investors Corporation, (877) 275-6242

with as few as two, but the NAIC reports that the average club has 16 members, and some have as many as 40 participants. More important than membership numbers to a club's success is its commitment to learning. Members must be motivated to learn about the financial markets and be willing to investigate together to increase their knowledge.

All members should be prepared to contribute time as well as money. Set regular monthly meetings, collect monthly dues (which provide the capital for the club's investment forays) and assign each member specific responsibilities. Your club's success hinges on the level of each member's participation. The more information you can find, the better decisions you will make

Investment clubs need a legal structure that allows them to act as a single entity. Most choose a partnership format, but some prefer to form a corporation. While there are pros and cons to each, the NAIC recommends going with a partnership to cut down on the legal and filing requirements, paperwork and taxes. Your partnership agreement should outline how your club will function, what roles partners will play, how people who leave the club will be paid, and how new members may enter. Be sure to have your agreement reviewed by an attorney, and give a copy to every member for review before it is signed.

While you're free to reinvent the wheel, if you'd rather spend your time researching companies, the NAIC provides a sample partnership agreement in its membership kit. Membership in the NAIC is not mandatory, but it certainly gives clubs a head start. In addition to informative brochures on how to form and maintain your club, the annual membership dues ($35, plus $11 per member) provides information on stock selection, fundamental analysis, and tools to help computer techies and pencil pushers alike become stock market mavens. The monthly magazine alone is worth the dues, even if you decide not to join or start a club.

Dipping Your Toe

Ready to try out the investing waters with your new club? First, here are a few tips to get you acclimated. Diversify the club portfolio by selecting companies from several industries and market sectors. Defensive businesses, such as food, drug, alcohol, health-care and entertainment companies, usually hold their own in economic downturns. Cyclical stocks include companies that do better when the economy is booming, like autos, airplanes, travel, chemicals and paper. A diversified portfolio might include both types of stocks.

Whatever you do, never put all your club's money into one stock. This may seem impossible to avoid if you want to focus on blue-chip or Internet stocks that have a per-share price almost as much as your membership dues. But don't be disheartened: Investing is a long-term affair. If you rush into decisions too fast, it may take a while for your portfolio to get over its burns.

At each meeting, members should report the research they have done on a number of companies. Information sources abound—from the smallest daily paper and glossy monthly magazines to a host of newsletters, daily and weekly investment papers, and the Internet. But remember, investment clubs are meant for learning, so be thorough: Before you accept a secondhand opinion on a company's value, go directly to the source. Request a 10K and an annual report from companies your club finds interesting, and review these carefully. Keep a file of applicable news clippings, and use opinions from a variety of printed sources to round out your club's selection.

Club decisions are group decisions, and not everyone will agree or be happy with every selection. If you find that no one likes your idea, consider investing on your own. John Markese, president of the American Association of Individual Investors (AAII), believes that one of the biggest

Ask The Lifeguards

How do you find stocks to research in the first place? Investment newsletters are a great source of info from the pros. Request samples from Select Information Exchange, 2315 Broadway, New York, NY 10024, (212) 874-6408. For a nominal fee, your club can try several different newsletters from their collection.

For further information on newsletters you think might suit your needs, subscribe to *The Hulbert Financial Digest*, 316 Commerce St., Alexandria, VA 22314, (800) 443-0100, ext. 459.

Finally, use any of the Web sites mentioned in Day 8 to check recommendations.

investing mistakes people make is buying into things they don't really understand. "Instead of looking at a company's management and earnings history," Markese says, "they select a company simply because they like it and buy its product." While this can work, more often than not you could have done better elsewhere.

For its $49 annual membership fee, the AAII provides materials to study the market and learn more about investing. The AAII Journal, issued 10 times a year, features articles by leading financial advisors. Unlike the NAIC, which only provides research on how to invest in stocks, the AAII provides information on many aspects of financial planning.

Lessons From A Pro

Once you've decided on a stock, you'll need someplace to buy or sell. Most trades go through a broker, and selecting the right type of broker can be immensely helpful to your club. For clubs that really want to do it all on their own, a discount broker may be sufficient, as they do not provide advice. If you require research materials from a discounter, you may incur a charge. Full-service brokerage firms offer advice, guidance and research—with higher fees. Some clubs use a certified financial planner or an insurance agent. Whichever route you choose, be sure to be clear when placing orders, and always review your trade confirmations as soon as they are received.

Group Effort

Take some tips from Laura Starnes, treasurer of Tuckaway Investors:

- **Bring together a group of people who are similar but different.** For example, our club is a mix of older and younger women. The difference in age makes decision-making easier.

- **Decide how the club will make decisions.** When we vote to buy or sell a stock, majority rules, no matter how many members attend.

- **Pay yourselves a dividend occasionally.** This really makes it fun. Over our 20 years, our members have been paid out more than they've put in!

- **Put people in charge of certain things.** That has helped our club be more consistent.

- **Don't day trade.** We've made our best returns by using a buy-and-hold philosophy.

How often do you need to check in with your financial advisor? Many clubs find that an advisor's visits are most helpful when made quarterly. And while a fledgling club is not a big source of commission, it's a source of potential new clients for your advisor, so you should be able to find quality help no matter what the size of your organization. (For more information on choosing a financial planner, see Day 44.)

And Ladies Of The Club

They say it's a man's world, and Wall Street is certainly one of the last bastions of male-dominated society. But this is not so with investment clubs. According to the NAIC, 60 percent of all clubs are comprised entirely of female members, up from 25 percent only 25 years ago. Performance also seems to be bent toward the fairer sex: In 10 of the last 13 years, all-female clubs outperformed exclusively male clubs.

Why? Murphy notes that women are highly communicative, discussing companies tirelessly and taking longer to make a decision—and often their final decision is better than one made more rapidly. "When they get lost, women are the ones who ask for directions," says Murphy. "They don't make assumptions about companies they investigate." Not to worry, guys: Co-ed clubs beat the performance of single-sex clubs, and in eight of the past 10 years, they beat the S&P 500.

How can club members, many who are new to the vicissitudes of the stock market, beat the pros? The key is patience. According to Markese, investment club members have long-term goals and are willing to wait a stock out. Clubs also often mix investing styles, buying growth and value and large and small companies. The NAIC handbook suggests a program of buy and hold, and many clubs follow this maxim religiously.

Don't give up if your club loses money for a while in the beginning. Some clubs take several years to turn a profit. Remember, the reason you're there is to learn. After all, Rome wasn't built in a day. So whatever your vacation plans, spend some time down at the investment club. By the time you go back to the grind, you may have improved a lot more than your backstroke.

Personal Trainer

How to select a financial advisor

> "Some extremely sharp investment advisors can get you in at the bottom of the market. Some extremely sharp ones can get you out at the top. They are never the same people."
>
> —Gary North

P hyllis, a recent widow, was referred by her attorney. The first visit was fun: Having discussed the stock and bond markets and talked about her late husband, his investment philosophy, and her needs and goals, she asked how to transfer her accounts. I asked if she wanted to know anything else—like what my services would cost. Suddenly, she burst into tears, and between sniffles, she told me about her experience with her late husband's broker.

Since her husband's death, the broker had assured her repeatedly that he would take care of everything and not to worry about a thing. When pressed for the reasons behind several transactions, he again assured her that he knew what he was doing and not to worry about all those slips of paper. Finally, she asked him what all these transactions were costing, to which he replied, "If you have to ask what it costs, then you can't afford to work with me." I have to agree . . . no one can afford to work with such a jerk!

Fortunately, not all financial advisors are out to take you or your money for a ride. "A good industry is getting tarred by the conduct of a few bad apples," contends Elisse Walter, executive vice president of legal and regulatory policy for the National Association of Securities Dealers (NASD). Most financial advisors value their clients and strive to help them reach their financial goals. How do you separate the wheat from the chaff? Surprisingly, it's a lot easier than learning how to do a sit-up. It just takes a little perseverance.

There are hundreds of ways to find the right financial advisor. From referrals to attending seminars, opportunities abound. Of course, thanks to the time-honored method of telemarketing, you don't even have to look for them—they'll seek *you* out. Ah, yes, there's nothing like sitting down to dinner accompanied by a chorus of calls from every brokerage firm in the country. Some callers do have great ideas, are respectful of your time and send appropriate information; it can be the start of a beautiful relationship. If you're not interested, most interlopers won't call back. Just don't forget: If something sounds too good to be true, guess what? "It probably is." Don't let fear or greed get the best of you. Another "once in a lifetime" idea will come along—never fear.

Who Goes There?

Stockbroker, registered representative, CFP, ChFC, CFA . . . the titles alone are enough to make your eyes glaze over. But understanding what they mean can help you know what type of service to expect. According to the Certified Financial Planner (CFP) Board of Standards' definition, a personal financial planner (who may possess any of the above titles) is "an individual who uses the financial-planning process to help a client determine whether he or she can meet life's goals by addressing a host of interrelated issues like budgeting and saving, tax planning, investments, and insurance, or by focusing on a single or limited number of financial concerns."

Financial planning is a process, not a product. The term "financial advisor" covers a broad spectrum of financial professionals. A chartered financial consultant (ChFC) has earned this designation by completing a program covering economics, insurance, taxation and real estate. Registered representatives, or stockbrokers, have passed an NASD-administered licensing exam and are affiliated with a stock exchange member broker/dealer firm. CFA stands for chartered financial analyst and

Money Missteps

Be skeptical of an advisor who:

- guarantees a big return

- tells you that an investment is a sure thing

- recommends obscure investments and can't or won't explain how they work

- doesn't listen to you

- is argumentative

- suggests putting all your money into one investment

- won't tell you their fees or charges

designates primarily securities analysts. A CFP, or certified financial planner, has fulfilled specific certification and biannual licensing requirements.

Just because your broker has passed the licensing exam doesn't mean he or she is the right one for you. The NASD publishes a free booklet, *Invest Wisely* (call 301-590-6500), that can give you a few tips. Before talking to any professionals, the publication recommends thinking through your financial objectives and preparing a financial profile, (which, of course, you have prepared by now). Then talk to potential advisors at several firms and learn about their investment experience, professional background and education.

Ruthann Niosi, a former assistant U.S. attorney and ex-SEC staff attorney who heads her own firm, suggests that investors use all the materials at hand to check an advisor's credentials, including brochures on the broker's firm, information from the NASD and referrals from friends. But don't succumb to the herd mentality. "Ask the advisor to profile their type of trading and investment strategy before you tell them yours," recommends Niosi. "You may meet an excellent broker who likes stocks when you like bonds. Make sure your broker's strategy is consistent with the level of risk you're comfortable with."

Track records are often used to persuade investors to sign up. While past performance is not a guarantee of future returns, it can be helpful. Large swings from quarter to quarter may be more than you are willing to handle. If you're conservative, make sure the record you're being shown is equally conservative. Niosi also recommends meeting with a potential advisor in their office, not your home. "This is especially important if you've never heard of the firm," she says. "If it's a boiler room operation, you need to know that going in."

Money For Nothing?

Everyone wants to get the most for their money, but remember, you get what you pay for. While "discount broker" has a nice ring to it, after reading the fine print, you may find yourself getting scalped by miscellaneous fees; charges for setup, handling and research reports; and lower interest rates on money-market funds. Add to that the well-publicized difficulty investors sometimes have reaching their discount broker when the markets are excessively active, and you may be ready to throw in the towel. But these firms have their place. Experienced, knowledgeable investors who do their own research and just want a place to execute trades can save money and time here. Before you get involved, make sure the firm can meet your expectations.

Online brokerage houses can also be a nifty option. If you're a bargain-loving investor, print ads touting "stock trades for $10" and TV commercials whose participants claim to have "plowed in 1,000 shares of Deere for 15 bucks" may make you do a double take. But before you fire your broker, make sure you can get the kind of service you need. Remember that no frills still means, well, no frills. For example, your full-service broker may research trades at tax time as a courtesy, but online firms charge either an hourly or per-transaction fee.

For absolute reliability, e-brokers may fall short. Despite claims of 24-hour trading capability, most have been unable to keep up with demand on heavy-volume days. While some online services tout access to full-service Wall Street firms' research, be sure you read the fine print before you get too excited. In most cases, information *does* come directly from major firms . . . a few hours to a few days later. In an industry where immediate access to information can make or break an opportunity, such delays can be costly.

Looking for opportunities to invest completely on your own? Many companies provide direct share purchase programs and direct reinvestment programs (DRIPs). These programs allow investors to start with a direct purchase and continue purchases via bank draft or mailed-in periodic payments. Commissions are nominal, shares are usually held by the company's transfer agent, and reinvestments are often free. Minimum and initial investments vary. Get more information by calling the company's investor relations department.

And Your Tips For Free

With advice running the gamut from practically nonexistent at discount firms to experienced at full-service companies, why bother at all when you can get a newsletter, pick your mutual funds from a rating service, dial up the Internet, and go merrily on your way? Successful naviga-

Trainer's Tip

To get the right advisor:

- Start slowly and add as you go . . . trust must be earned!

- Look for compatibility (risk tolerance/education/ process).

- Assess compliance records and ask for references.

- Visit his or her office.

- Ask what investment choices are offered.

- Make sure he or she elicits the information needed about you.

- See if he or she is technologically literate.

—Hardwick Simmons, president and CEO, Prudential Securities

tion of today's markets takes more than luck. Anyone can randomly pick a stock, bond or fund, but a comprehensive, personalized package is more likely to help you reach your goals.

Although many investors are comfortable investing a few thousand dollars on their own, hundreds of thousands of dollars is another story. But that doesn't mean giving an advisor full control. According to Ruthann Niosi, the most frequent complaints against brokers are unauthorized transactions and unsuitable recommendations. Preventing these problems is easy . . . read your confirmations and statements as soon as they arrive. If there is a discrepancy that is not quickly corrected, call your financial advisor with questions and follow up with a letter to the advisor and his or her supervisor.

Good, Better, Best

It used to be easy to tell the good guys from the bad—good guys rode in on a white horse, and they always got the girl. Evaluating a financial advisor is a little more complicated, so don't be too quick on the draw. Make sure any candidate's record is free of customer and regulatory complaints. "The percentage of people in the industry who have had trouble or are in trouble is a very small percentage of those who are registered," says Elisse Walter. "But it's also a very large number of people."

Records of customer complaints against a registered representative is public information and can be accessed through the NASD Central Registration Depository (CRD) report. Here you can find out about regulatory disciplinary actions and arbitration results. Remember, though, when reading these reports, that anyone can make a complaint; just because it's there doesn't mean it's justified. Don't decide against an advisor solely because of these very abbreviated reports. Ask the broker about your findings and take into consideration his or her experience and over-all career.

More than 31,000 individuals have earned the right to use the CFP designation, but you don't have to choose one blindly. Bob Goss, executive director of the CFP Board of Standards, notes that the board uses a clipping service that alerts them any time a CFP is mentioned in print, and a planner's record is checked to make sure that he or she is properly registered. "Written complaints received by the board against a CFP must be answered in writing within 20 days," Goss explains. "Failure to respond or cooperate is grounds for suspension or revocation of the CFP license." To learn more about CFPs and to check on an individual under consideration, check out the board's Web site at www.cfp-board.org.

Most Favored Customer Status

There's no such animal as the perfect financial advisor. No one can control or predict the markets, and financial advisors are governed by strict rules—rules that have been set up to protect the investor. While most financial advisors will bend over backward to get and keep your business, it's a fact that some clients are favored over others . . . and believe it or not, it's rarely those who generate the most commission or the highest fees.

Bye-Bye, Baby

Firing your broker? Here are some simple steps to make it easy:

- Have your new broker accomplish the transfer; to do so, you'll have to sign transfer forms.

- If your brokerage account includes check-writing provisions, stop writing checks and return unused checks and debit cards.

- Be patient. Brokerages that use the ACAT (Automated Customer Account Transfer) system need a minimum of five business days to receive securities accounts and 14 days for retirement accounts.

- Before you move, ask about any fees associated with the transfer. Most firms charge a fee per account transferred in addition to charges to liquidate proprietary investments that will not transfer.

- Close out any open orders to buy or sell securities before you submit transfer papers.

Background Check

Investigating your broker? Here's where to start:

- **State securities agency.** Obtain the entire Central Registration Depository (CRD) report, containing the complete employment history and disciplinary actions against all registered representatives. Look for your state agency in the government section of the phone book.

- **National Association of Securities Dealers (NASD).** Here you can get a CRD report for both a firm and a broker. Call (800) 289-9999 or log on to www.nasd.com for investor protection information.

- **National Council of Individual Investors (NCII).** Ask for their booklet, *How to Check out a Broker*, to help you make sense of the CRD report. Send $4 and a self-addressed, stamped envelope to NCII, 1828 L St. NW, #1010, Washington, DC 20036.

To get the most from your financial advisors, treat them with the respect you'd expect in return. Don't call them with questions on paperwork; that's a job for their assistants. If you have a complicated question, consider calling when the stock market is closed; your financial advisor will have more time to devote to you. Most of all, be nice to your financial advisor's staff. They're the ones who do the paperwork that makes your account work. If you plan to dance with bulls, make sure to start out on the right foot.

DAY 45

False Moves

Investment mistakes to avoid

Recently, a new client came in to see me. About to retire, he wanted to be sure he could maintain his lifestyle with his current investments. As he pulled out his retirement plan statement, his whole demeanor changed. "I can't believe I left all this money in a money-market fund for the past six years," he said. "I could have done so much better if only I had invested a little of it in the stock market. I was just so afraid of losing it that I didn't do anything."

Certainly, this investor was justified in his fear of stock market fluctuations. There's always some measure of risk when investing in stocks, and there's a chance you'll lose money. Unfortunately, however, thanks to the bite taken by inflation and taxes, you can also lose purchasing power in money-market funds and other similar investments. Our investor didn't realize his money-market fund was neither insured nor guaranteed by the U.S. government. Further, there's no assurance such a fund will maintain a stable net asset value of $1 per share.

The moral of the story? To retire in the style to which he's accustomed, our investor may be forced to work longer or to invest more aggressively than he might have had he included a partial investment in stocks in his portfolio from the start.

Wouldn't it be nice to learn from someone else's mistakes for a change, or to at least avoid making the same mistakes twice? With that in mind, here are eight of the most common errors made by astute (and some not-so-astute) investors. Tally up how many you've made, and review those sections. If you tick off fewer than two, consider yourself an expert; three to five, you need some help; six to eight, go directly to Day 1! Read on to see how you fare.

1. **Taking stock.** Everyone's heard the one about the stock inherited from Grandma that began as a few measly shares and, through dividend reinvestment (and divine neglect), is now worth hundreds of thousands of dollars. The stock shares are like the Energizer bunny . . . they just keep going and going, and presumably they always will. Or will they?

   Whether you're holding shares of a tobacco company, a soft-drink purveyor or a software developer, if this is the dominant position in your portfolio, consider selling a few of those wonderful shares and diversifying a bit. (Before you do, however, be sure to check with your tax advisor.)

   It's a strange but common phenomenon that the person doing the selling usually values an item at a higher price than the one doing the buying. If you're holding shares of a stock because you can't bear to part with them, consider what might happen if their value was cut in half. If you could still reach your goals without a pause, hold on, but if that idea is making you sick, consider lightening up your position (and review Day 18).

2. **Hot fund, cold fund.** If you're seeking a few good funds and have set your sights on a few of last year's hottest properties, look before you leap. In many cases, last year's top performers will be funds of similar style and market sector, which means they'll probably all move in the same

Healthy Habit

Have too much riding on one stock? Variations on this theme include keeping too much company stock in your 401(k) plan or holding off too long to exercise options. The key to avoiding this mistake is "diversifying to conquer."

direction—not bad if that direction continues to be up, but no fun if things go the other way. That old saying, "past performance is not an indication of future returns," is especially meaningful here, as the performance of investments over time shows a regression toward the mean. In other words, investments that show far superior performance will tend to cool off while less-than-stellar funds may pick up the pace over time. Worse yet, a hot fund could cool off just as you're getting into it.

Instead, consider looking for fund managers with good long-term track records, whose funds are out of favor (and therefore aren't winning any popularity contests). By selecting funds that are out of sync with the current best and brightest, you'll have the chance to get in early on a trend. While every dog has its day (we hope), avoid selling at the wrong time by taking another look at Day 23.

> **Smart Stretch**
>
> Though you may not agree with all his ideas, check out *25 Myths You've Got to Avoid If You Want to Manage Your Money Right* (Simon & Schuster) by Jonathan Clements. Clements breaks open many cherished theories on managing personal finances, and his style will make you alternately cringe and laugh.

3. **Buy low, sell high.** How difficult can that be? For many of us, it's next to impossible. It seems that lots of folks can tell you when to buy a stock (your brother-in-law, your golf buddy, even your broker), but few can tell you when to sell. See if this sounds familiar: You buy shares in a stock you like, and the price begins to rise. It continues to rise until you have a profit of more than 20 percent. You're now faced with a classic dilemma: Do you stay or do you go? Unfortunately, no one has a crystal ball. You may have a pharmaceutical company with the cure for cancer on your hands—or maybe it's just a rash. There's no way to know for sure.

    One possible strategy? When buying, set a target price at which you'd be happy to sell. When your shares get there, re-evaluate your decision. If you'd buy the stock anew at the higher price, there may still be some room left for more appreciation. If you sell, don't look back unless the price falls to a point where you want to pick it up again.

4. **Mistaken identity.** If you lean toward value investing, one of the things you look for is a low P/E ratio—but it may not make sense to find those stocks whose P/Es are at their lowest historical level. Such

There are several ways to consolidate IRA accounts. Rollovers, allowed once per year, entail taking receipt of the funds and transferring them to another institution within 60 days. This method of consolidation generates a notice to the IRS, so be sure that you keep your paperwork in order; you'll need it if questioned.

With a direct transfer from one custodian to another, assets never touch human hands (at least not yours), and the IRS does't usually receive a notice. Make your life easier and let your new custodian's fingers do the walking.

stocks may have sunk for a reason, and they may be slow in returning to health. Instead, consider stocks with P/Es that are low relative to companies in the same industry, but that have had positive earnings surprises in recent quarters. These stocks are more likely to rebound and make money than those that are really in the bargain basement. For a review, check out Day 16.

The same goes for evaluating a mutual fund. While the names of some funds suggest that they are value types, they may be investing in many momentum stocks (anyone whose fund performed well in 1998, for example, had a large dose of technology stocks in them, no matter what they were called). Check the fund's annual report to be sure it provides the style you seek.

5. **I want my stock TV.** What's the first thing you do in the morning? If you switch on CNBC, get your fix of *The Wall Street Journal* or check your stocks on the Internet before you pour your coffee, you might be obsessing over the stock market. It's true such diligence could lead to profits, but it could also lead to needless worry, panic, and way too much trading. It's important to pay attention, but it's bad to be too anxious.

Worse still is letting those talking heads go to your head. By the time you've heard it on the national news, you're hardly the first to act. A lot of financial information is just that—information. Interpreting that information is what separates winners form losers. Unless you're a very experienced trader or plan to make trading your full-time occupation, resist the temptation to day trade. This isn't investing; it's gambling. And while it may be an avocation for some, it can become a dangerous addiction for others.

6. **Where do you want to go today . . . and tomorrow?** If Bill Gates hadn't known where he wanted to go, he probably would have ended up somewhere else. The same goes for your portfolio. If you're saving for a goal that's five, 10 or 20 years away, your reactions to the market's fluctuations will likely be different from those of someone whose focus is on speculation and short-term gains. If the lofty levels of stocks have you spooked, consider dollar-cost averaging into investments you'd like to own. By making smaller purchases on a consistent schedule, you could be in a better position to take advantage of the market's fluctuations without a lot of headaches (see Day 36).

At the same time, avoid an all-too-common mistake: ignoring your IRAs. Many investors pay too little attention to these beautiful accounts. Some people scatter them about, earning a meager interest rate because the bank or brokerage firm had an offer that was too good to pass up at the time. That toaster you got is probably obsolete, but so might be the IRA that came with it. Consider consolidating these accounts and making them a vital part of your financial fitness program (review Days 39 and 40).

7. **Ain't nothin' like the real thing.** Despite what the pundits say, average annual returns of 20 percent are not an inalienable right. The past several years have proved to be remarkable, but that doesn't mean the bull will run forever. It also doesn't necessarily mean the market will crash and the Dow will return to 6000 either. To paraphrase Yogi Berra: Investing is 90 percent mental—the other half is monetary. Babe Ruth had one of the finest batting averages in history, and even he struck out sometimes. So if you expect your portfolio to swing for the fences every year, you'll probably end up demoted to the minor leagues.

Give your portfolio a break by periodically rebalancing your assets (see the workbook exercise for Day 35 for help). This forces you to prune positions that have performed well and add to positions that have stagnated. The key here is to keep your percentages the same.

8. **Where's your advice coming from?** While a stockbroker may have an insurance license and an insurance agent may be fluent in mutual fund lingo, these areas are too complicated

> **Money Missteps**
>
> Got a hot tip from a voice on the radio? A talking head on TV? A nom de plume on the Internet? Be wary of "expert advice" and "inside tips" from these sources. Just because it's financial advice doesn't mean it's appropriate for everyone.

and change too quickly for anyone to be an expert in both. Think of it this way: If you broke your arm, would you call the veterinarian? While he could probably set your limb, your fur may never grow quite the same way. By acting as a consultant, your financial advisor can help you reach your goals more efficiently and with a lot fewer mistakes than a specialist.

That goes for investment newsletters as well. While some provide substantial expert advice, others are worth less than the paper they're written on. Check a writer's track record (see Day 43) before "subscribing" to their ideas.

Glossary

Accelerated benefit: A rider that allows a terminally ill person to cash in a policy before he or she dies and collect up to 95 percent of the policy's face value.

Accumulation fund: The savings component of a universal life insurance policy. The money in the fund earns interest and goes to pay the higher cost of the mortality charge as you age.

Addendum: Any addition to, or modification of, a contract; also called an amendment or rider.

Adjusted gross income (AGI): The income on which a person pays income tax; this amount is determined by subtracting out deductions such as deductible IRA contributions, unreimbursed business expenses, etc.

Adjustable-rate mortgage (ARM): A type of loan whose prevailing interest rate is tied to an economic index (like one-year Treasury bills) that fluctuates with the market. ARMs can adjust at varying rates, including every one, three and five years. ARMs are considered far riskier than fixed-rate mortgages, but their starting interest rates are extremely low.

Asset allocation: The process of determining what percentage of your investment portfolio should be placed in particular types of investments based on your risk tolerance, financial objectives and time frame.

Beta: A measure of risk based on a stock or mutual fund's fluctuations; a beta of more than one means the security is more volatile than the market.

Bear market: A period of falling securities prices. A bear market in stocks is usually brought on by the potential of declining economic activity; a bear market in bonds is caused by the anticipation of rising interest rates; the opposite of a bull market.

Beneficiary: The recipient of the proceeds of an investment vehicle; a beneficiary can be a person, company or organization.

Blue chip: A solid stock of a well-known company with a reputation for consistent earnings despite market fluctuations whose record is expected to continue.

Bond: A loan to a government (federal or municipal) or a corporation. You earn interest on your money as well as a promise to get your principal back.

Bond fund: A shorthand way of talking about a mutual fund made up of bond issues.

Book-entry: Applies to securities not represented by a certificate; a record of ownership of this type of security is on a customer's account only; especially common in the case of municipal bonds; also called "certificateless."

Bull market: A period of rising securities prices. In general, a "bull" is a person who is optimistic about the future, so you can be bullish about an individual stock, a market sector or about the economy as a whole.

Capital gain: The difference between what you paid for something and what you received when you sold it. Tax is payable on this net amount when the item is sold.

Cash value: The amount available in cash upon voluntary termination of a policy by its owner before it becomes payable by death or maturity. This amount is typically paid in cash or paid-up insurance.

Cash value policy: A category of life insurance including whole life, universal life and variable universal life that combines a death benefit with a savings component.

Common stock: A share of ownership in a company.

Compound interest: Interest figured on principal and interest earned during the preceding period; interest may be compounded daily, weekly, monthly, semiannually or annually.

Confirmation: The notice from the brokerage firm to the client that a security has been purchased; confirms the date, price, sales charge, and other information about the purchase or sale of securities.

Consumer price index (CPI): A measure of the relative cost of living for a family of four compared with a base year; considered an indication of the rate of inflation.

Convertible bond: A bond that can be converted into shares of stock.

Corporate bond: A bond issued by a corporation.

Correction: The reversal of the movement of a stock, bond, commodity or index of stocks, usually in the downward direction.

Coupon: The interest rate payable on a bond.

Crummey Letter: A written notification to the beneficiaries of an irrevocable life insurance trust that a gift has been received on their behalf. When the beneficiaries have declared the gift, it can be used to purchase insurance on the grantor's life.

Current yield: The coupon interest rate divided by the bond's price. This fluctuates based on where interest rates are and what you could currently sell your bond for in the marketplace.

Custodial account: An account that a parent or guardian sets up for a minor.

Debt service: The total amount of debt that an individual is carrying at one time.

Deferred compensation plan: Employees put a limited portion of their pretax earnings into this plan, such as a 401(k) plan. The earnings are excluded from taxes and grow tax free until the funds are withdrawn at retirement.

Dependent: An individual for whom the taxpayer provides more than half of his or her support for a calendar year.

Discount: Newly issued bonds typically sell at a discount; for example, a bond with a face value of $1,000 that sells for $925 has a $75 discount.

Diversification: Dividing assets among different investments to reduce risk.

Dividend: The portion of net earnings paid to stockholders by a corporation; may be fixed (as in preferred securities) or variable (as in common stock).

Dog: Slang term for a security whose price is expected to lag the market; also known as a "turkey."

Dow Jones industrial average (DJIA): A weighted average of the stocks of 30 companies; considered a market bellwether.

Earned income: Salary, wages and self-employment income; dividends and interest are not earned income.

Equity: Another word for "stock."

401(k) plan: A defined-contribution plan for employees.

Fiduciary duty: A relationship of trust between a broker and a seller or a broker and a buyer.

Growth stock: The stock of a company focusing on growing above all else. All profits are typically reinvested into the company to keep it growing quickly, so little if any dividends are paid.

Hard-asset funds: A mutual fund that holds a portion of its assets in commodities like gold or silver or in indices that are based on hard assets.

Income-replacement policy: A category of private disability insurance that covers the difference between what you earned prior to the disability and what you now earn doing a different job.

Income stock: The stock of a company that tends to pay out more of its profits to shareholders (in the form of dividends) and put less resources toward growth.

Index funds: Mutual funds designed to mimic the movements of a particular index. For example, a fund trying to mimic the movement of the S&P 500 will either purchase every stock in the S&P 500 in the same ratio that those stocks appear in the index, or will purchase a representative sample of companies that closely approximates the index. Since index funds rarely change their holdings, they are relatively cheap to hold.

Inflation: An increase in the price of goods and services.

Individual retirement account (IRA): a personal, tax-deferred retirement account that individuals with earned income can contribute to annually, within certain limitations.

Interest: Money charged for the use of borrowed funds.

Interest-rate cap: The total number of percentage points that an adjustable-rate mortgage (ARM) might rise over the life of the loan.

Letter of intent: A formal statement, usually in letter form, from the buyer to the seller, stating that the buyer intends to purchase a specific piece of property for a specific price on a specific date.

Liquidity: The ability to convert assets into cash without significant loss.

Limit order: An order to buy or sell a security at a particular price or better; can only be executed within certain parameters.

Load: A sales charge that can range from 1 percent to 7 percent. It might be a front load (payable when you buy into a fund) or a back load (payable when you cash out). You typically pay this because you want the service of a financial professional selecting and building your portfolio. Your load may decrease the longer you hold the fund.

Loan origination fee: A onetime fee charged by a mortgage company to arrange the financing for a loan.

Market price: The price your bond is worth in the current market. On any given day, your bond will be worth more or less than the face value. That's because the bond market is always active, with traders bidding up and down the value of bonds based on the day's current interest rate. When interest rates rise, bonds are worth less (because it takes a smaller amount of capital to earn the same amount of interest). When interest rates fall, bonds are worth more (because it takes a greater amount of money to earn the same amount of interest).

Market sector: The categorizing of companies based on the industry in which they operate.

Matured bond: A bond that has been paid back in full.

Municipal bond: A bond offered by a local municipality; munis, as they are commonly known, are not taxed by the federal government.

Net asset value (NAV): In mutual funds, the value of one share, also known as the "bid price," calculated at the end of the day; those selling shares of a fund receive this price. In no-load funds, the bid, ask and NAV are the same; load funds offer shares at NAV plus a sales charge.

New York Stock Exchange (NYSE): The oldest and largest stock exchange in the United States (1792); also known as "the Big Board" and "the exchange."

Nikkei Stock Index: An index of 225 stocks trading on the Tokyo Stock Exchange.

No load: Funds that charge no fees to buy in or cash out; there are other charges, however. (Check the *OER* to see how much you're being charged.)

Operating expense ratio (OER): Also known as the expense ratio, the OER is the cost of administering and managing a mutual fund.

Origination fee: Fee charged by the lender for allowing you to borrow money or purchase property; also referred to as points, it is usually expressed as a percentage of the total loan amount.

Over the counter (OTC): A security that is not listed and traded on an organized exchange such as the NYSE; OTC stocks are usually those of smaller companies. Symbols for these stocks are usually more than three letters. Exceptions to the smaller-company rule include Microsoft and Cisco Systems, both of which are traded OTC.

Par: The bond's face value; a $1,000 bond will have a par value of $1,000. Par also refers to 100, as in 100 percent of a bond's value. So you may hear that your bond costs 95, which means 95 percent of par. That means you'll get a 5 percent discount and pay $950 for every bond with a $1,000 face value. If the bond costs 116, that means it's 116 percent of par, or it costs you $1,160 for a bond with a face value of $1,000.

Partial disability coverage: A benefit sometimes found in disability income policies providing for the payment of reduced monthly income in the event the insured cannot work full time.

PITI: An acronym for principal, interest, taxes and insurance; these are generally the four parts of your monthly mortgage payment.

Point: *Stocks:* a change of $1 in share price.
  Bonds: a change of 1 percent of face value.
  Real estate: 1 percent of the total principal amount of a loan.

Portfolio: The total assets held by an investor.

Preferred stock: A special class of stock that may have certain voting privileges; companies typically pay a fixed, high dividend whose return is similar to what you'd get on a bond.

Prepayment penalty: A fine imposed when a loan is paid off before it comes due.

Price-to-earnings (P/E) ratio: The price of a stock divided by its earnings per share; gives investors an idea of what they are paying for the company's earning power. The higher the P/E, the more they are paying, thus the more earnings are expected; also known as the "multiple."

Pretax return: The return on an investment before the tax situation of the investor is considered.

Principal: In a home loan, the principal is the amount of money you borrow. When buying a bond, the principal is the amount you're lending. If you buy a bond with a $1,000 face value, your principal is $1,000.

Rider: An addendum to an insurance contract that provides specific coverage for an additional fee.

Roth IRA: A retirement account that allows nondeductible, after-tax contributions of up to $2,000 per year. If you meet certain requirements, the gains are tax free. You are not required to make a minimum contribution each year, and there is no age limit for additional contributions.

Round lot: 100 shares of a stock; $25,000 face value of a bond.

Savings bonds: Backed by the U.S. government, savings bonds (which come in different series like EE and HH) can be purchased in small amounts, either from a bank, the Treasury Department, or through a broker.

Standard & Poor's Composite Index of 500 stocks: A measurement of changes in the prices of a group of 500 widely held common stocks; also known as the "S&P 500."

Security: An instrument that signifies ownership in a corporation (stock), a creditor relationship with a corporation or governmental body (bond), or the right to such relationship (option).

Settlement: When a customer completes a securities trade by either paying for it (when buying) or providing the shares (when selling); stock transactions must be settled in three business days, called a "regular way settlement."

Tax deferred: An investment on which income tax is payable only when withdrawals are made; tax-deferred asset classes include annuities, traditional IRAs, 401(k) and 403(b) plans, etc.

Tax shelter: Investments entered into for the sole purpose of lowering your tax burden.

Taxable income: Your gross earnings minus deductions and exclusions.

Term bonds: Short-term bonds run up to three years in length; intermediate bonds run from three to 10 years; long-term bonds run up to 30 years.

Total return: Capital gain plus dividends earned from an investment.

Transaction fees: The costs mutual funds incur when they buy and sell shares of stock on the open market.

Transfer agent: The corporation, usually a commercial bank, that oversees and maintains the records of fund, stock or bond owners and that is responsible for issuing certificates and resolving problems that arise from lost, stolen or destroyed certificates.

Treasury Bills (T-Bills): Government-backed securities with a minimum purchase price of $1,000; they are offered in three-, six- and 12-month terms.

Trust: A form of property ownership in which legal title to assets is held by someone (trustee) for the benefit of someone else (beneficiary).

12b-1 fees: A mutual fund's marketing expenses.

Universal life insurance: A flexible premium life insurance policy under which the policyholder may change the death benefit, vary the amount or timing of premium payments, and choose the investment vehicle for his or her premiums.

Variable interest rate: An interest rate that rises and falls according to a particular economic indicator such as Treasury bills.

Wrap accounts: Your broker might offer to wrap your mutual funds in with other investments you own and manage all of it for a 1 percent to 3 percent wrap account fee. Another wrap account is a mutual fund that has no upfront load but charges a fixed percentage of assets each year to cover the costs of commission, management and expenses.

Yield: The dividends or interest paid by a company on its stock as expressed as a percentage of its current price.

Yield to maturity: If you hold your bond until it matures and reinvest every interest payment at the interest rate on your bond, you would end up with your yield to maturity. If you spend your interest payments or reinvest them at a lower interest rate, your yield to maturity will be lower; if you invest them at a higher rate, your yield to maturity will be higher.

Zero-coupon bonds: Bonds that pay no interest throughout the bond term.

Mental

Gymnastics

Workbook

Day 1

What comes to mind when you say the words "If only I had enough money, I would . . ."? Use these lines (and any other pages you'd like to add) to list your dreams in unedited fashion. Be as specific as possible, painting a picture of the goal you have in mind. No erasures, no editing, and no help from the peanut gallery, please.

Day 1

Now take a look at your list from the previous page—what pops out at you first? What makes your pulse quicken, makes you chuckle, makes you feel like a kid again? Put your goals in order according to how they make you feel, placing the ones that will make you most happy at the top (that doesn't mean they are the most realistic—they just give you the biggest charge).

Day 1

Go over your list one more time. Categorize your dreams into short-, intermediate- or long-term goals; estimate what they will cost; decide by what date you want to achieve them and what steps you will do monthly to obtain them.

Short-Term Goal	What It Costs	Needed— By Date	Monthly Savings Required
1.			
2.			
3.			
4.			
5.			
6.			
7.			
8.			
9.			
10.			
Intermediate-Term Goal	**What It Costs**	**Needed— By Date**	**Monthly Savings Required**
1.			
2.			
3.			
4.			
5.			
6.			
7.			
8.			
9.			
10.			

Continued on next page

Continued from previous page

Long-Term Goal	What It Costs	Needed— By Date	Monthly Savings Required
1.			
2.			
3.			
4.			
5.			
6.			
7.			
8.			
9.			
10.			

Day 2

Work Sheet 1

Where do your dollars go? Keep track of them for several weeks with the following chart to get a handle on "where your money's at."

Monday	Tuesday	Wednesday	Thursday	Friday	Saturday	
						Cost
						Description
						Cost
						Description
						Cost
						Description
						Cost
						Description
						Cost
						Description
						Cost
						Description
						Cost
						Description
						Cost
						Description
						Cost
						Description
						Cost
						Description
						Cost
						Description
						Cost
						Description
						Cost
						Description
						Cost
						Description
						Cost
						Description
						Cost
						Description
						Cost
						Description
						Cost
						Description
Total	Total	Total	Total	Total	Total	Grand Total

Day 2

After looking over your week's expenses, list some steps you can take to get your savings plan started.

Where Can I Cut Back?	What Cheaper Alternatives Can I Find?

Day 2

Work Sheet 3

Things I Would Like To Have But Don't Need

Item	Store Seen At	Month Will Go On Sale	Do I Have Actual $ To Buy It?	Original Price	Price Paid	$$$ Saved	1/2 of $$$ Saved Into Account

Day 2

Income			Outgo		
Source	$$$/month	X 12	Description	$$$/month	X 12
Bonds			Association dues		
CDs			Auto maintenance		
Checking			Car payment		
Her paycheck			Charity		
His paycheck			Child care		
Life insurance			Clothing		
Money market funds			Commuting		
Mutual funds			Dining out		
Rental property			Dry cleaning		
Retirement account			Education		
Savings			Food		
Stocks			Gasoline		
T-bills			Gifts		
			Health care		
			Hobbies		
			Home maintenance		
			Housekeeping		
			Insurance		
			Personal debt		
			Property tax		
			Recreation		
			Rent or mortgage		
			Subscriptions		
			Utilities		
			Vacation		
			Other		
			Other		
Total:			Total:		

Go back to the "Where Can I Cut Back" chart. What can you add to it now that you see where your pennies are going?

Day 3

Quick . . . before you lose your resolve, jot down the locations of your precious papers and records on today's handy-dandy work sheet. Can't think of all your important records? Maybe our categories will jog your memory.

Item	Contact/Location*	Phone
Bank accounts/ account # (savings, checking, etc.)		
Credit cards/ account # (include loan agreements)		
Securities (stocks/ bonds/mutual funds/ unit investment trusts/etc.)		
Employee retirement plan (Pension/401(k)/profit sharing/etc.)		
Other retirement plans (Keoghs/SEPs/IRAs/ annuities)		
Will and trust documents		
Tax returns and backup materials		
Canceled checks		
Copies of credit cards		
Safe deposit box		
Insurance policies		

*Name of financial institution

Day 4

Take a few minutes to figure your net worth. Once you figure out your current financial position, you have a tool to measure your progress toward your financial goals. Don't worry—no one will see your answers, so be honest. Remember to put down your assets in terms of their current value, not what you paid for them.

Your Net Worth As Of _____

ASSETS

Cash Equivalents

Checking accounts	$ _____
Savings accounts	_____
Money market accounts	_____
Money market fund accounts	_____
CDs	_____
Treasury bills	_____
Cash value of life insurance	_____
Total	$ _____

Investments

Stocks	_____
Bonds	_____
Mutual fund investments	_____
Partnership interests	_____
Other investments	_____
Total	$ _____

Retirement Funds

Pension (present lump-sum value)	_____
IRAs and Keogh accounts	_____
Employee savings plans (e.g., 401(k), SEP, ESOP)	_____
Total	$ _____

Continued on next page

Continued from previous page

Personal Investments

Principal residence $ _____

Second residence   _____

Collectibles/art/antiques   _____

Automobiles   _____

Home furnishings   _____

Furs and jewelry   _____

Other assets   _____

       Total $ _____

       TOTAL ASSETS $ _____

LIABILITIES

Charge account balances $ _____

Personal loans   _____

Student loans   _____

Auto loans   _____

401(k) loans   _____

Investment loans (margin, real estate, etc.)   _____

Home mortgages   _____

Home equity loans   _____

Alimony   _____

Child support   _____

Life insurance policy loans   _____

Projected income-tax liability   _____

Other liabilities   _____

       TOTAL LIABILITIES $ (_____)

       NET WORTH $ _____

Day 5

Looking for a mortgage can be exhausting, so save some time and use this form before starting your search. Mortgage calculators are available free at the HSH Web site, www.hsh.com.

STEP ONE

To start, figure out how much money you can borrow.

1. Gross monthly salary $ _____

2. Bonuses, commissions, overtime (previous two years) $ _____

3. Divide line 2 by 24. $ _____

4. Add lines 1 and 3. *This is your total monthly "qualifying" income.* $ _____

5. Estimated monthly property-tax payments and homeowner's insurance on new home (Call local tax assessor's office for property-tax estimate; for homeowner's insurance, use the national average of $35 per month.) $ _____

6. Multiply line 4 by 0.28. $ _____

7. Subtract line 5 from line 6. *This is how much you can afford to pay per month under the "household ratio."* $ _____

8. Multiply line 4 by 0.36. $ _____

9. Monthly debt: credit cards, car loans, student loans, child support/alimony $ _____

10. Subtract lines 5 and 9 from line 8. *This is how much you can afford to pay per month under the "total obligation ratio."* $ _____

11. Compare lines 7 and 10. The lesser amount is the approximate monthly mortgage payment for which you can qualify. To see how big a loan you can get with that payment, use the table on page 300 and enter the amount here. $ _____

Continued on next page

Continued from previous page

STEP TWO

Naturally, the bigger the down payment you make, the more house you can afford. But don't worry. Many lenders will take less than 20 percent.

1. Estimated equity in your current home (today's value minus your mortgage balance; if you're a first-time homebuyer, skip to line 6.) $ _____

2. Repairs needed before selling $ _____

3. Closing costs (these vary widely; multiply selling price by 3 percent for a rough estimate.) $ _____

4. Broker's commission on sale of your current home (ranges from 5 percent to 8 percent of sale price) $ _____

5. Subtract lines 3, 2 and 4 from line 1. $ _____

6. Additional savings you're prepared to put toward your down payment $ _____

7. Add lines 5 and 6. *This is the total amount you have available for a down payment.* $ _____

8. Maximum amount you can borrow, from line 11 in Step One $ _____

9. Divide line 8 by 0.80. *This is how much house you can afford right now, assuming a 20 percent down payment. For a 10 percent down payment, divide line 8 by 0.90. If you're only putting 5 percent down, divide by 0.95.* $ _____

10. Subtract line 8 from line 9. *This is the down payment you'll have to come up with for the house on line 9. If this amount is greater than the amount on line 7, you'll have to find a lender who will let you put less than 20 percent down. If line 10 is less than the amount on line 7, add lines 7 and 8. This is how much you can afford to spend on a house.* $ _____

Continued on next page

Continued from previous page

Match your maximum monthly payment (from Step One) as closely as possible with a dollar amount shown at the bottom of the columns. Then choose a term—15 or 30 years—and the current interest rate. Where those three variables intersect is the amount you can borrow, in thousands. *Note:* If your maximum monthly payment is off the chart—say $3,500—you can still use the table. In this case, simply find the term and interest rate you want at $1,750 per month, and multiply the amount you find by two.

Rate	$750 15 YR	$750 30 YR	$1,000 15 YR	$1,000 30 YR	$1,250 15 YR	$1,250 30 YR	$1,500 15 YR	$1,500 30 YR	$1,750 15 YR	$1,750 30 YR	$2,000 15 YR	$2,000 30 YR	$2,250 15 YR	$2,250 30 YR	$2,500 15 YR	$2,500 30 YR	$2,750 15 YR	$2,750 30 YR	$3,000 15 YR	$3,000 30 YR
5.00	89	125	119	167	148	208	178	250	207	292	237	334	267	375	296	417	326	458	355	500
5.25	89	125	119	167	148	208	178	250	207	292	237	334	267	375	296	417	326	458	355	500
5.50	89	125	119	167	148	208	178	250	207	292	237	334	267	375	296	417	326	458	355	500
5.75	87	122	117	162	146	203	175	244	204	284	233	325	262	365	291	406	321	447	350	487
6.00	89	125	119	167	148	208	178	250	207	292	237	334	267	375	296	417	326	458	355	500
6.25	87	122	117	162	146	203	175	244	204	284	233	325	262	365	291	406	321	447	350	487
6.50	86	119	115	158	143	198	172	237	201	277	230	316	258	356	287	395	315	435	344	475
6.75	85	116	113	154	141	193	170	231	198	270	226	310	254	347	282	385	311	424	339	462
7.00	83	113	111	150	139	188	167	225	195	263	223	301	250	338	278	376	306	413	334	451
7.25	82	110	110	147	137	183	164	220	192	257	219	293	246	330	274	366	301	403	329	440
7.50	81	107	108	143	135	179	162	215	189	250	216	286	243	322	270	358	297	393	324	429
7.75	80	105	106	140	133	174	159	209	186	244	212	279	239	314	266	349	292	384	319	419
8.00	78	102	105	136	131	170	157	204	183	238	209	273	235	307	262	341	288	375	314	409
8.25	77	100	103	133	129	166	155	200	180	233	206	266	232	299	258	333	283	366	309	399
8.50	76	98	102	130	127	163	152	195	178	228	203	260	228	293	254	325	279	358	305	390
8.75	75	95	100	127	125	159	150	191	175	222	200	254	225	286	250	318	275	350	300	381
9.00	74	93	99	124	123	155	148	186	173	217	197	249	222	280	246	311	271	342	296	373
9.25	73	91	97	122	121	152	146	182	170	213	194	243	219	273	243	304	267	334	291	365
9.50	72	89	96	119	119	149	144	178	168	208	192	238	215	268	239	297	263	327	287	357
9.75	71	87	94	116	118	145	141	175	165	204	189	233	212	262	236	291	260	320	283	349
Monthly Payment	**$750**		**$1,000**		**$1,250**		**$1,500**		**$1,750**		**$2,000**		**$2,250**		**$2,500**		**$2,750**		**$3,000**	

Source: HSH Associates

Day 6

Some experts (and lots of TV commercials) suggest that you have *at least* five times your mortgage in life insurance. Whew! Use this work sheet to figure out how much coverage you *really* need.

Determine Your Household Income Shortfall

1. Current Monthly Household Income .... $_____

2. Future Monthly Household Income .... $_____

     Surviving spouse's income .... $_____

     Social Security .... $_____

     Pension (monthly) .... $_____

     Other income .... $_____

3. Household Income Shortfall (line 1 minus line 2) .... $_____

4. Current Monthly Expenses .... $_____

5. Surviving Spouse's Expected Monthly Expenses* .... $_____

     Regular expenses .... $_____

     Retirement .... $_____

     Extras .... $_____

6. Monthly Household Income Shortfall
(line 2 minus line 5) .... $_____

7. Annual Income Shortfall (line 6 times 12) .... $_____

8. Lifetime Shortfall (line 7 times number of years)** .... $_____

Determine Your Total Additional Expenses

9. Survivor's Future Expenses .... $_____

     Additional child care .... $_____

     Debt repayment .... $_____

     Mortgage payoff .... $_____

     College tuition .... $_____

     Emergency fund .... $_____

10. Survivor's Final Expenses .... $_____

Continued on next page

Continued from previous page

11. Total Future and Final Expenses
(line 8 plus line 9 plus line 10)*** $_____

Determine How Much You Have

12. Assets

      Investment portfolio $_____

      Retirement accounts $_____

      Real estate equity
        (current value minus mortgage) $_____

      Life insurance proceeds
        (what the surviving spouse
        would receive today) $_____

      Other assets $_____

    Total Assets $_____

13. Total Amount of Life Insurance Needed
(line 11 minus line 12) $_____

*When you're estimating your expenses after the death of a nonworking spouse, don't decrease your needs if you have young children. You'll probably need full-time help. If your spouse or partner works, keep your monthly expenses about the same if you don't want your standard of living to change.

** "Lifetime Shortfall" is your annual shortfall multiplied by the number of years you'll need the extra income. If you have children, figure these expenses until the youngest graduates from college.

*** Final expenses are funeral expenses—figure a minimum of $5,000, plus about $10,000 to probate an estate of more than $600,000.

Day 6

Use this work sheet to estimate how much income you could expect if you became disabled tomorrow. "Benefit duration" refers to how long you will receive any benefit. Your goal is to be covered by savings until your policy kicks in. Most affordable policies kick in after 90 days. Your "disability income shortfall" is the amount of disability insurance your policy should provide.

From Where	Monthly Amount	Waiting Period	Benefit Duration
Sick leave*	$		
Short-term disability*	$		
Group long-term disability*	$		
Social Security	$		
Other government programs	$		
Investment income	$		
Savings	$		
Spouse's income	$		
Other	$		
Current monthly disability benefits	$		

Current monthly salary $ _____

Current monthly disability benefits
(from the above chart) – $ _____

Disability income shortfall $ _____

*These are disability benefits from an employer. They do not apply to those who are self-employed.

Day 7

If you can answer the questions and match up this tricky column, you've learned a lot about fixed income investments. More than one answer may be correct.

1. Bonds are:
   a. rated by Moody's
   b. debt securities issued by organizations to finance projects
   c. rated by Standard & Poor's
   d. considered most highly rated with a AAA rating

2. You should receive higher interest on a bond:
   a. with a longer maturity
   b. with a lower rating
   c. from a corporation with a low quality rating
   d. with a AAA rating

3. Bonds may be issued by which of the following:
   a. corporations
   b. lions clubs
   c. state, local, and federal governments
   d. foreign governments

4. Coupon _____

5. Interest rates _____

6. Maturity date _____

7. Treasury bonds _____

8. Face/par value _____

9. Collateral trust obligations _____

10. Municipal bonds _____

11. Equipment obligations _____

12. FHLMA _____

13. Debentures _____

14. Treasury bills _____

15. FNMA _____

16. Yield curve _____

17. Mortgage-backed bonds _____

18. GNMA _____

19. Coupon bonds _____

20. Treasury notes _____

Continued on next page

Continued from previous page

a. Backed by the U.S. Government
b. Short-term securities with maturities of one year or less
c. Secured by equipment
d. Secured by real estate
e. Can indicate whether a bond is good deal or not
f. Maturities range one-10 years
g. Interest rate paid by a bond
h. Backed by a government agency
i. Bond prices vary inversely to them
j. Very liquid investments
k. Issued at a discount from face value
l. Secured by stocks and bonds
m. Date when the bond comes due
n. Interest is tax free to state residents
o. Denominations range from $1,000 to $1 million
p. What the bond holder gets when the bond matures
q. Secured by the general credit of the company
r. Issued in the denominations of $10,000
s. Maturities of 10 years or more
t. Plots interest rates vs. time
u. Minimum denomination of $25,000

Day 8

If you can complete today's exercise on stocks, you'll be ready to take on mutual funds tomorrow.

Match the lettered columns with the numbered terms:

1. Income stocks _____
2. Cyclical stocks _____
3. Capital appreciation _____
4. Growth stocks _____

5. Blue-chip stocks _____
6. Defensive stocks _____
7. Dividend _____
8. Seasonal stocks _____

a. Stocks whose sales, earnings and market share are expanding faster than the industry average and general economy

b. Stocks attractive to people seeking immediate income

c. Stocks providing a degree of stability during periods in which the economy is declining

d. A quarterly payment that represents a percentage of the company's earnings

e. The difference between purchase price and current market value

f. Stocks whose performance fluctuates with the seasons

g. Stocks whose earnings are tied to the business cycle

h. Stocks paying little, if any, dividends

i. High-quality stocks of major companies

j. Stocks providing necessary services, essential goods or staples

k. Stocks with long, unbroken records of earnings and dividend payments

Circle all those that are correct:

9. Which of the following are mistakes made in stock market investing?
   a. Selecting securities that are inconsistent with your objectives

   b. Taking profits too soon

   c. Buying a stock based on a tip alone

   d. Adjusting to changing market cycles

   e. Minimizing losses promptly

   f. Purchasing too many securities

   g. Establishing clear objectives

   h. Following a disciplined approach

Continued on next page

Continued from previous page

i. Investigating the merits of a stock before buying

j. Purchasing too few securities

k. Fully exploring alternative investments

10. What are the right things to do? (Hint: What's left?) Write the answers here:

Day 9

There's a lot to learn about mutual funds, and after today's chapter, you should have a handle on the basics. Test your recall by placing the following letters in the proper column. Some letters go in more than one column.

a. Strive for maximum capital appreciation

b. Invest in large, well-established companies, a.k.a. blue-chip funds

c. Risks they are subjected to include currency fluctuation and social and political changes abroad

d. Their share prices move in the opposite direction of interest rates

e. Can invest in well-established markets in Europe

f. Seek high current income

g. Dividends accrued daily, often credited monthly

h. Focus on investing in a particular section of the market

i. Invest in a mixture of different types of bonds or invest in a single category of bonds

j. Invest in higher grade securities, hope to give moderate returns and lower risk

k. May use short sales or leverage to achieve the highest possible returns

l. Invest in companies whose price compared to book value is low

m. Seek to have low price volatility

n. Considered by some to be the riskiest of funds

o. Seek long-term appreciation investing in securities that provide dividends and capital gains

p. Share price is more volatile with longer average maturity of the bonds

q. Provide access to markets outside the United States

r. Invest in companies with low prices compared to earnings, paying a relatively high dividend

s. Invest in short-term IOUs from industries and government agencies

t. Provide capital appreciation by investing in companies whose earnings are growing at a rate higher than that of other companies in their industry or higher than that of the stock market as a whole

Continued on next page

Continued from previous page

u. Concentrate on a particular industry

v. Not guaranteed or insured by the U.S. government

w. Manage risk by allocating investments in stocks, bonds and cash

x. Invest in securities that pay dividends and interest

y. Frequent choices for retirement plans

z. Invest in emerging markets

1 Money-Market Funds	2 Income Funds	3 Growth Funds	4 Value Funds	5 Aggressive Growth Funds	6 Balanced Funds	7 Int'l. & Global Funds	8 Total Return Funds	9 Bond Funds	10 Sector Funds

Day 10

Today, you can test your understanding of preferred stocks by working this crossword puzzle.

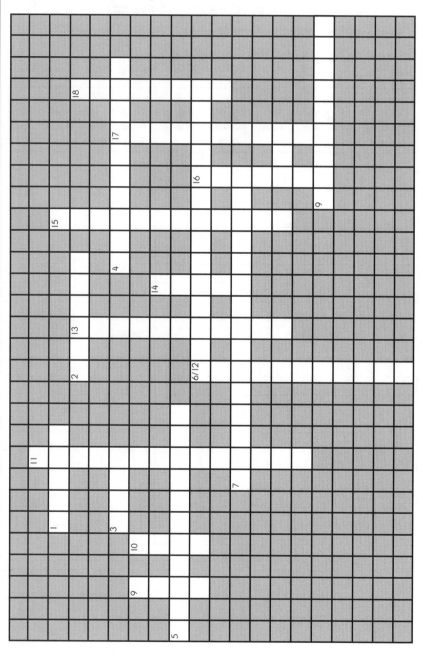

Continued on next page

Continued from previous page

Box-O-Words			
QUIDS	redeem	MIPS	cumulative
convertible	call protection	preferred stocks	inflation
bond	owed	adjustable rate	corporation
debt holders	TOPRS	common stock	cushion
traditional	dividend		

ACROSS

1. The acronym for one of two types of preferred securities that consist of subordinated debentures; _____ stands for quarterly income debt securities.

2. When dealing with callable preferreds, the call date indicates when the issuer can call, or _____ , the shares at a predetermined price.

3. This is the acronym for securities that represent a limited partnership interest in a company that exists solely for the purpose of issuing preferred securities and lending the proceeds of the sales to its parent company; it stands for monthly income preferred securities.

4. _____ preferred stock must pay its shareholders all owed interest before it can resume its dividend payments on common shares.

5. _____ preferreds convert into a set amount of the underlying common stock, at the company's convenience.

6. The time period during which the issuer of callable preferreds cannot redeem their shares is _____.

7. _____ are a cross between a common stock and a bond, paying a set dividend.

8. Many preferreds offer little protection from _____, making them vulnerable to rising interest rates.

DOWN

9. A _____ makes a set interest payment in the same way a preferred stock makes a set dividend payment.

10. Before an issuer can resume dividend payments on common shares, it must first pay all the shareholders of its preferred stock all _____ interest.

11. _____ preferred stock is a type that tries to counteract the effects of inflation.

12. Owning preferred stock represents ownership in a _____ in the same way owning common stock does.

Continued on next page

Continued from previous page

13. If a company's assets are liquidated, _____ are paid first, and then the preferred stockholders.

14. This is an acronym that represents a special-purpose business trust; it is similar to MIPS and QUIPS, except that holders will receive a 1099 at year-end.

15. Preferred stock issues are not traded as widely as _____ issues are.

16. When you purchase higher coupon issues with a larger dividend payments and desire the increased chance your security will be called, you are dealing with _____ preferred stock.

17. Most _____, or standard preferred stocks, are perpetual in their dividend payments and do not have a set maturity as bonds do.

18. Preferred stocks usually pay higher _____ than their common cousins.

Day 14

Have you mastered today's topic? If you can work this crossword and not be puzzled about the properties of stocks, you're on your way!

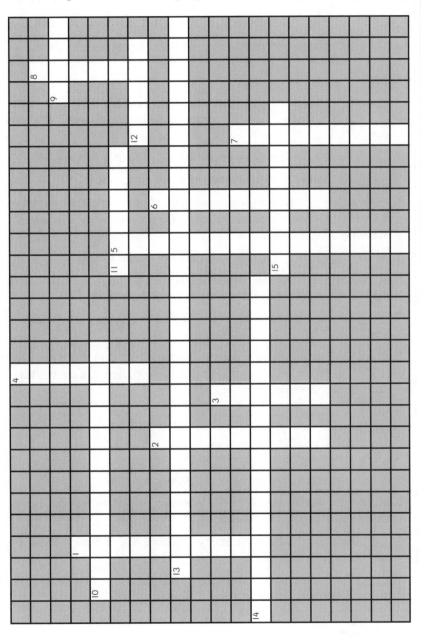

Continued on next page

Continued from previous page

Box-O-Words

management	utilities	growth	reverse
positive	replacing	dividends	buybacks
bull	shareholders	past performance	stock
real estate investment trusts		distribution date	splits

ACROSS

1. Stock splits have seen positive market reaction since they often signal that the company's _____ 15. (across) is feeling _____ about the company's future.

2. _____ usually distribute a large part of their earnings in dividends.

3. _____ companies tend to not distribute any dividends.

4. At times, a _____ split is used by companies whose share price is low to increase the price of a share, yet decrease the number of shares outstanding.

5. Never forget that _____ is no guarantee of future returns.

6. Some companies borrow heavily to buy shares, thus _____ equity with debt, leaving investors with a more leveraged company.

7. _____ are important to investors and the performance of their portfolios.

8. Stock _____ are sometimes seen by investors as a sign that a company's stock is undervalued, often resulting in a rise in the share price after such an announcement.

DOWN

9. _____ markets often mean more splits.

10. Long-term, stock splits are rewards given to longtime _____.

11. Stock _____ are a form of lowly dividend, often increasing a stock's liquidity and dropping the share price.

12. _____ dividends increase the ability of a company to grow if these are a substitute for a cash dividend.

13. _____ distribute almost all their earnings in the form of dividends. (Hint: It's an investment vehicle.)

14. The day the dividend is paid, which may be several weeks after the date of record.

15. See clue above under #1 down.

Day 18

Anyone can tell you when to *buy* a stock, but if you can answer these questions properly, you'll know when to *sell*. Some questions may have more than one answer.

1. Your relationship with the stock market should be a _____ one. (long-term, short-term)

2. The price-to-earnings ratio is a reliable determinant of a stock's value, except in the case of _____ . (utility stocks, cyclical stocks, Internet stocks)

3. _____ seems to be the secret to Internet stocks. (high earnings, momentum)

4. Which of the following are red flags, indicating it may be time to sell your beloved?

   a. Its quarterly earnings are lower than last year's.

   b. Its quarterly earnings are lower than anticipated for two or three consecutive quarters.

   c. The price varies by more than 10 points one trading day to the next.

   d. It receives a negative review in *The Wall Street Journal.*

5. Which of the following are things you can do to help shed light on a changing stock price?

   a. Do a comparison of its earnings with others in the industry and a similar index.

   b. Look at whether the industry is still viable.

   c. Determine whether economic and interest-rate changes or trends may be affecting the company and/or industry positively or negatively.

   d. Check buying and selling patterns of insiders.

6. Some experts counsel: "If you would still buy an equity at today's price, keep it." T/F

7. One strategy that may help evaluate a stock is to decide how long you can wait for its price to increase and then sell it after the deadline has been reached. T/F

Continued on next page

Continued from previous page

8. A good time to buy equities you've always wanted to own is during a market correction. T/F

9. In all cases, you should sell a stock that has appreciated 20 percent. T/F

10. Poor earnings eventually translate into lower stock prices. T/F

11. In the case of employing a _____ order, your stock will sell at an exact price. (stop-loss, sell-limit, stop-limit)

12. It is a good idea, with a _____ order, to set your price at least 10% below the stock's support. (stop-loss, sell-limit, stop-limit)

13. You may miss the chance to sell your stock if the market should open below the price stated in your _____ order. (stop-loss, sell-limit, stop-limit)

14. With a _____ order, your stock will usually sell at the price selected or higher. (stop-loss, sell-limit, stop-limit)

Day 21

Are index funds for you? If you can complete this chart correctly, you'll have learned enough to decide.

```
                              I  __ __ __ __
__ __ __ __ __ __ __ __   N  __ __ __ __ __
              __ __ __  D  __ __ __
                              E  __ __ __ __ __ __ __ __
        __ __ __ __  X

              __ __ __  F  __ __ __ __ __ __ __ __ __ __
              __ __ __  U  __
              __ __  N  __ __ __ __
              __ __  D  __ __ __
__ __ __ __ __  S  __ __ __ __
```

Box-O-Words			
managed	trading	mid-cap	self-fulfilling
index	aggressive	opportunities	
value	efficient	mirror	

1. Index funds either _____ their benchmark index or comprise a group of stocks that are close to the underlying index.

2. Index funds don't offer the _____ for savvy managers to overweight a portfolio in an undervalued sector that will be the next to take off.

3. Investment management fees and _____ costs are generally lower than with actively managed funds.

4. Low portfolio turnover may make index funds more tax _____ than other managed portfolios whose holdings change more frequently.

5. Many people don't realize the S&P 500 _____ fund is capitalization-weighted.

6. The higher the fund mentioned in #5 goes, the more money it attracts, making the fund go even higher and attract even more money—it's a _____ prophecy.

Continued on next page

Continued from previous page

7. Continuing to buy as prices increase is not the mantra of the _____ investor.

8. Because they hold some cash, _____ funds offer, in theory, less volatility than index funds.

9. If someone is only invested in the S&P 500 index fund, they have minimal exposure to small-cap, _____, overseas and bond markets.

10. Even the most _____ investor should have no more than 25 percent allocated to funds that mirror the S&P 500.

Day 22

If you can answer all these questions on fund-evaluation systems correctly, you'll rank at the head of the class. Better yet, you'll be clued in on how to use these valuable sources of information to help you reach your financial goals.

1. According to Lipper Inc., funds should be:
   a. rated
   b. ranked
   c. divided into quartiles
   d. none of the above

2. Fund-ranking systems provide information designed to help investors predict which funds will be the best funds of the future.
   T/F _____

3. Morningstar's star-rating system consists of:
   a. a risk-adjusted return
   b. a return component and a risk component
   c. an in-depth editorial analysis
   d. a quadruple fund bypass

4. A smart fund investor should only buy funds given five stars by Morningstar. T/F _____

5. Morningstar fund information includes:
   a. written fund analysis
   b. performance over time vs. an appropriate index
   c. a style box that shows what style of management the fund follows
   d. all of the above

6. Fund evaluation system information is available:
   a. only in your broker's office
   b. only for a lot of money directly from the fund
   c. on the Internet
   d. at the library
   e. other
   f. c and d

7. Financial advisors can help investors select funds
   a. for a fee
   b. by selling them load funds
   c. for free
   d. to the best of their ability
   e. all of the above

Continued on next page

Continued from previous page

8. After researching a fund, before you buy it, you should:
   a. call your broker and ask if his or her firm owns it
   b. read the prospectus
   c. ask your rich uncle what he thinks
   d. close your eyes and send a check

9. A fund with a high standard deviation means that annual returns will likely:
   a. be very consistent
   b. vary considerably
   c. returns are not affected by standard deviation
   d. it doesn't matter because funds are a long-term investment

10. The Sharpe ratio calculates the level of performance a fund provides vs. its:
    a. sales charge
    b. expense ratio
    c. level of risk
    d. number of stars

11. A higher Sharpe ratio means that a fund delivers _____ (more/less) performance for its level of risk.

Day 23

You've learned when to sell a stock. If you can master today's exercises, you'll have a good idea when to jettison that losing fund as well.

1 Expenses Are Rising	2 Change In Management	3 Performance Decreases	4 Change In Your Objective

Which follow-up questions belong to which potential red flag? Place the letters in the appropriate columns; some may go more than one place.

   a. When compared to similar indexes, how does your fund fare?
   b. Does the new manager have a similar style?
   c. Are more investors selling out than buying in?
   d. Is your fund at the bottom or consistently lagging when compared to funds in the same market sector with a similar style?
   e. Have your investment needs changed since you began investing in the fund?
   f. Is the fund advised by an investment team?
   g. Are sales and management charges increasing or excessive?
   h. Is the size of the fund, its asset base, dwindling?
   i. Have you added something similar to your portfolio that may replace your current fund?

What have you learned? Are these statements true or false?

5. Mutual funds should not be judged on short-term performance. T/F _____

6. A hot fund always handles a huge influx of cash from new investors well. T/F _____

7. Sector funds have more investment choices than a typical growth and income fund. T/F _____

8. A fund's prospectus contains complete information on the investment. T/F _____

9. Annual and quarterly reports will indicate the departure of a fund's manager. T/F _____

10. Reallocating your assets periodically is sure to wreak havoc on your portfolio. T/F _____

11. Bond funds are the best long-term vehicle to save for far-off objectives. T/F _____

12. Be patient waiting for a fund with declining assets to turn around. T/F _____

Day 26

If you're considering taking your portfolio abroad, think of today's exercise as a way to "get your shots" before you leave. If you can answer all of them correctly, your passport will be waiting!

1. Equity markets outside the United States have _____ (grown/shrunk) over the past 25 years.

2. Studies have shown that over time, investing in markets outside the United States can be:
   a. illegal
   b. lucrative
   c. impossible if you don't speak the language
   d. difficult

3. International mutual funds invest in securities of governments and companies outside the United States only. T/F

4. Global investments include some exposure to U.S. markets. T/F

5. American companies that have significant presence abroad are called:
   a. multinational
   b. co-educational
   c. foreign
   d. cross-investing

6. The riskiest foreign investments are considered those made in:
   a. the new Europe
   b. emerging markets
   c. Scandinavian countries
   d. those that are not made at all

7. Individual shares can be purchased in foreign companies:
   a. through their respective stock markets
   b. through ADRs
   c. through mutual funds
   d. American investors cannot invest directly in foreign shares
   e. a and b

8. ADRs are available in a variety of forms, including:
   a. common stock
   b. preferred stock
   c. convertible securities
   d. all of the above

9. American investors cannot invest in the bonds of foreign corporations or governments. T/F

10. Multi-asset funds are those that allocate money to both stocks and bonds. T/F

Continued on next page

Continued from previous page

Match the following terms with their most appropriate definitions:

11. American depository receipts   15. portfolio diversification

12. market risk   16. currency risk

13. interest rate risk   17. differences in accounting practices

14. political and economic risk

        a. _____ risk associated with international investing

        b. _____ risk associated with any kind of investing

        c. _____ represent shares of foreign companies

        d. _____ benefit of international investing

Day 27

Looking to land some real estate for your portfolio? If you can match these attributes with the correct asset class, you're ready to move. Some attributes belong to more than one asset class.

a. High dividends

b. Apartment complexes

c. Liquid investments

d. Illiquid investments

e. Shopping centers

f. Oil and gas properties

g. Low dividends

h. Momentum investments

1. _____ Utility stocks

2. _____ REITs

3. _____ Limited partnerships

4. _____ Technology stocks

Whew! Now some specific questions on REITs. Circle the correct answers:

5. REITS can invest in:
   a. animal hospitals
   b. massage parlors
   c. casinos
   d. lemonade stands

6. Unlike other types of real estate investments, REITs:
   a. require a small investment
   b. require a real estate agent
   c. must be closed before January 1 of the year in which you retire
   d. provide a guaranteed income stream

7. Unlike limited partnerships, REITs:
   a. trade like stocks
   b. are debt financing
   c. are illiquid
   d. distribute K-1 forms

True or false?

8. The best thing about REITs is their tax advantage. T/F

9. REITs are examples of equity financing. T/F

10. REITs are considered by some to be in a different asset category than stocks. T/F

Day 28

Are you interested in socially conscious investing? If you can complete today's crossword, you'll have mastered some important aspects of this approach.

Box-O-Words			
tax deduction	restrictive	jury	fewer
positive	on	criteria	good
negative	return	interpretation	environment
labor			

Continued on next page

Continued from previous page

DOWN

1. You can always donate to your favorite charitable organization and get a _____.

2. Avoid becoming too _____ so that you will be able to reach your social *and* financial goals.

3. Given the short track record of socially conscious mutual funds, one should note that the _____ is still out.

4. Companies that treat their employees well, don't pollute the environment, or produce products and services that better the lives of their customers face _____ regulatory problems, lawsuits and strikes.

5. A _____ screen helps build a portfolio by looking for companies with above-average records in a particular area.

6. In most cases, the opposite of "off" is _____.

ACROSS

7. Define your own personal _____ to be able to build a portfolio as you like it.

8. Increasingly, investors are choosing investments that make them feel _____ as well as those that make them money.

9. A _____ screen helps build a portfolio by avoiding particular companies or industries.

10. Some choose to look only at the best possible _____ for their investments without regard to their investments' social consequences.

11. What an investor considers socially responsible or irresponsible is subject to _____.

12. & 13. These are two of the hottest issues to emerge in the field of social investing.

Day 29

Now that you've learned *how* to save for your children's education, here's how to figure out *what* you'll need to save:

How Much You Can Expect In Total College Bills

1. Expected cost for four years. Check Table A on page 330 for an estimate of four-year college costs, including tuition, room and board, books and other expenses. Separate projections are supplied for public, private and elite colleges. For more than one child, add the appropriate amount for each child. $_____

How Much You Can Afford To Save

2. Enter your current monthly income after taxes. $_____

3. Retirement-account savings per month. This should be the maximum allowed by the IRS, not necessarily the amount you are currently saving. For each adult in the household using IRAs only, enter $283. For each adult with a 401(k), enter 7 percent of the amount on line 2 or $554, whichever is less. Those with Keogh, SEP or other retirement plans should enter only the after-tax cost of their maximum contributions. (To estimate after-tax cost, multiply the maximum by 0.7.) $_____

4. Subtract line 3 from line 2. $_____

5. Household expenses on a monthly basis. (Remember to include all insurance, food, clothing, car payments, loan and credit card payments, medical costs, travel, entertainment and so on.) $_____

6. Subtract line 5 from line 4. This is the maximum you can save for tuition per month. $_____

How Much Your Savings Will Grow

7. Multiply the amount on line 6 by the Monthly Savings Factor in Table B on page 331 that corresponds to your child. This is how much your future tuition savings, plus the after-tax investment returns, will be worth when your child reaches college age. The table assumes that you invest your savings and that you increase the amount of your monthly savings by 5 percent per year. If you are saving

Continued on next page

Continued from previous page

for more than one child, divide line 6 by your number of children. Then multiply each portion by the appropriate figure from Table B. Keep the results for each child separate. (If you want to see how much in monthly savings is necessary to cover all your tuition goals, divide line 1 by the corresponding Monthly Savings Factor.) $_____

8. Existing tuition savings. Reduce what you've set aside by whatever taxes you would owe if you sold the investments today. Enter the result here. $_____

9. Multiply the amount on line 8 by the appropriate figure in the third column in Table B. This estimates how much your existing savings will compound, on an after-tax basis, by the time your child reaches college, assuming you follow our investment plan. If you have more than one child, divide the amount on line 8 by your number of children and multiply each portion by the appropriate factor from Table B. Keep the results separate. $_____

10. Total estimated tuition savings. Add line 7 and line 9. Keep each child's figures separate. $_____

How Much You Can Expect In Financial Aid

11. Enter the value of your current assets—cash, stocks, bonds, mutual funds and real estate—excluding your home equity and retirement-account savings. (If you plan to send your children to a private or elite college, add your home equity back in.) $_____

12. Divide line 7 by the amount in the Present-Value Divisor column in Table B that corresponds to your child. For more than one child, use the appropriate divisor for each child. Then add the results for all children. This calculation will put your future savings in today's dollars. $_____

13. Total assets available for tuition. Add the amounts on lines 11 and 12. $_____

14. Percentage paid by financial aid. Refer to Table C on page 332 using the information on line 13 and your family's current pretax income.   _____%

15. Multiply line 14 by 0.01.   _____%

Continued on next page

Continued from previous page

16. Estimated amount of financial aid you can expect based on today's aid standards. (This figure may include government-guaranteed student and parent loans, depending on the type of aid awarded by the school.) Multiply line 1 by line 15. $_____

If you will have two children in college at once:

a. Subtract the amount on line 15 from 1.0. _____%

b. Multiply line a by 0.5. _____%

c. Add line b and line 15. _____%

d. If the children will be in college together all four years, repeat the entry from line c. If they will be together for one year, multiply line c by 0.25; for two years, by 0.5; for three years, by 0.75. _____%

e. If the children will be in college together all four years, enter zero. If they will be together one year, multiply line 15 by 0.75; for two years, by 0.5, for three years, by 0.25. _____%

f. Add line d and line e. _____%

g. Multiply line 1 by line f. Replace line 16 with this amount. $_____

How Much You May Need To Borrow

17. Add the amounts on line 16 and line 10. (Combine any separate figures from line 10.) $_____

18. Subtract line 17 from line 1. This is the estimated amount you may have to borrow (in addition to any loans in your aid package) to pay for four years of college. If the number is negative, it means you're in the clear. $_____

Continued on next page

Continued from previous page

Table A: Four-Year College Costs

Years Until College	Public College*	Private College**	Elite College**
1	$43,561	$90,973	$129,372
2	$45,703	$95,052	$135,356
3	$47,956	$99,317	$141,623
4	$50,326	$103,780	$148,185
5	$52,818	$108,447	$155,057
6	$55,440	$113,330	$162,253
7	$58,198	$118,439	$169,790
8	$61,100	$123,783	$177,683
9	$64,153	$129,374	$185,949
10	$67,366	$135,224	$194,607
11	$70,746	$141,345	$203,675
12	$74,303	$147,750	$213,173
13	$78,047	$154,452	$223,121
14	$81,988	$161,464	$233,542
15	$86,136	$168,803	$244,457
16	$90,502	$176,483	$255,891
17	$95,098	$184,520	$267,868
18	$99,936	$192,931	$280,416

Includes tuition and fees, room and board, and other expenses
*Assumes a 5.5 percent annual increase in tuition and fees, 5.6 percent in room and board and 3 percent for all other expenses.
**Assumes a 5 percent annual increase in tuition and fees, 3.8 percent in room and board, and 3 percent for all other expenses

Source: The College Board

Continued on next page

Continued from previous page

Table B: How Your Savings Will Grow

Years Until College	Monthly Savings Factor*	Existing- Savings Multiplier	Present- Value Divisor
1	12.47	1.04	1.04
2	26.02	1.08	1.04
3	40.77	1.13	1.12
4	56.89	1.17	1.17
5	74.47	1.22	1.22
6	93.78	1.27	1.27
7	115.09	1.33	1.32
8	138.68	1.41	1.37
9	164.74	1.51	1.42
10	193.44	1.61	1.48
11	225.20	1.73	1.54
12	260.04	1.85	1.60
13	298.67	1.97	1.67
14	341.37	2.11	1.73
15	388.45	2.26	1.80
16	440.64	2.42	1.87
17	498.20	2.59	1.95
18	562.23	2.77	2.03

*Assumes you increase your savings by 5 percent per year.

Continued on next page

Continued from previous page

Table C: How Much Will Financial Aid Cover?

Total Family Assets*	Annual Family Pretax Income							
	$30,000		$50,000		$70,000		$90,000	
	Public	Private & Elite	Public	Private & Elite	Public	Private & Elite	Public	Private & Elite
$20,000	87%	94%	45%	74%	0%	45%	0%	16%
$40,000	87%	94%	44%	73%	0%	44%	0%	15%
$60,000	87%	94%	33%	68%	0%	39%	0%	9%
$80,000	87%	94%	21%	63%	0%	33%	0%	4%
$100,000	87%	94%	9%	57%	0%	28%	0%	0%

*Excluding retirement-account savings and home equity. Assumes a family of four, with one child in college.

Source: T. Rowe Price

Source: Smart Money Magazine

Day 32

Prenuptial agreements are all about telling the truth. Can you tell the truth from the falsehoods? Circle the correct answers for today's exercise, and you'll be on your way to knowing your rights.

1. With respect to prenuptial agreements, there are two classes of property: marital and separate. T/F

2. Prenuptial agreements are only for the wealthy. T/F

3. Prenuptial agreements can outline disposition of both property and child custody. T/F

4. Community property states divide property in a fair, but not necessarily equal, way. T/F

5. Equitable distribution states divide property down the middle. T/F

6. In a divorce, most people are concerned about dividing assets, but dividing debt can be as important. T/F

7. If you're a business owner living in a community property state, half your business could go to your spouse. T/F

8. Prenuptial agreements can be written on the way to the altar and still be valid. T/F

9. When writing a prenuptial agreement, the parties involved should disclose the appropriate assets. T/F

10. You should allow your spouse to sign you name on little things, like bills and checks. T/F

11. It's OK to sign a tax return with your spouse:
    a. if you are in agreement about what is in it
    b. no matter what because of the "innocent spouse" defense
    c. when your accountant says to
    d. after the tax deadline

12. Gifts given to a couple before the wedding are considered:
    a. property of the couple
    b. property of the bride
    c. property of the groom
    d. property of the mother-in-law

13. Children from a marriage are:
    a. under the jurisdiction of the court
    b. are divided by a prenuptial agreement
    c. can choose who they like better
    d. are not an issue in divorce

Day 33

After 33 days of working out to the max, you may be really doggin' it. Circle the correct answer to these multiple-choice questions, and you can give your tired dogs a rest:

1. Yield =
    a. price ÷ dividend
    b. price ÷ earnings
    c. dividend ÷ price
    d. none of the above

2. The Dow Dividend Strategy (DDS) is an investment strategy that buys the 10 stocks of the DJIA that have:
    a. the lowest price
    b. the highest dividend
    c. the highest yield
    d. the lowest cost
    e. the highest cash flow

3. The "Low 5" portfolio is a variation on the DDS that invests in:
    a. The five stocks in the Dow with the lowest price
    b. The five stocks in the DDS with the lowest price
    c. The five stocks in the Dow with the lowest yield
    d. The five stocks in the S&P 500 with the highest yield

4. Part of the success of the DDS is due to all of the following *except:*
    a. buying low and selling high
    b. the compounding effect of dividends
    c. a portfolio of large, stable companies
    d. option strategies

    True or false?

6. The DDS can be invested only in January. T/F

7. The DDS is a guaranteed investment. T/F

8. Investors who seek growth and income might want to learn more about the DDS. T/F

9. One way to invest in the DDS is through a unit trust. T/F

10. You need a lot of money to invest in the DDS. T/F

Day 34

What does risk mean to you? After you've completed today's exercises, you should be able to answer that question.

Match the type of risk with its associated manifestation:

1. Market risk _____   a. Rising interest rates

2. Purchasing-power risk _____   b. A company could go bankrupt

3. Liquidity risk _____   c. Increasing inflation

4. Interest-rate risk _____   d. Inability to sell an investment

5. Business risk _____   e. Stock market volatility

6. The older you are, the more:
   a. stocks you should own
   b. mutual funds you should own
   c. you should consider conservative investments
   d. money you should leave to your financial advisor

7. The younger you are, the more:
   a. you should save now
   b. you should spend now while you're making money
   c. you should count on an inheritance
   d. conservative your investments should be

8. When the stock market corrects, you should:
   a. call you broker and threaten to sue him/her
   b. sit tight and remember that you're a long-term investor
   c. sell everything and get out before there's nothing left
   d. none of the above

Day 35

Based on your current financial situation, risk tolerance and time frame, the following work sheet will help you create a strategy to allocate your assets to meet your investment needs.

Investment Type

1. Is your investment for retirement?
   ❏ Yes *(4 points)*   ❏ No *(0 points)*

2. Have you ever invested in stock or bond mutual funds (or in individual stocks or bonds)?
   ❏ Yes *(4 points)*   ❏ No *(0 points)*

   If yes, how long have you been investing?
   ❏ Less than 1 year *(0 points)*
   ❏ 1–5 years *(2 points)*
   ❏ More than 5 years *(3 points)*

3. Do you have an emergency fund that you can use to meet short-term (next six months) cash flow needs?
   ❏ Yes *(4 points)*   ❏ No *(0 points)*

4. Do you feel that your overall financial situation is secure?
   ❏ Yes *(4 points)*   ❏ No *(0 points)*

Risk Tolerance

5. Which of the following best describes your attitude toward investing?
   ❏ I like to keep my money in the bank where I know it's safe. *(0 points)*
   ❏ I'm interested in stocks and bonds, but I don't know very much. *(3 points)*
   ❏ I'd like to invest in the market, but I'm still concerned about its ups and downs. *(5 points)*
   ❏ I want to participate in the economy's growth, and I realize there will be market volatility. *(7 points)*

6. If you could raise your chances of improving your returns by taking more risk, would you be:
   ❏ Unlikely to take much more risk *(0 points)*
   ❏ Willing to take a little more risk with some of your money *(2 points)*
   ❏ Willing to take a little more risk with all your money *(4 points)*
   ❏ Willing to take a lot more risk with some of your money *(6 points)*

Continued on next page

Continued from previous page

7. Where would you place yourself on the following risk tolerance scale?

Most Cautious ——————————————→ *Least Cautious*

Scale:	1	2	3	4	5	6	7	8	9	10
Points:	(1)	(1)	(2)	(2)	(3)	(3)	(4)	(6)	(8)	(10)

Figuring Your Score: Add the points you checked for questions 2-7, and write your total below:

Total: _____

What Does It All Mean?

If you answered no to question 1, please refer to "Your Nonretirement Investment" below. If you answered yes to question 1, refer to "Your Retirement Investment" below. Using the appropriate chart, identify the expected time frame of your investment, and find the asset allocation model that corresponds to your score.

Your Nonretirement Investment

Investment Time Frame	*Recommended Asset Allocation Model**	
	Score	**Model**
Less than 3 years:	Any	Income
Between 3 and 5 years:	0–15	Income
	16–25	Growth & Income
	26–35	Growth
	36–40	Aggressive Growth
More than 5 years:	0–10	Income
	11–20	Growth & Income
	21–30	Growth
	31–40	Aggressive Growth

Your Retirement Investment

Investment Time Frame	*Recommended Asset Allocation Model**	
	Score	**Model**
Less than 3 years:	Any	Income
Between 3 and 7 years:	0–15	Income
	16–25	Growth & Income
	26–35	Growth
	36–40	Aggressive Growth
More than 7 years:	0–10	Income
	11–20	Growth & Income
	21–30	Growth
	31–40	Aggressive Growth

*Remember the Recommended Asset Allocation Model mix is based on your responses. As your situation changes, you should review your investment strategy.

Continued on next page

Continued from previous page

Your Investor Profile

Read the Investor Profile below for the model that was recommended for you.

Aggressive Growth
Aggressive Investor

Willing to take high levels of risk for the potential high returns. Understands that market volatility accompanies higher-risk investments.

Growth, Growth & Income
Moderate Investor

Willing to take increased risks to realize possible higher returns. Understands that market volatility will impact investments but will be reduced by a balanced mix of asset classes.

Income
Conservative Investor

Uncomfortable taking on increased risk, even for the possibility of higher returns. Understands that limiting the impact of market volatility also limits the potential for higher long-term investment returns.

Day 36

Don't snooze off and let your portfolio get complacent. Today, you'll test your newfound knowledge of how to safeguard your portfolio from the market's ravages.

True or false?

1. Dollar-cost averaging is an investment strategy that allows investors to invest in a fund and have their money matched dollar for dollar. T/F

2. One key to investing successfully is time spent in the market, not trying to time the market. T/F

3. IPO stands for initial public offering. T/F

4. All IPOs go up for the first few days after release. T/F

5. To be successful at dollar-cost averaging, you must be able to continue making systematic investments no matter what the market does. T/F

6. Zero-coupon bonds pay no current interest. T/F

7. Convertible securities have considerably more downside risk than do their underlying stocks. T/F

8. A hedge-wrapping strategy is a conservative way to safeguard your portfolio. T/F

9. Cash can be a good place to invest if you're worried about the direction of the stock market. T/F

10. Hedging strategies guarantee that you won't lose any money. T/F

11. Short-term capital gains rates take effect on sales of securities within all the following except:
    a. 12 months and one day
    b. six months
    c. 10 weeks
    d. nine months

12. The long-term capital gains tax rate for someone in the 28 percent federal tax bracket is:
    a. 28 percent
    b. 20 percent
    c. 15 percent
    d. there is no capital gains tax; it has been repealed

13. Dollar-cost averaging is a conservative way to:
    a. buy stock a little at a time
    b. buy bonds a little at a time
    c. buy funds a little at a time
    d. a and c

Day 37

What should you do when interest rates rise? If you can answer today's questions properly, you won't have to run for cover. Good luck!

1. Rising interest rates are great for:
   a. Alan Greenspan
   b. stock prices
   c. bond prices
   d. no one
   e. CD investors

2. GDP is a measure of:
   a. the value of goods and services produced in the United States over a specific time period
   b. the value of goods produced by major manufacturing concerns in one calendar quarter
   c. inflation
   d. the money supply

3. The Federal Reserve tightens the money supply by:
   a. increasing the discount rate
   b. raising the federal funds rate
   c. increasing the required level of banks' reserves
   d. all of the above
   e. none of the above; the Federal Reserve has nothing to do with the money supply

4. CDs are:
   a. guaranteed by the FDIC up to $100,000 plus interest
   b. guaranteed by the FDIC up to $100,000
   c. guaranteed by the bank that issues them
   d. backed by the U.S. Treasury

5. Funds that invest in adjustable-rate mortgages can be beneficial if:
   a. you seek an insured, guaranteed investment
   b. you're looking for a liquid alternative to money-market funds
   c. you want to replace lower-yielding short-term investments of one to three years
   d. you want an investment whose share price is fixed at $1

6. Prime-rate income funds can be a good investment when:
   a. the prime rate is low
   b. the prime rate is high
   c. you're looking for something guaranteed
   d. interest rates fall

Continued on next page

Continued from previous page

7. Before investing in a fund, make sure you *always:*
   a. pay your beloved broker a big commission
   b. read the prospectus before you invest
   c. have dividends sent to your home address
   d. read the brochure and make a decision based solely on that information

Note: If you got this one wrong, you must run five times around the block, repeating the correct answer at the top of your lungs.

8. The best time to pay off credit cards is:
   a. when you have the money
   b. when interest rates are high
   c. when you win the lottery
   d. when you receive an inheritance
   e. when you have a balance
   f. monthly
   g. all of the above

9. Simple interest is:
   a. interest paid monthly and compounded annually
   b. interest paid at the end of the year
   c. interest paid daily and compounded annually
   d. not so simple, really

10. If bonds must be sold when interest rates have risen, the price you get for your bond may be:
   a. more than what you paid
   b. less than what you paid
   c. equal to what you paid
   d. any of the above, depending on who issued the bond

Day 38

Can you recall what sort of investments to make when interest rates fall? Circle the correct answers:

1. Low interest rates are generally:
   a. great for stock investors
   b. great for holders of utility stocks
   c. great for people who want to refinance their mortgage
   d. all of the above
   e. none of the above

2. Short-term variable mortgage interest rates are:
   a. usually lower than 30- or 15-year fixed rates
   b. are a good choice for homeowners who plan to pay their mortgage off
   c. reset after 20 years
   d. have no closing costs

3. "Points" should be considered if:
   a. you plan to stay in your house for more than five years
   b. you plan to stay in your house for fewer than three years
   c. you can't get a 30-year mortgage
   d. you don't have enough money for a down payment

   True or false?

4. When interest rates are low, you should pay off your credit card. T/F

5. When interest rates are high, you should pay off your credit card. T/F

6. Floating-rate securities have fixed interest rates. T/F

Day 38

Before you decide to take advantage of temptingly low refinance rates, use this work sheet to make sure your new payments won't bust your budget.

This work sheet shows how many months it will take you to break even on a refinancing loan. To illustrate how this works, the work sheet shows numbers for a hypothetical borrower with a $210,000 mortgage who's going from an 8.75 percent rate to 7 percent.

This work sheet assumes that you will be refinancing into a 30-year mortgage. If you've already lived in the home for a few years, part of the monthly savings you get from refinancing comes from the fact that you are extending the loan's term.

Section A: Your Refinanced Mortgage

1. Discount points		1%	_____ %
2. Cost of points	($210,000 × 1%) $2,100	$ _____
3. Origination fee	0	$ _____
4. Application fee	$150	$ _____
5. Credit check	$55	$ _____
6. Attorney fee (yours)	$150	$ _____
7. Attorney fee (lender's)	0	$ _____
8. Title search	0	$ _____
9. Title insurance	$275	$ _____
10. Appraisal fee	$300	$ _____
11. Inspections	0	$ _____
12. Local fees (taxes, transfers)	$200	$ _____
13. Document preparation	$200	$ _____
14. Other miscellaneous fees	0	$ _____
15. Prepayment penalty on current mortgage	0	$ _____
16. Total	$3,430	$ _____

Continued on next page

Continued from previous page

Section B: Your Monthly Expenses

17. Your current monthly mortgage payment
    (Don't include insurance or taxes.) $1,652 $ _____

18. Amount you are refinancing $210,000 $ _____

19. Using the table on page 345, find the
    amount you'll be paying per $1,000. $6.653 $ _____

20. Divide line 18 by 1,000.   210 $ _____

21. Monthly payment for your new loan.
    (Multiply line 19 by line 20.) $1,397 $ _____

22. Your monthly savings (Subtract line 21
    from line 17.) $255 $ _____

23. Number of months it will take to recoup
    the cost of your new loan (Divide line 16
    by line 22, rounding up.)   14   _____

Is A "No Cost" Loan For You?

Discount fees, or "points," used to be a fact of life in mortgages. Now many lenders will allow you to choose. You can pay points and other costs up front, or you can pay no costs and accept a slightly higher interest rate. Here's how to figure out which alternative makes more sense for you.

1. Your mortgage amount $210,000 $ _____

2. Rate you'll pay without costs   7.50%   _____ %

3. Rate you'll pay with costs   7.00%   _____ %

    a) Costs with this loan (including points) $3,430 $ _____

4. Monthly payments with rate on line 2

    a) Payment per $1,000 (see table on
       page 345) $6.992 $ _____

    b) Divide line 1 by 1,000.   210 $ _____

    c) Multiply line 4a by line 4b. $1,468 $ _____

5. Monthly payments with rate on line 3

    a) Payment per $1,000 (see table on
       page 345) $6.653 $ _____

    b) Divide line 1 by 1,000.   210   _____

    c) Multiply line 5a by line 5b. $1,397 $ _____

Continued on next page

Continued from previous page

6. Monthly savings from lower rate (Subtract line 5c from line 4c.)	$71	$_____
7. Amount you could earn each month on the money you spent to get a lower rate.* (Multiply line 3a by 0.00487.)	$17	$_____
8. Total monthly savings (Subtract line 7 from line 6.)	$54	$_____
9. Number of months it will take to recoup the costs of the loan with a lower rate (Divide line 3a by line 8, rounding up.) *If you expect to own your home longer than the number of months on line 9, pay the costs and grab the lower rate.*	64	_____

*Assumes a conservative annual return of 6 percent

How Much Will You End Up Paying?

Loan Rate	Monthly Payment Per $1,000**	Loan Rate	Monthly Payment Per $1,000	Loan Rate	Monthly Payment Per $1,000	Loan Rate	Monthly Payment Per $1,000
4.50%	$5.06	6.00%	$5.996	7.50%	$6.992	9.00%	$8.046
4.625	5.141	6.15	6.067	7.625	7.078	9.125	8.136
4.750	5.216	6.25	6.157	7.75	7.164	9.25	8.227
4.875	5.292	6.375	6.239	7.875	7.251	9.375	8.317
5.00	5.368	6.50	6.321	8.00	7.338	9.50	8.409
5.125	5.445	6.625	6.403	8.125	7.425	9.625	8.50
5.250	5.522	6.75	6.486	8.25	7.513	9.75	8.592
5.375	5.60	6.875	6.569	8.375	7.601	9.875	8.683
5.50	5.678	7.00	6.653	8.50	7.689	10.00	8.776
5.625	5.757	7.125	6.737	8.625	7.778	10.125	8.868
5.75	5.836	7.25	6.822	8.75	7.867	10.25	8.961
5.875	5.915	7.375	6.907	8.875	7.956	10.375	9.054

**Assumes a 30-year mortgage

Source: HSH Associates

Day 40

Not sure how much you should be saving for retirement? Today's assignment can help you decide how much to put away to reach your goals. Don't put this off for tomorrow.

Make a copy of these pages before you fill them in, and re-evaluate your progress annually. If you're not meeting your objectives, you may have to increase your savings rate, lower your goals, plan to retire later or change your investment allocation. But if you don't take the first step and figure out what you'll need, you'll never know . . . so whip out that pencil and get a-figurin'.

Financial planners estimate that individuals generally need to replace 60 percent to 80 percent of their pre-retirement income to maintain their standard of living after retirement. Social Security currently provides 45 percent of pre-retirement income for those earning $20,000, but less than 25 percent for those earning more than $50,000. The balance must come from your savings or your employer's pension plan.

The retirement savings work sheet below can help you estimate how much of your salary must be saved annually to accumulate enough assets to provide 50 percent of your salary after retirement. The work sheet takes into account your current savings in taxable and tax-deferred accounts, as well as the rate of return you expect to earn on your savings before and after retirement. The work sheet also assumes that your income before and after retirement keeps pace with a 3.1 percent inflation rate and an 8 percent pretax rate of return.

Keep in mind this is a simplified work sheet that only provides a rough estimate of your retirement savings needs.

	Example	Your Calculation
1. Enter your current salary.	$50,000	$ _____
2. Enter the factor from Table A that corresponds to the rate of return you expect to earn on your retirement savings *after* you retire and the number of years until you retire. (You might earn a lower rate of return after retirement, reflecting a more conservative investment strategy.) For example, if you expect to retire in 20 years and earn 7 percent on your savings after retirement, the factor to use is 15.86.	× 15.86	× _____

Continued on next page

Continued from previous page

3. Multiply line 1 by line 2. This is the total assets you will need at retirement to generate 50 percent of your salary. =$793,000 =$ _____

4. Enter any current investments in taxable income. $20,000 $ _____

5. Enter factor from Table B that corresponds to the rate of return you expect to earn on your current taxable investments between now and retirement and the number of years until you retire. If you expect to earn a 9 percent annual rate of return and retire in 20 years, the factor to use is 3.51. x 3.51 x _____

6. Multiply line 4 by line 5. This is the value of your taxable investments at retirement (assuming a 28 percent tax rate). =$70,200 =$ _____

7. Enter your current assets in tax-deferred accounts. $100,000 $ _____

8. Enter factor from Table C that corresponds to the rate of return you expect to earn on your tax-deferred assets between now and retirement and the number of years until you retire. If you expect to earn a 9 percent annual rate of return and retire in 20 years, the factor to use is 5.60. x 5.60 x _____

9. Multiply line 7 by line 8. This is the value of your tax-deferred investments at retirement. =$560,000 =$ _____

10. Add line 6 and line 9. This is the projected value of your current investments at retirement. $630,200 $ _____

11. Subtract line 10 from line 3. This is the additional amount you need. (If line 11 is negative, you are well on your way to meeting your retirement goal, but monitor your program to make sure your savings are meeting your expectations.) $162,800 $ _____

12. Enter your salary from line 1. $50,000 $ _____

13. Divide line 11 by line 12. = 3.25 = _____

Continued on next page

Continued from previous page

14. Enter the factor from Table D that
corresponds to your expected rate of
return before retirement and years until
retirement. If you expect to earn 9 percent
and you have 20 years until retirement, the
factor is 1.57.

 <u>x 1.57</u> x <u>_____</u>

15. Multiply line 13 by line 14. This is the
percentage of your salary you need to
invest each year to meet your retirement
goal.

 = 5.10% = <u>_____</u> %

Table A: Factors For Total Capital Needed At Retirement

Investment Returns	Years Until Retirement					
	10	15	20	25	30	35
4%	17.30	20.16	23.48	27.35	31.87	37.12
5	15.06	17.55	20.44	23.81	27.74	32.31
6	13.22	15.40	17.94	20.89	24.34	28.35
7	11.69	13.61	15.86	18.47	21.52	25.07
8	10.41	12.12	14.12	16.45	19.17	22.33
9	9.33	10.87	12.67	14.76	17.19	20.02
10	8.43	9.81	11.43	13.32	15.52	18.07

Table B: Factors For Future Value Of Taxable Savings

Investment Returns	Years Until Retirement					
	10	15	20	25	30	35
4%	1.33	1.53	1.76	2.03	2.34	2.70
5	1.42	1.70	2.03	2.42	2.89	3.45
6	1.53	1.89	2.33	2.88	3.56	4.39
7	1.64	2.09	2.67	3.42	4.37	5.59
8	1.75	2.32	3.07	4.06	5.37	7.10
9	1.87	2.56	3.51	4.81	6.58	9.00
10	2.00	2.84	4.02	5.69	8.05	11.40

Continued on next page

Continued from previous page

Table C: Factors For Future Value Of Tax-Deferred Savings

Investment Returns	Years Until Retirement					
	10	15	20	25	30	35
4%	1.48	1.80	2.19	2.67	3.24	3.95
5	1.63	2.08	2.65	3.39	4.32	5.52
6	1.79	2.40	3.21	4.29	5.74	7.69
7	1.97	2.76	3.87	5.43	7.61	10.68
8	2.16	3.17	4.66	6.85	10.06	14.79
9	2.37	3.64	5.60	8.62	13.27	20.41
10	2.59	4.18	6.73	10.83	17.45	28.10

Table D: Factors For Additional Savings Required

Investment Returns	Years Until Retirement					
	10	15	20	25	30	35
4%	7.30	4.09	2.57	1.73	1.21	0.87
5	6.99	3.81	2.34	1.53	1.04	0.73
6	6.68	3.56	2.12	1.35	0.89	0.61
7	6.39	3.31	1.92	1.19	0.76	0.50
8	6.11	3.08	1.74	1.04	0.65	0.41
9	5.84	2.86	1.57	0.91	0.55	0.34
10	5.58	2.66	1.41	0.79	0.46	0.27

Exhibits showing market performance are for illustrative purposes only and are not intended to represent the performance of any T. Rowe Price fund. Past performance does not guarantee future results.

Source: T. Rowe Price

Day 41

Now that you know all the ins and outs of will-planning, here's a work sheet to help you start planning your own will.

Names Of Executors (to administer the estate):

Names Of Guardians (and all alternates) **Of Minor Children** (you can have one guardian over the child and another guardian over the child's property):

Provisions For Payments Of Debts And Taxes:

Specific Bequests Of Money And Tangible Property

Name of person or organization	Amount or Item

Disposition Of The Remainder Of The Property

Names of primary beneficiaries (including trusts)	Percentage

Names of contingent beneficiaries	Percentage

Day 43

Investment clubs can be fun and profitable, but don't get any help answering today's questions!

1. You can find members for your investment club:
   a. in the local bar
   b. at the office
   c. at the country club
   d. anywhere people already have some affiliation

2. The key to a successful club is:
   a. making a killing by day trading
   b. paying low commissions
   c. a commitment to learning
   d. a lot of money to invest

3. Clubs need a structure that allows them to act. The most popular is:
   a. a corporation
   b. a sole proprietorship
   c. a partnership
   d. a limited partnership

4. Successful clubs are made up of:
   a. men
   b. women
   c. both men and women
   d. bulls and bears

5. To get information on a company before you buy its stock, get its:
   a. 10K report
   b. annual report
   c. Value Line report
   d. S&P report
   e. all of the above if available

6. Successful clubs never:
   a. debate the value of a stock picked by their president
   b. put all their money into one stock
   c. buy and hold
   d. do research

7. Clubs can trade stocks:
   a. through a full-service broker
   b. on the Internet
   c. through a discount broker
   d. all of the above

8. Successful investment clubs often:
   a. lose money for a few years
   b. mix styles of investing
   c. meet quarterly
   d. leave the stock-picking to their brokers

Day 44

The perfect financial advisor probably doesn't exist (with the exception of myself, of course!). But if you can answer today's quiz accurately, at least you'll know who to avoid.

1. A registered representative is someone who may:
   a. be a stockbroker
   b. be a certified financial planner
   c. have passed an exam administered by the NASD
   d. all of the above

2. Before you meet with a financial advisor, it is wise to do all of the following except:
   a. consider your financial goals
   b. think about your risk tolerance
   c. prepare a financial profile
   d. liquidate all your assets

3. Discount brokers and online trading are appropriate for:
   a. neophyte investors
   b. people who don't have time to deal with their money
   c. experienced investors who are prepared to do it themselves
   d. widows and grandmothers

4. DRIPs are:
   a. investment programs that are good to the last drop
   b. dividend reinvestment programs available in initial public offerings
   c. direct reinvestment programs available directly from some publicly traded companies
   d. a systematic method of investing

5. DRIPs provide all the following except:
   a. nominal commissions
   b. dividend reinvestment
   c. easy acess to trading
   d. low minimum investments

6. The most frequent legal complaints against brokers include:
   a. a strong New York accent
   b. unauthorized transactions
   c. unsuitable recommendations
   d. using too much jargon
   e. talking too fast
   f. a, b and c
   g. b and c

Continued on next page

Continued from previous page

7. A record of complaints against a registered representative can be accessed through:
   a. the firm's home office
   b. the state regulator's office
   c. the CFP board
   d. the NASD
   e. the Central Registration Depository (CRD)

8. To get the best service from your financial advisor, do all the following except:
   a. be nice to his/her assistant
   b. call frequently with questions on your dividends
   c. refer your friends to them if you think they do a great job
   d. call them after or before market hours when you have a complicated, nonmarket-related question

9. You should never:
   a. open and check confirmations of trades as soon as you receive them
   b. toss all your statements into a drawer or to open at tax time
   c. confirm trades with your broker
   d. immediately let your financial advisor know about any trade that looks incorrect in your account

10. According to the CFP Board of Standards, a certified financial planner is:
    a. an individual who addresses budgeting, savings, taxes and other issues to help people reach their financial goals
    b. an individual who uses insurance products exclusively to help people save for retirement
    c. an individual who focuses on a limited number of financial concerns
    d. an individual who is certified to lead the board of a NYSE-listed company

Day 45

This is it! Answer these last few questions, and you've made it! I promise they aren't too hard.

1. The best place to look for a good fund to invest in is:
   a. last year's best performing funds
   b. Morningstar rating sheets
   c. the fund's prospectus
   d. a fund with a good long-term track record that is currently out of favor

2. The key to success in investing in stocks is:
   a. buy low, sell high
   b. buy on the bad news, sell on the good
   c. you never go broke taking a profit
   d. none of the above; any of these would be great if only they were predictable

3. The best way to select a value stock is to look for one with:
   a. a low P/E ratio
   b. a low P/E ratio compared to similar companies in the same industry
   c. a high P/E ratio
   d. a high price-to-book ratio

4. To find out more about a fund you might be considering, check its:
   a. annual report
   b. prospectus
   c. ratings by various magazines
   d. all of the above

5. If you've learned *anything* at all from this book it has become obvious that:
   a. past performance is not an indication of future returns
   b. you should read the prospectus before you invest in a mutual fund
   c. anyone can become financially fit if they really want to
   d. all of the above, especially the last one!

Workbook Answer Key

Day 7
1. a, b, c, d
2. a, b, c
3. a, c, d
4. g
5. i
6. m
7. a, o, s
8. p
9. l
10. n
11. c
12. h
13. q
14. a, b, k
15. h
16. e, t
17. d
18. a, u
19. j
20. a, f, o

Day 8
1. b
2. g
3. e
4. a, h
5. i, k
6. c, j
7. d
8. f
9. a, b, c, f, j
10. d, e, g, h, i, k

Day 9
1. g, m, s, v
2. d, f, j, m, v, x, y
3. t, v, y
4. b, l, r, v
5. a, k, n, t, v
6. j, v, w, y
7. c, e, q, v, z
8. b, o, v, y
9. d, i, p, v, x
10. h, n, u, v, z

Day 10
1. QUIDS
2. redeem
3. MIPS
4. cumulative
5. convertible
6. call protection
7. preferred stocks
8. inflation
9. bond
10. owed
11. adjustable rate
12. corporation
13. debt holders
14. TOPRS
15. common stock
16. cushion
17. traditional
18. dividend

Day 14
1. management
2. utilities
3. growth
4. reverse
5. past
   performance
6. replacing
7. dividends
8. buybacks
9. bull
10. shareholders
11. splits
12. stock
13. real estate
    investment
    trusts
14. distribution date
15. positive

Day 18
1. long-term
2. Internet stocks
3. momentum
4. a, b
5. a, b, c, d

6. T
7. T
8. T
9. F
10. T
11. stop-limit
12. stop-loss
13. stop-limit
14. sell-limit

Day 21
1. mirror
2. opportunities
3. trading
4. efficient
5. index
6. self-fulfilling
7. value
8. managed
9. mid-cap
10. aggressive

Day 22
1. b
2. F
3. b
4. F
5. d
6. e
7. e
8. b
9. b
10. c
11. more

Day 23
1. c, g, h
2. b, f
3. a, c, d, h
4. e, i
5. T
6. F
7. F
8. T
9. T
10. F

Continued on next page

Continued from previous page

11. F
12. F

Day 26
1. grown
2. b
3. T
4. T
5. a
6. b
7. e
8. d
9. F
10. F
11. a, c
12. a, b
13. a, b
14. a
15. d
16. a
17. a

Day 27
1. a, c
2. a, b, c, e
3. d, f
4. c, g, h
5. c
6. a
7. a
8. F
9. T
10. T

Day 28
1. tax deduction
2. restrictive
3. jury
4. fewer
5. positive
6. on
7. criteria
8. good
9. negative
10. return
11. interpretation
12. environment
13. labor

Day 32
1. T
2. F
3. F
4. F
5. F
6. T
7. T
8. F
9. T
10. F
11. a
12. b
13. a

Day 33
1. c
2. c
3. b
4. d
5. b
6. F
7. F
8. T
9. T
10. F

Day 34
1. e
2. c
3. d
4. a
5. b
6. c
7. a
8. b

Day 36
1. F
2. T
3. T
4. T
5. T
6. T
7. F
8. F
9. T
10. F
11. a

12. b
13. d

Day 37
1. e
2. a
3. d
4. b
5. c
6. b
7. b
8. g
9. b
10. b

Day 38
1. d
2. a
3. a
4. T
5. F
6. F

Day 43
1. d
2. c
3. c
4. c
5. e
6. b
7. a
8. b

Day 44
1. d
2. d
3. c
4. c
5. c
6. g
7. e
8. b
9. b
10. a

Day 45
1. d
2. d
3. b
4. d
5. d

Index

Current titles from Entrepreneur Press

Business Plans Made Easy:
It's Not as Hard as You Think

Gen E: Generation Entrepreneur is Rewriting
the Rules of Business—and You Can, Too!

Get Smart: 365 Tips
to Boost Your Entrepreneurial IQ

Knock-Out Marketing: Powerful Strategies
to Punch Up Your Sales

Start Your Own Business:
The Only Start-Up Book You'll Ever Need

Success for Less: 100 Low-Cost Businesses
You Can Start Today

303 Marketing Tips Guaranteed
to Boost Your Business

Young Millionaires: Inspiring Stories
to Ignite Your Entrepreneurial Dreams

Where's The Money? Sure-Fire Financial Solutions
for Your Small Business

Forthcoming titles from Entrepreneur Press

April 2000:
Ben Franklin's 12 Rules of Management:
The Founding Father of American Business
Solves Your Toughest Problems

May 2000:
Radicals & Visionaries: The Entrepreneurs Who
Revolutionized the 20th Century

About The Author

Lorayne Fiorillo is a senior vice president at a major brokerage firm. A financial advisor since 1986, she currently manages over $120 million in assets for more than 600 clients. She is a registered investment advisor. She also has been a contributing editor at *Entrepreneur* magazine for six years and was a market analyst for National Public Radio for 11 years as well as the personal finance commentator for the ABC affiliate in Charlotte, North Carolina.

Lorayne Fiorillo conducts seminars and workshops on personal finance. To contact her, write to Lorayne Fiorillo, P.O. Box 212, Scarsdale, NY 10583-0212.

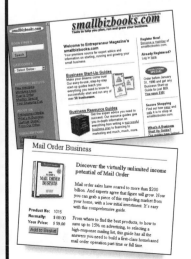

FREE ADVICE

When was the last time you got **free** advice that was worth something?

free issue!

Entrepreneur Magazine, the leading small business authority, is loaded with free advice—advice that could be worth millions to you. Every issue gives you detailed, practical knowledge on how to start a business and run it successfully. Entrepreneur is the perfect resource to keep small business owners up-to-date, on track, and growing their business.

Get your **free issue** of Entrepreneur today!

Call 800-274-6229 Dept. 5G9J9,
or fill out and mail the back of this card.

Entrepreneur MAGAZINE

BREAK OUT

Business Start-Ups helps you **break** out of the 9–5 life!

free issue!

Do you want to get out of the 9–5 routine and take control of your life? Business Start-Ups shows you the franchise and business opportunities that will give you the future you dream of. Every issue answers your questions, highlights hot trends, spotlights new ideas, and provides the inspiration and real-life information you need to succeed.

Get your **free issue** of Business Start-Ups today!

Call 800-274-8333 Dept. 5HBK2,
or fill out and mail the back of this card.

Entrepreneur's **Business Start·Ups**